YARRA

It was John Wedge, Batman's private surveyor, who named the Yarra Yarra. In September 1835 he was at the Turning Basin with some Kulin and heard them identify the river as it came over the Falls as, he wrote, 'Yarrow Yarrow'. It was only some months later that Wedge discovered they had been referring to the pattern and movement of water over the Falls, not the river itself.

~

And ever since, it has been the Yarra's fate to be misunderstood: maligned for its muddiness, ill-used as sewer and tip; scooped, sculpted, straightened and stressed, 'cleaned up' to the detriment of its natural inhabitants; built-over, -under and -beside; worked mercilessly and then bridged almost to maritime extinction.

In Kristin Otto's superbly entertaining new history, the whole sorry tale is laid bare. From the creation stories of Kulin owners and geologist blow-ins (and Robert Hoddle's bad-tempered expedition to the headwaters) to the twenty-first-century waterside building boom, Otto traces the course of Melbourne's murky river.

Erudite, affectionate and witty, with more meanders and diversions than the river itself, *Yarra* is both a fascinating read and a fitting tribute to the 'noble stream'.

Kristin Otto lives in the Yarra Valley.
She has a degree in fine arts and has worked as a bookseller and curator. *Yarra* is her first book.

KRISTIN OTTO

Yarra

A diverting HISTORY

TEXT PUBLISHING MELBOURNE AUSTRALIA

The Text Publishing Company acknowledges the Traditional Owners of the country on which we work, the Wurundjeri people of the Kulin Nation, and pays respect to their Elders past and present.

The Text Publishing Company
Wurundjeri Country, Level 6, Royal Bank Chambers, 287 Collins Street,
Melbourne Victoria 3000 Australia
www.textpublishing.com.au

First published in 2005 by The Text Publishing Company
This edition 2009
Reprinted 2021, 2023

Designed by Chong
Typeset in Granjon by J&M Typesetting
Printed and bound in Australia by Griffin Press, a member of the Opus Group. The Opus Group is ISO/NZS 14001:2004 Environmental Management System certified.

National Library of Australia Cataloguing-in-Publication data:

Otto, Kristin, 1958-
Yarra : a diverting history / Kristin Otto.
ISBN 9781921520006 (pbk.)
Rivers—Victoria—Melbourne—History. Stream conservation—Victoria—Melbourne. Yarra River (Vic.)—History. Melbourne (Vic.)—History
551.483099452

This project has been assisted by the Commonwealth Government through the Australia Council, its arts funding and advisory body.

The paper this book is printed on is certified against the Forest Stewardship Council® Standards. Griffin Press, a member of the Opus Group, holds chain of custody certification SCS-COC-001185. FSC® promotes environmentally responsible, socially beneficial and economically viable management of the world's forests.

Contents

Measures

one foot = 0.3 metre

100 links = 1 chain = 66 feet = 20.1 metres

10 chains = 1 furlong

8 furlongs = 1 mile = 1.6 kilometres

10 square chains = 1 acre = 0.4 hectare

one ounce = 28 grams

one pound = 0.45 kilogram

1 cusec = 1 cubic foot of water passing per second = 0.028 cumec
= 0.028 cubic metres of water passing per second

or

1 cumec = 35.3 cusecs

Author's note

Spelling and usage are based on the document sighted: where I saw an original document, that spelling has been used. If only a later, tidied-up transcript has been seen, I have had to use that spelling and capitalisation.

In the interests of simplicity, the Botanic Gardens have been referred to by that name regardless of whether at a particular period they were known as the Botanical Gardens, any variations thereof or by their current appellation, Royal Botanic Gardens Melbourne. Similarly, Baron von Mueller is given his title despite the fact that it was not applicable during the entire historical period.

Kulin words are spelt as an average approximation of oral language.

~

The information in this book is drawn from the sources listed at the end of the text. Any errors, glaring omissions or instances of over-opinionated speculation found within the text are mine.

Also, the biblical rollcall of creeks that appears on pages 50–3 does not claim to be complete or correct. It includes some creeks that have 'disappeared' by becoming below-ground drains, and also some that are intermittent or discontinuous and originally ended in an adjacent wetland rather than the river itself.

Additions and corrections are welcome—please direct them to the author care of the publisher.

The shape of this river echoes in its stories.
There are meanders in the telling, billabongs,
islands, snags, floods…

The River

Around the same time someone explains the mechanics of an Australian hoop snake to you,* you might also hear how the Yarra flows upside down. The explanation for the river's famous muddiness, they'll tell you, is that it carries its bed turgidly on the surface, the clear water flowing underneath. Too thin to plough, they'll say; too thick to drink.

This particular tall tale is eerily similar to the way fresh and salt water do actually layer themselves in the lower reaches of the river: the fresh—that is, the warm, muddy—water flowing down on top and the heavier seawater flooding in clear and cold below. You can see it in the wake of big ships in the Port of Melbourne as their propellors churn up clear water from the bottom. It's noted occasionally by police divers, getting two metres of good visibility underneath half a dozen of suspended river sedimentary darkness.

We are antipodean—upside down at the bottom of the world—only to people from somewhere else. (And the Danube isn't blue, either.) Australian rivers are noted for their turbidity—that is, they are silt-filled; i.e. muddy—and the Yarra is an Australian river. The

---

* It takes its tail in its mouth and forms a rigid circle that enables it to roll speedily after its prey.

colours of the Yarra are the colours of our country, literally, being suspended earth from the upstream and middle-reach banks. This is our real world. Richard Twopeny, writing for the English visitor to Melbourne in the nineteenth century, noted in a discussion of the names of suburbs, 'Yarra is the only native name.'*

We have rowed on it, drunk it, dammed it, washed with it, ignored it, sewered into it, gazed at it, drowned in it, swum it, built factories and cities because of it.

Several million years ago hot lava from volcanic fields laid out the western plains of Victoria, which reach right in to the present-day western suburbs of Melbourne. That hot lava became magma, then

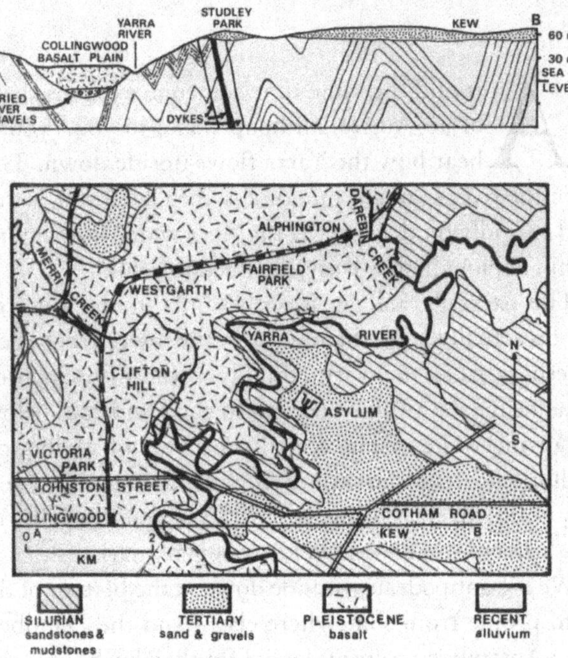

The basalt hot-rock flow that shaped the river through the inner suburbs, as rendered in 1940.

---

* Although he was not strictly correct: Prahran would be another example.

solid rock: basalt, bluestone. Another wave of volcanic activity north of Melbourne, maybe 800,000 years ago, poured a huge lava flow south to cover the old river's bed, which lay to the north and west of where it is now.* The huge mass of lava flowed down the river and creek valleys in its path, cooling in some places into rock tens of metres deep. The Yarra was dammed, blocked from Gardiners Creek to Darebin Creek, making a huge lake of the river flats above, upstream to Templestowe.

Eventually the river wore its way downstream again, cutting and curving a new bed around the southern edges of the lava flow against the old river valley's escarpments. You can drive through that old hot rock north of the river along the Eastern Freeway and glance south, to take in the sandstone ramparts opposite Deep Rock and the escarpment above Dights Falls on the other bank. Yarra tributaries the Darebin, Merri and Moonee Ponds creeks, and the Maribyrnong River—all of these cut through volcanic flow. The volcanic hills of Kangaroo Ground also flowed over the earlier bed of the river (later re-excavated for gravel). The big lake in the middle reaches of the river drained eventually, leaving rich river flats.

The sandstone, siltstone, mudstone strata that reveal themselves by Dights Falls, among other places, are four-hundred-million-year-old seabed that's folded, faulted and eroded. Three hundred-something million years ago the ancient Yarra started to form in it, and the eruptions of Corhanwarrabul (the Dandenongs), Blacks Spur and Donna Buang positioned the flow of the Upper Yarra River to the south and west. Ten or twenty million years ago, Port Phillip and the lower Yarra Valley were sinking into the sea while the upper valley pushed up. The river cut down deeper into Yering Gorge. It only took another few million years for that whole bay and valley area to lift above sea level again. From about a million years ago, up until the second volcanic wave that shifted the river's path, its fast

---

* Apparently, according to some nineteenth-century prospectors, part of it is under the Collingwood Town Hall. Goldminers can dig deep looking for prehistoric river and creek beds. It's there that ancient gold-bearing gravel eroded from mother lode quartz reefs settled heavily after being washed away.

flow laid down masses of gravels on the lower reaches, which can be found more than thirty metres below current ground level.

During the last Ice Age, maybe twenty thousand years ago, the sea level dropped very much lower again because of all the seawater held up, frozen, around the Arctic and Antarctic. The Yarra ran all the way down across a dry Port Phillip Bay and out through the heads. It was joined by the Barwon River and then met the now-Tasmanian Tamar River in an equally dry Bass Strait, before eventually flowing into the Southern Ocean west of King Island. As the world gradually warmed, the sea level rose until finally the plains of Bass Strait, and the River Yarra running through them, were inundated. The island of Tasmania emerged.

The cold, wet river landscape at Melbourne then was similar to late-nineteenth-century descriptions of the country around Yarra Falls at the river's headwaters. The moss-laden beech forests described by Baldwin Spencer grew then around the canyon of the river at the location of the present city. The Yarra turned south from there, to flow down through Port Melbourne. It joined the Maribyrnong River off Williamstown, meeting the Werribee and Barwon rivers further down the still-dry bay.

With the global warming, more of the ice caps melted and the sea level rose, creating Port Phillip and Westernport Bays about eight thousand years ago, and covering the old river bed and its canyons.* The sea got higher and higher, making a shore for itself and depositing seashells as far upriver as Cremorne and South Yarra, before starting to drop back to its current level about five thousand years ago. At its height, the river must have been tidal to Dights Falls—as it is again today, due to human intervention.

In another version of the same story, Billibellary, a Kulin leader at the time of Melbourne's colonial settlement, told how the Yarra's course was formed by two Woiwurrung headmen. A long time ago, when

---

* Now part of the South Channel for shipping. What would then have been a huge waterfall is now an element of the Rip, the intensely narrow maelstrom at the entrance to Port Phillip Bay.

Port Phillip Bay was still a lush plain, the Boonwurrung and Wathawurrung hunted there while the Woiwurrung were stuck in the mountains by the waters of the Yarra massed in one huge pool. Bar-wool, a headman, used his axe to carve a way through for the water to fall west past Baw Baw, then past Donna Buang, another mountainous barrier. He continued west, through the softer hills to Warrandyte where he met Yan Yan, headman from Morang, who was cutting a way with his axe for the Plenty River. The two of them kept going, resting at Warringal/Bolin-Bolin. Between the Darebin and Merri creeks they had to slow down and cut tight around hard ground, a longer way. When they finally hit the flats of Port Phillip—the Boonwurrung, Wathawurrung hunting grounds—the water behind them flooded out, flowing the length of the new rivers they had made. The great pool of water in the mountains emptied, and Port Phillip filled.

Anyway, the old river canyon and those areas later to become the river delta filled with more layers of sediment, sands and silt. These, combined with the silts, gravels and underground saline around what had accumulated earlier, give engineers on heavy building projects in Docklands and Southbank huge problems by tilting high-rise cores and leaking into road tunnels. Coode Island Silt, geologically the most recent, is probably the most notorious and treacherous material they have to deal with. Apart from the fact that it's structurally unstable, when it contacts oxygen through air or water some of its components may turn to sulphuric acid. Parts of the Arts Centre foundations have to have a continuous electric current conducted through them to counter possible corrosion.

At the beginning of the delta's formation the river met the sea where Princes Bridge is now. It covered what became Albert Park Lake (a salt lagoon later sealed and refilled with Yarra riverwater), South and Port Melbourne, Docklands, Coode Island, Fishermans Bend, Southbank and St Kilda Road (except for the old volcanic hills, like Emerald Hill). The river has joined the sea through all these points at various times. Silt coming down would eventually block up the mouth, fill the waterway and a new course would form further west. One old course was east of Emerald Hill (roughly the direction of Kingsway to Albert Park Lake), entering the sea at West St Kilda.

At settlement, in the early to mid-nineteenth century, the sands, silts and clays of the south-west of Melbourne were clothed in 'dense, snaky, scrubby jungle' (as described by Garryowen): teatree scrub punctuated by intermittent marsh, swamps and lagoons.

The river has always been turbid, but the degree has varied with the degradation and erosion of river soils, banks, flats and catchments. Sediment loads in rivers across Australia are now many times greater than they were before settlement. The uses made of the river and the areas draining into it affect the state of the water: intensive agriculture, vegetation removal, anywhere with exposed or disturbed earth—these are all factors. Frightening amounts of runoff, in the order of tonnes, have been measured coming from roads alone (think how many hundreds and thousands of kilometres there are in the catchment).

Tributaries coming across basalt (as in the middle and lower north) can be quite clear compared to those joining from clayey country (south, upper reaches), just as rivers in other parts of Australia, such as those flowing over Sydney sandstone, may appear cleaner.

The river's geological formation and structure and certain of its extremely turbid tributaries (eroding high amounts of mudstone and siltstone, and central alluvial flats) cause its characteristic appearance. Above those unstable, sometimes overagitated, soils of the Yarra Valley, the upstream Yarra can generally be found crystal clear, flowing through the mountain bushland over rounded river pebbles. This also reflects the normal river process produced by the higher gradient in the mountains: the lower the gradient, the slower the current, the siltier a stream.

Activities that took place in the catchment many decades before can still affect the river. Sand slugs—bodies of gravel and sand—from events that set off erosion, such as goldmining or heavy rain after bushfire, can be found moving down the river even a century later. Time of year and seasonal flow are another factor. The more rain, the more water coming down the river; the bigger and faster a body of water coming down, the more silt is picked up and moved along. You can see this in the middle reaches: along shallow edges with no flow the water is transparent above soft mud. As soon as the current is evident, fast and deep in the middle, it's rendered completely opaque by the amount of sediment carried. Even in the centre of the city, there may be clear golden sunlit water at the river's edge, until wash from passing traffic explodes the superfine silt.*

The microscopic clay particles that make the Yarra look so muddy are an unusual disc-like shape. They reflect much more light than normal mud particles so the water becomes even more opaque. The water in the Yarra may look dirty even when, in terms of pollutants or harmful bacteria, it is comparatively 'clean'. Australian river silt is fine; much finer than mud from elsewhere. It comes from soil and earth so old, so weathered and worn down, buffeted into such small particles, that it stays suspended in the water for a long, long time before it settles.

As with many Yarra stories, there are riverbank views—parallel but opposing—on the turbidity question. Core samples taken from nine-hundred-year-old billabongs such as Bolin-Bolin show no typically brown muddy deposits. If anything, it seems that the water in the billabongs was black, implying that comparatively clear water flowed in from the river replenishing them and was later coloured dark by surrounding vegetation. There would have been turbidity during flood, but not otherwise. Perhaps one factor to consider is the amount of mud and silt disturbed by, say, a thousand people who 'touch the earth lightly' as compared to a million people in the same space who sit down hard on it, churn it, use it, readying it to wash away.†

---

* This visual effect, one solid-coloured liquid exploding within another, was used in Hollywood special effects before everything went digital. Glass tank footage was run upside down, to become apocalyptic, alien, cloud-roiling sky.

† A report to government in the late 1990s put the amount of sediment going past at 30,000 tonnes annually, in the water, just about all of which was ripped off the disturbed land by major storms.

The appearance of Yarra water is something people have been dealing with for a long time. It was once known as one of the filthiest rivers in the world. Yet over the past hundred years its catchment has provided some of the world's best drinking water. Most of us have spent our lives confusing turbidity with dirtiness and wondering why our messy natural bushscapes weren't Derwent coloured-pencil sketches.

We are only just getting used to being Australian, instead of our sensibilities being attuned to the ideas of another place.

The Source

The Yarra's water has defined territory for everybody, but differently. For Wurundjeri people the river's watershed described their country, which centred on its flow. Where rain fell, its droplets hitting manna gum, fern, wattle and teatree, running off to soaks, creeks, down to the river; wherever water ran—downstream from the Yarra's source west of Baw Baw and south of Mount Gregory—in that direction was their land. They camped close to the river or tributary and drank directly from it. They were born near it and buried near it. They made water containers from hollowed-out tree burls, or bark. Waterbags were possibly made of tied and sealed possum skins turned inside out, fur filtering the muddy water en route. Anthropological descriptions of Wurundjeri territories, when plotted out on a map, show the river's catchment.

Wurundjeri were Woiwurrung, and Woiwurrung was one of five languages within the Kulin nation.* The others were Wathawurrung to the west (Geelong, Ballarat); Boonwurrung in the south (the Peninsula and the bays), Daungwurrung, north-east over

* Each language had slight variations—how the word 'no' (*woi*) was said, with *wurrung* being lip/tongue/speech. *Kulin*, the word for man, was the same in each language.

the Great Divide (Goulburn watershed) and Djadjawurrung to the north-west. There was fighting; outsiders were seen as barbarians and black snakes.

One day in 1835, somewhere on a tributary of the Yarra (the exact location is open to much conjecture), eight 'chiefs' reportedly signed a piece of paper. They included Bebejern, headman of the Wurundjeri and one of three to 'sign' against the name Jagajaga; Billibellary, Bebejern's brother, also 'signed' against Jagajaga. The paper was John Batman's 'deed to Melbourne' and he claimed to have got all the headmen to make their marks, which coincidentally all looked very much the same, their lines neat and contained. Perhaps he showed them the papers, these pieces of stiff skin more like paperbark or melaleuca with lots of other little marks already on, like tiny tracks.

The headmen didn't know Batman's language. They didn't use paper, or writing: they talked, knew, remembered. The Sydney Aborigines Batman brought with him very likely spoke more than one of the other two hundred and thirty or so Aboriginal languages in use at that time, but not the tongues of the south. Batman certainly didn't know them. It was a meet 'n' greet, a gift exchange—knives, mirrors and hankies for possum-skin cloaks and boomerangs.

John Batman was Sydney born and more recently resident in Van Diemen's Land, a Tasmanian flock-holder who crossed Bass Strait with the specific purpose of securing half a million acres of land in the Port Phillip area from the local people. He had a contract for them to sign and proposed to pay them with goods such as blankets, flour and axes. He reckoned everybody would be happy with this. The Aborigines would be; as a grazier he certainly was; and the British colony's government in Sydney would also, he 'confidently trusted', see this and think it rather good.

The exact terms were…

> Twenty Pairs of Blankets, Thirty Tomahawks, One Hundred Knives, Fifty Pairs Scissors, Thirty Looking-Glasses, Two Hundred Handkerchiefs, One Hundred Pounds of Flour, and

> Six Shirts,...for...about Five Hundred Thousand more or less Acres...to...John Batman, his Heirs and Assigns for ever.

The bonus was 'One Hundred Pairs of Blankets, One Hundred Knives, One Hundred Tomahawks, Fifty Suits of Clothing, Fifty Looking-Glasses, Fifty Pairs Scissors, and Five Tons Flour...as Yearly Rent or Tribute' to the 'real owners of the soil', as described in Batman's official report to Sydney.

Batman wrote in his journal what fine-looking men the chiefs were, interesting people; and how, after a full explanation of what he wanted, they had agreed. At the signing of the deed he got the Kulin to pour a handful of their soil into his hands to represent the ancient legal title to land 'with livery of Seisin endorsed', in which the contract is sealed by passing over something of the land itself. For example, if you were a feudal Englishman, an oak twig.*

Bebejern's son, Barak, was with them, eleven years old. He'd never seen a white man.

It's been reported that the first thing John Batman said when he got back to Van Diemen's Land and walked into a Launceston pub was, 'I am the greatest landowner in the world!' Certainly when writing to John Wedge, his surveyor, he crossed out his own name and signed himself 'Dutigalla'. After all, he had the paperwork: what became known as the deed to Melbourne was actually 'Grant of the Territory called Dutigalla', and he reckoned it made him lord of that vast piece of country. (The name Dutigalla was another picked up erroneously in the linguistic confusion.)

The *MAP of PART of NEW HOLLAND Showing the Territory of GEELONG and DUTIGALLA Acquired by Treaty with Native Chiefs, 6 June 1835* shows a double dotted line heading vaguely eastward from the site reserved for a township, labelled *Batman's River Supposed Course*. Batman's party had actually spent more time north-north-east and on the saltwater river, now the Maribyrnong.

---

* Using this as inspiration, about a century and a half later the Prime Minister of Australia, Gough Whitlam, poured a handful of sandy soil into the palms of Gurindji headman Vincent Lingiari at the first Aboriginal land hand-back, at Wattie Creek in the Northern Territory.

In Sydney, the colonial government refused to recognise Batman's deed on the grounds that they already owned the country anyway. In August 1835,

> His Excellence Major General Sir RICHARD BOURKE, KCB, Commanding His Majesty's Forces, Captain General and Governor in Chief of the Territory of New South Wales and its Dependencies, and Vice Admiral of the same &c. &c. &c. PROCLAIMED that divers of His Majesty's subjects have taken possession of vacant lands of the Crown...under the pretence of a treaty, bargain, or contract, for the purchase thereof, with the Aboriginal Natives [*and so on and so forth*] all persons who shall be found in possession of any such Lands...will be considered as trespassers, and liable to be dealt with in like manner as other intruders upon the vacant lands of the Crown...GOD SAVE THE KING!

This is actually the document that underpinned the doctrine of *terra nullius*—the fiction that the entire continent was a land with no owners until the Crown arrived—which was the legal basis for British occupation of Australia until the High Court overturned it in the Mabo case of 1992.

Batman was not, however, the first white man in the Port Phillip District. Back in 1803 the Surveyor-General of the Colony of New South Wales, Charles Grimes, and his party (including diarist James Flemming) sailed down from Sydney with the express purpose of seeing whether there was a site worth settling. London was worried about long-time enemy France claiming land in Westernport Bay, and decided the south coast of New South Wales* needed a new settlement for defence if nothing else.

After meeting up with a French scientific expedition led by Nicolas Baudin on the *Geographe* at King Island, Bass Strait, and

* The colony of Victoria was not proclaimed until 1851; until then, the area was known as the Port Phillip District of NSW.

passing on notice from Governor King officially warning the French off,* Grimes' party carried on up to Port Phillip Bay. They left their vessel anchored near the mouth of the river and proceeded by boat, exploring over several days, and in the process creating the first map of the Yarra River. They first rowed up the saltwater river (the Maribyrnong) a little way, then back down and up the freshwater river (the Yarra), which Flemming described in his diary as 'the Great River…a few miles up found it excellent water'. The ship's captain filled some of his casks there. They went as far as what is now Dights Falls, which was as far as they could get the boat, then ventured inland another half mile on foot before turning back. Flemming walked through part of what is now Studley Park.

The report to the Governor of New South Wales stated, 'the most eligible place for a settlement that I have seen is on the Freshwater River', and that was exactly where both Batman and Fawkner eventually turned up some decades later. But in 1803 the government that mattered, in London, didn't get Grimes' information until after they'd ordered settlement at Sorrento, much further down the Bay and closer to the Heads.

It was bad news all round: Sorrento failed, partly because of lack of water, after barely six months. Apart from William Buckley passing through during his thirty-year escape from penal servitude there, on his way to the Bellarine Peninsula, no white man lived in the Port Phillip District until 1835.

Batman went back to Van Diemen's Land after his treaty expedition, planning to return with the Port Phillip Association and settle his newly acquired lands. Before that happened, the schooner *Enterprize* arrived, also from Launceston, carrying a small group of people organised by John Pascoe Fawkner. They, too, initially went up the more easily navigable saltwater river, before taking high tide to pass over a mud bar and marking a channel up the freshwater river. And so began the enduring historical dispute as to who was

---

* 'Solemnly proclaimed by England, all these countries form an integral part of the British Empire' your activities had better not be 'any kind of invasion of British territory' etc. etc.

there first: which of the two parties, Batman's or Fawkner's, was the first to settle and therefore truly 'found' Melbourne.

Soon after the first settling parties arrived on the river, Barak's father, Bebejern, one of those signatories of Batman's treaty, died. He was buried near the Yarra and its confluence with the Merri Creek.

It was John Wedge, Batman's private surveyor, who named the Yarra Yarra. In September 1835 he was at the Turning Basin with some Kulin and heard them identify the river as it came over the Falls as, he wrote, 'Yarrow Yarrow'.* It was only some months later that Wedge discovered they had been referring to the pattern and movement of water over the Falls, not the river itself. Hugh McCrae, in annotations to the diary of his grandmother Georgiana McCrae, translates *yarra yarra* as 'flowing flowing', giving also examples of *yarrain* meaning 'tide rolling up on the beach' and *yarragondook* being 'the beard'. *Yarrabing* has also been recorded as the word for 'white gum', and *yarraga* for 'swim'.

The Anglified word Birrarung now used as an approximation of the Kulin name has also in the past been noted as Berrern, Barrern, Barraring, Burerring, Bayrayrung, *brrering* (as the general Kulin word for river) and Boorearn. Spelling out the sounds of an unknown language without an alphabet—and one that is pronounced differently, with its own multiple variations—is an interesting exercise for anyone. A suggestion is that it was said *Brahrang* and therefore falls closest in contemporary location names to Prahran ('p' and 'b' tending to be interchangeable in Aboriginal languages; 'ng' becoming 'n' in common usage). In the early days Prahran was apparently also spelt and sounded 'Purraran', the Kulin name for a specific location on the river.

Over the decades and centuries varied opinions have been given as to the original name of the river. One is that there was no single name, but that each location on it was named individually: for

* As surveyors, both Wedge and later Hoddle did use original Kulin names, Hoddle being instructed to do so by his superior in Sydney.

example, the *Dictionary of Aboriginal Place Names of Victoria* lists Ngindabil, Nurtpubbellekoorun, Wongete, Tichunggorruc and Warringal, of which only the last has survived.

Parallel realities don't always stick. Virtually nothing Batman himself named is still called the same.

One of Batman's Sydney Aborigines (Gilg-bang from Shoalhaven) was found dead, drunk, in the Yarra Yarra in March 1839. The body was pulled out of the water by surveyor Robert Russell. Batman himself died alone in May of that year. A few years later the only child of his born in Melbourne drowned at the Falls. The boy had slipped, fallen, hit his head on the rocks and been swept away.* He was Batman's only son, the only child to carry his name. Next morning, Benbow, a Kulin elder, dived in the Yarra to recover the little body.

The low Falls rockily crossed the river where Queen Street Bridge is now, stopping seawater going any further. Below was a natural pool or widening of the tidal river, later named as a Turning Basin for ships and perfect for mooring. On the other side of the Falls, upstream, was continual fresh water for drinking, at least in low tide. The combination of saltwater access and freshwater supply at this juncture, with higher land on the north side, made it the logical place for all to stake claims and notions of settlement and territory: Grimes' 'most eligible place for a settlement', Batman's 'This will be the place for a village', Fawkner's getting on and doing just that. It's because of the Yarra River that the city of Melbourne has to be precisely where it is, and eventually even the colonial government realised it.

In 1836 Captain William Lonsdale brought government from Sydney to Port Phillip. Official surveyors also arrived, and their convict work gang who were used lugging stores and baggage up from the beach at Point Gellibrand (Williamstown), where Lonsdale

* The reason for the boy's death, as recalled seventy years later, was that he'd overbalanced while drowning puppies or kittens. The more orthodox version is that he was fishing.

had decided the official settlement would be. A week or two later he realised the town actually needed to be on the Yarra Yarra River, since humans could not survive without a constant supply of fresh water; so he switched the official site of the settlement to where most of the settlers already were. More lugging for the lags, this time from the beach directly opposite Point Gellibrand, Sandridge (later Port Melbourne), overland to the settlement, a journey judged quicker and certainly closer than taking a boat up a heavily rain-freshed river.

After bringing Lonsdale from Sydney, William Hobson, the captain of HMS *Rattlesnake*, charted the way into the river from Port Phillip Bay. From the open water to the point where the Saltwater and Freshwater rivers joined, the river was then known as Hobsons River. The little curve Port Phillip Bay makes into Point Gellibrand, its northernmost part, where the river flows in, is still called Hobsons Bay. It was gazetted in March 1837 at the same time as William's Town and Melbourne.

The government had sent a survey team, comprising Assistant Surveyors Robert Russell, Frederick D'Arcy and William Darke, but

'Melbourne from the Yarra' by George Henry Haydon, 1841. When the artist returned to London from Melbourne in 1845, aged 22, he is said to have taken with him water from the Yarra to christen any future offspring.

they didn't seem to get much done. When Governor Bourke arrived in March 1837 on the 'Rattler', he brought Robert Hoddle with him to take over as Surveyor in Charge. Hoddle noted later,

> It was truly amusing to hear of the panic caused among the assistant surveyors by the unexpected appearance of the Governor; as these gentlemen had principally been amusing themselves kangarooing, and one produced some excellent caricatures of their flight into the bush, seemingly employed at their duty.

Hoddle did have trouble with staff—Charles La Trobe remarked in his 1839 diary how severe Hoddle was with his aides. Some years earlier, in Sydney, Hoddle described, 'The arduous and laborious life of a Surveyor in this Colony; who in the discharge of the duties of his Profession, must sacrifice, almost every comfort of civilized life' and his maxim in preparation for Port Phillip was, 'Surveyors and soldiers should always be ready to march.'

It was a long way from Robert Russell's earlier incarnation as a young architect employed under John Nash, the King's Architect, on the renovation of Buckingham Palace.

Hoddle's superior, the Governor, seemed able to whip through the laying out of Melbourne with him quite quickly in March 1837. Bourke recorded,

> Disembarked and proceeded by water to the Settlement (as it is now called) by the Salt Water River and the Yarre Yarre which receives the tide as a low fall near to where the first Settlers Huts were placed. In the afternoon rode over the ground adjacent to the Huts with Surveyor Hoddle, and traced the general outline of a Township upon a beautiful and convenient site. It does not, however, promise to afford water, which must be provided (at first at least) entirely from the River. A good Dam will require to be constructed here to keep up the fresh water and effect its entire Separation from the Salt.

The water, the river, the town: the grid of Melbourne was lined up with the river, its fulcrum in many senses (Turning Basin and Falls, fresh water and salt). The ideal city planned by Surveyor Hoddle and Governor Bourke was bounded south by river and billabong, west by hill then swamp, north by burial ground, all laid on a standard city grid drawn earlier by the artistic Russell and ink-blotched later by some anonymous government clerk. Russell placed his grid parallel to the river but—as Grimes, Batman, Fawkner and Lonsdale had already realised—where else was it going to be?

And the water? Hoddle stated, 'Water is excellent in the River Yarra Yarra.' The Governor 'proceeded early on a ride up the bank of the Yarra'. He went as far as Plenty Creek, and opined,

> The Yarra continues a fine full stream of clear water in places bubbling over ledges of rock, at others forming fine deep reaches...It is perhaps the finest river I have seen in New South Wales...The Yarra abounds in fine fish and the water is of very good quality.

Hoddle had business in Sydney for a few months, during which Russell and Darke were supposed to survey the Yarra Yarra River. By the time he got back, each of them had completed about seven miles. Hoddle's annotations on a report of Robert Russell's to the Surveyor General include comments such as 'about five miles not fit to be received', and, 'from March 1836 to May 1837 13 miles of creek surveyed, miles of promises'. In July Hoddle described how,

> In three weeks [Darke] surveyed 18 miles of the Yarra Yarra River. During that period I surveyed about 60 miles, including sections of land...to the amount of 15,000 acres ready for sale. I am going to proceed myself with the Yarra Yarra River, which appears to be a very important river, and contains excellent water, not generally the case, the water being of Chalybeate quality [*flavoured with iron*]...I am on the eve of tracing that river. I shall be able to tell...more about the country in two or three months, if the weather will permit, and no mishaps.

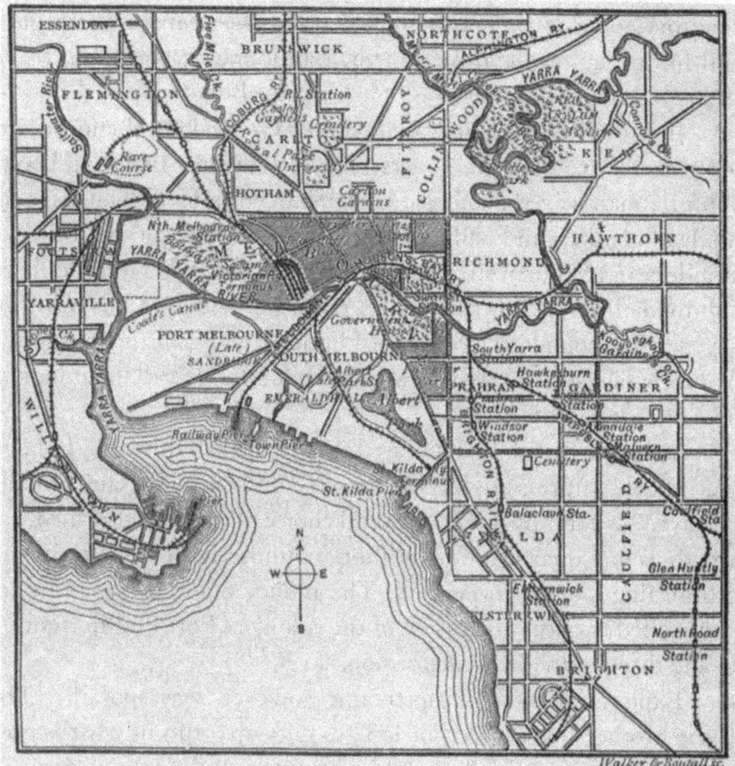

Greater Melbourne, 1886. The section of the river designated 'Yarra Yarra' here has been filled in. 'Coode's Canal' is now known as the Yarra River and the lowest section of the present Maribyrnong River was actually originally the Yarra. See also 'Connor's Creek' upper right. You won't see it anywhere else, as it is now an underground drain—a good example of the waterway/tip/drain/ progression (see pages 90–1).

Hoddle did take over, and by the end of the year Russell had been recalled, and D'Arcy had left as well, the situation between all protagonists quite ill-natured.

Surveying was not just about describing territory but claiming it: taking the land, possessing it. The priority was cutting up real estate as fast as possible. The point of exploring was not the wonder of going into the unknown, but the business imperative of ascertaining territory and assessing economic usefulness—access to water, good soil for agriculture and settlement. Land, once it was 'found' and measured, could be sold.

In June 1837, Hoddle was appointed Crown land auctioneer (on a 1.5 percent commission) overseeing Melbourne's first land boom. John Batman waved goodbye to his dream of half a million acres for a pile of blankets and half a dozen Pelaco.* He bought the corner of Flinders and William streets, the very block (although it's since been subdivided) on which this book's publishers now do business, for seventy-five pounds, the corner of Flinders and Swanston streets (the Young & Jackson's site) for a hundred pounds. He got about half an acre in each of his eight lots.

Since the British had declared they owned all this land, London was hugely impressed with the massive returns on its sale. Hoddle parlayed his commission into several choice blocks, one of which was worth some quarter of a million pounds upon his death—an astonishing sum in those days. The money made from land sales bankrolled the administration of the colony at Port Phillip right up to and through the 1840s depression.

Exploration further upstream, however, was sporadic. The Ryrie brothers overlanded in 1837 to take up a run in what is now known as the Yarra Valley, and became part of the squattocracy. In February 1838 Hoddle travelled up that way; through the roos at the Kangaroo Ground and along the ridge down to what he called Billanook, commenting on what a fine piece of country it was, about 30,000 acres of good land, good soil but scarce of water.

Supposedly the beginning of the expedition to find the source of the Yarra, the trip lasted about as long as a weekend at the Ryries'. The government as developer was calling, and Hoddle had to get back for the more urgent task of cutting up land for sale. He had been told to skip marking sections sixty miles up the river, and get on

---

* In the twentieth century, Pelaco was a well-known brand of shirts manufactured in Melbourne. Richmond Football Club acquired the legendary full forward Royce Hart from his Tasmanian club in 1965 for 'a new suit and half a dozen Pelacos'.

with the nitty-gritty of subdivision. The only parts not thought particularly good to sell were flood-prone, and sometimes even they were tried.

Thomas Nutt, who arrived from Sydney in 1838 to join Hoddle's team as a draughtsman in the field, did a big survey of the Yarra in 1839, going upriver 112 miles, passing Ryries' Station (Yering). He was less than fifty miles from Melbourne as the crow flies (a popular Surveyor-in-Charge phrase), the river curved and looped so much. Nutt was already noting, 'The mountains past Mr Ryrie's are next to impassable, and I understand farther up they are so much worse.' He'd initially been ordered to survey the Yarra to its source. However,

> The banks are covered with almost impenetrable scrub, the ranges are very steep and thickly timbered, and the roads are very bad...when I get fifty or sixty miles further up...it will not be safe for me to leave less than two men at a time with the dray in an uninhabited part of the country where no European has ever been, and of course not knowing what tribe of Natives inhabit that part of the country.

There was another false start in 1842 when Mr Darke was ordered to survey the Yarra Yarra River up to its source, after working in the Yarra Ranges.

Hoddle, meanwhile, was laying out other settlements, busily subdividing (St Kilda 1842, Sandridge/Port Melbourne 1839), working round town and in the country, and signing off a large number of surveys. His return to Survey to the Source of the Yarra Yarra did not come until late 1844.

~ ~ ~

> Sky country, Tharangalk-bek, manna-gum country, up there is where Bunjil went in a whirlwind with all his people, on the other side of the sky. There are trees up there, too. And Bunjil the great one, old headman, eaglehawk, looking down on us, Kulin/men all. He has two wives himself: Ganwarra, black swans. Bunjil, he made the first men, took clay from the riverbank, made them, put his breath into their nose, mouth, bellybutton. His brother, Pallina, always everything of water, brought women up from the creek to be their wives: first the hands came up from the mud, then the heads, the bosoms. Bunjil's son, Binbeal, the rainbow, his son's wife is the second rainbow you sometimes see. Bunjil, he made the earth, trees, men. Bunjil is wisdom, knowledge. In the sky land, you see him, he's the star Altair, Aquila, Eagle. And he sees you.

Barak, an eleven-year-old boy at Batman's treaty signing, knew the beginning of the Yarra Yarra, and told the story.*

> Playing in the bush, a boy climbed an old wattletree looking for some gum. He threw the lumps he found down to his mate, but they kept disappearing. The boy below poked around in a hole there with his toy spear. Then a growl came, shaking the earth. An old man had been asleep underground, his mouth hanging open. He angrily snatched up the scared boy and made off with him. The boy was a dead weight, and the man was so old he could could do no more than shuffle as he carried this heaviness; deeper his feet scuffed into the dirt,

* Barak's stories were not notated in his voice, but that of the nineteenth-century man transcribing them (A.W. Howitt, the man who led expeditions to rescue Burke and Wills in 1861 and corroborated some of the giant tree measurements given later on). The stories here have been retold.

Barak, Wurundjeri headman, tells their story.

> deeper like a mark, deeper like a rough crack, like a creek, like a river, Birrarung, Yarra Yarra River. The little boy cried so much that Bunjil eventually heard. He put stones down to trip the old man, and cut his feet so he dropped the boy, who ran off home. Before the old man died Bunjil told him this was a lesson for all old men: be good to little children.

Barak also knew the story of the sun and the moon:

> The flat earth was dark until one of the old spirits made the Sun. She, the Sun—sister of everyone—goes round by the sea, Bass Strait, Port Phillip, every night and comes back each morning the other side. She goes down into that bushfire-burnt tree-hole in sky country.

> The Moon was a man, once, too, friend of Sun. One night when they were travelling, there was a river they couldn't cross. Moon, that slow thing, he slept. But Sun found a fallen tree and crossed over. Next morning Moon saw her and tried to follow but the tree broke. The Moon, he's been following her—Sun—ever since.

In December 1844, Hoddle set out on the expedition to discover the source of the river, writing:*

> I have a rough journey before me and have made but little progress with the Survey of the Yarra Yarra my party have to cut through a dense scrub as sharp as needles and wade through swamps. I ought to have had ten men at least for such an undertaking I shall do the best I can with the means I have it is hard work to get a mile a day the men having to cut their way every inch. I have ascended a large mountain and the course of the Yarra Yarra appears to be North East...The river rose one night and washed me and my party out of the Tents, were obliged to ascend the high ground deluged with rain...Unless I get on better than at present I shall come to Melbourne at the end of next month.

Barak said once that before the white people arrived, the Wurundjeri heard about where the sky rests on the mountains in the Great Divide. (It was a widespread story. The Wathawurrung talked about it too, to William Buckley.) The poles there holding up the sky were rotting. Tomahawks would have to be sent straight away to cut new ones, otherwise the sky would fall, and burst. Everyone would drown.

---

* A microfilm copy of Hoddle's *Survey Office Letter Book Vol II 1843–1849* is in the La Trobe Library. The content of most letters is repeated in a second letter with occasional slight variations (one letter to the Office of the Surveyor-General in Sydney; the other to the Superintendent of the Port Phillip District, Charles La Trobe). The transcription here is a melding and eliding of the two, with notes also from the fieldbook of *1844 November to April 1845 Survey of the Yarra Yarra River towards its source by Robert Hoddle Surveyor*, held by the Office of the Surveyor General of Victoria. Hoddle did keep a personal diary or journal, but unfortunately the volumes relating to this period are missing.

Barak also said, dictating, 'Buckly say bring all the stone tomahoke and give it to Mr Bateman that stone-tomehoke go to England.'

In 1844 Barak joined the Native Police Corps. The uniform was impressive and highly valued; rations were the same as surveyors'. He went on various expeditions over the decades coming out of his policing career: in search of the Kelly Gang, far west with the Chief Protector of Aborigines; and in the Corps, manning Pentridge Stockade.

Hoddle wrote on New Year's Eve 1844,

> I beg leave to inform that my party is too small (7 persons) for the ~~purpose~~ arduous duty I am now engaged in…I left four chain men cutting their way through the scrub ready to chain on my return…I need not say much upon the importance of being made acquainted with the character of this part of the country, but even should no good country be found at the head of the Yarra Yarra its geographical features will form prominent objects in this District, a mountain near my last encampment being 2,786 feet above the level of the banks of the Yarra and the River as wide as at Melbourne…The summer is the only season that operations in the field can be carried on—as the swampy flats after rain are impassable. The dense scrubs are equally thick below & on the Ranges. I came to Melbourne for Assistance and supplies and return back immediately.

Coincidentally he was home for Christmas while his men were stuck in the scrub.

February 1845: 'Camp on yarra yarra…I have the honor to report the progress of the continuation of the Survey of this Australian River from which I date my letter, which bears nearly N 70°E. 30 miles from Mr Ryries Station and distant about 18 miles from Stewart's Cattle Station[*] as the crow flies.'

---

* Stewart's Cattle Station, later Steel's Flat, was 10,000 acres on Woori Yallock and Wandin Yallock creeks, overlooking the Yarra, taken up in October 1840 and running 500 head of cattle.

One of the two people he was reporting to, Charles La Trobe, had visited Ryries himself in 1839. He had gone kangaroo hunting there and made some fine sketches of this beautiful spot. Rolf Boldrewood, author of *Robbery Under Arms*, after visiting in the 1840s, described it as,

> A veritable oasis in this unredeemed stringy-bark desert... The cottage...was built upon a slight elevation overlooking a deep-grassed meadow, below which the Yarra, not much less wide and rapid than near Melbourne, ran its winding course. On the further side of the river, looking eastward, was a purple-shadowed mountain, apparently, though not in reality, overhanging the stream. In the dimmer distance rose the vast snow-summitted range of the Australian Alps. We walked about after our afternoon meal, admiring...the comfortable appearance of things generally.

Hoddle's progress, meanwhile, was 'tediously slow'.

> At my commencement last November, I was retarded by the moist state of the ground, having frequently to dig my dray out...In December the weather becoming settled and fine and occasionally sultry hot, I commence to cut through the scrub, using three pack Bullocks, and one pack horse to convey the Baggage and provisions, small as the number of animals are I have had great difficulty to keep them alive, being frequently obliged to employ three of my men to cut sufficient coarse grass which grows on the margin of the River banks, and occasionally to send the pack bullocks back to pasture near the Station.
>
> My progress rarely exceeds half a mile per day, and I am now within eight miles of the Dividing Range (as the Crow flies). The River here is about forty feet wide and runs rapidly.
>
> The scrub is principally willow, tea tree, prickly shrub, vines, sapling pines, and frequently boggy underground.
>
> The Trees are Gum, Box, Stringy Bark, and occasionally Iron Bark, Black Wattle and Silver Wattle, Honeysuckle.

> In portions of the Country the soil is good, but very heavily timbered.
>
> ...slate was found, also, White & Yellow Ochre...
>
> I propose returning with my party at the latter end of April as the agreements with the free men expire at that period, and the rations will be out. The men are in a ragged state.

Big one sulky. No wonder. These men were not travelling light like Wurundjeri. A surveyor with a work gang of seven convicts might be provisioned with '732 pounds Flour, 15¼ pounds tea, 96¼ pounds Sugar, 15¼ pounds Tobacco, 438 pounds Fresh Beef, 7¼ pounds Salt'. And the daily forage for a horse weighed in at over forty pounds.

Hard men, hard work, hard food. One surveyor's daily ration along with small amounts of tea, sugar, soap and tobacco, was '24 ounces Flour, 16 ounces Fresh or Salt Beef'. Hoddle's personal list in this fieldbook of 'Indispensables for a Journey with Pack Bullock or Pack Horses' ran:

> 1 Hammer. 2 Augur. 1 Hand Saw. Files. Felling Axes. Marking Axes. Tomahawks. Brush Hooks. Pack Saddles with extra Slinging Straps and Circingles. Each Horse Supplied with Tethers. Rope and Hobbles. Havre Sacks. Double Barrelled Gun. Brace of Holster Pistols. Gun Powder, Percussion Caps, Shot, Ball Cartridges.
>
> Pens. Indian ink. Parallel Ruler. Drawing & writing Paper. Ink. Wafers. Pen Knife. Pencils. Hone. Strap. Razor. Comb. Toothbrush. Soap. Protractor. Circumferentor or Theodolite. Katers Compass. Chain. Field Books. Form of Monthly Report of Progress. Thermometer. Barometer.
>
> Cloak, Opossum Rugs. Carpet bag to contain change of Linen.
>
> Tea. Sugar. Bacon. Flour. Salt meat. Salt. Pepper. 1 Bottle Vinegar, Brandy. Salts. Castor oil. Sticking Plaster.
>
> New Testament. Prayer Book. Chambers Information for the People. Outlines of Geology. Practical Mathematics...(Hutton)...Mineralogy.

On the Survey, three men would be employed 'transporting Baggage and Provision' and four cutting a way for the party through the scrub. 'The Scrubcutters, to facilitate their labours, fired the bush, which renders their appearance very similar to a party of Colliers or Sweeps,' commented their leader. The black-face scrubcutters were doing what the Wurundjeri before them had done for generations throughout the Yarra Valley: clearing the country and opening it up, making way, promoting pasture regrowth and smoking out wildlife by burning off.*

Barak's country was the Yarra's watershed, his birthplace—by relation to Yarra water—Brushy Creek, which joins the Yarra at what is now Wonga Park.

By the early 1840s Wurundjeri women had stopped having babies. Men were no longer being initiated. Barak himself wasn't fully initiated, though Billibellary ceremonially handed over certain traditional items to him at the mission on the old corroboree grounds downriver, near the Botanic Gardens site. Barak did get the body scarification, the lined tribal markings. 'I was a man,' he said, when asked by some white lady decades later about the pattern incised on his chest.

Hoddle wrote, in February 1845, 'The weather has been fine but hot. I have met with no Blacks but the hacking of the trees shew that one or two have passed a considerable period back.'

Some blacks were hooked on white bread.† Some were stuck on alcohol; many were dying miserably in town from syphilis, gonorrhoea, influenza, dysentery and typhus.

Some still camped at Ryries, along the billabongs. There were virtually no fences constraining them. They could hunt, fish, feed themselves, walk traditional routes. For them, as it became for the Ryries and their successors, the valley was a veritable paradise. There

---

* Firestick farming, as it is now described, was carried out with abandon by blacks and whites during early settlement of the colony. On his journey from the earlier Yarra reconnoitre in 1838 Hoddle had noted laconically, 'Returned from Billanook—the country on fire which renders travelling through burnt scrub disagreeable.'

† The eternal desire for the foods of the ruling culture, right down to *Heidi* and twentieth-century migrant children. But damn it can taste good.

were at least as many kangaroos as cattle and sheep, as well as fish, murnong, wild duck. People had no need to go up into the cold, wet, inaccessible ranges.

Sketches from the papers of William Thomas, Assistant Protector of Aboriginals for Port Phillip, Westernport and Gippsland 1839–49, show a panoramic view of the Valley, with its axis on 'Mr Ryrys House' and the Yarra Yarra River (as it curves two hundred degrees or so round the valley floor). Most of the locations named are labelled 'all gone dead', presumably referring to the original owners, but Mr Murry's country is shown at number one.

When Joseph Furphy, author of *Such is Life* and in 1843 the first white child born in the Yarra Valley, was a young boy at Ryries Station, he was treated by Dr Murray, aka Poen, a Wurundjeri healer and a brother of Bebejern, Barak's father. A Mr Murry was also a member of the Native Police Corps, along with Billibellary (actually Dr Murray's son); and it was a Kulin oral history, Murray's, that was quoted to a Select Committee in 1858 regarding the original course of the Yarra River along the Bay to its mouth at the Heads.

A James Murray was the first settler in Christmas Hills, locating down by the Yarra in 1840. Name swaps between English people and Kulin were made by Kulin as a gesture of friendship or respect. For example, Billibellary's cousin Murrem Murrem Bean was also known as Mr Hill, though it is not known whether the Mr Hill in question then went around referring to himself as Murrem Murrem Bean.

Down the river at what is now Lower Templestowe the Ruffeys had a station, on the creek that now bears their name. William Thomas wrote alongside his sketches,

> There can be no doubt from these names...taken from an old wandering black named Kurburra (alias Ruffy) how particular the Blacks are of giving names to every portion of Country. Even to the Ranges as correct (for their purpose) as Civilized Surveyors...every spot has its name.

Thomas stated much later in a government report, 'I have upwards of 200 names of mountains in the Australian Alps. Aborigines require neither latitude or longitude; plain nature by day and the stars by night.'

At the beginning of February 1845, Hoddle broke the glass of his surveying instrument, and from then on had to rely on his pocket compass. There was 'dense, thick scrub, high ferns and very large trees'. A week later he was at Starvation Creek, which was running rapidly. Further on was a 'black fellows Tree stringy bark barked ab. 3 years back'.

By the beginning of March, he'd passed 'lagoon flat... falls...high Ranges...Steep Range...Aboriginal black old encampment...Yarra Walpole's'. He was at Walshs Creek, that junction now submerged under the Upper Yarra Dam. By the 16th of March, 'The country very mountainous and scrubby. Pack animals nearly starved.' On the 19th the 'Water could be jumped over pebbles in the bed of the River'. He was nearing the end and drew 'High Range springs springs [*sic*] Blacks track'.

On the 28th of March the four scrubcutters took five hours to cut three-quarters of a mile. They'd been cutting scrub and getting

wet for a long time—now they were running out of food in the middle of nowhere.

> One weeks Ration left for myself and 6 men, at the foot of the Main Range which I am dubious of being able to ascend to complete my Survey of the Source of the Yarra, which would have been accomplished, had the men behaved with common prudence…upon my remonstrating against his consuming the Ration, 3 days before due, said he had not had his belly full for a long time past.

In drizzling rain on the 31st of March, with high ranges on both sides, Hoddle finished for the day after marking a 'branch of Yarra' with 'steep deep Waterfall' (which became known later as Yarra Falls). They were heading through 'heavily timbered and dense scrub'. There were wild oats (poa), kangaroo grass, fern trees, a 'white gum 48 feet in circumference…Sassefras, myrtle, and Dog wood scrub…remarkable large Gums 18 feet diameter'.

April Fool's Day passed and by now Hoddle was drawing the river as a single line accompanied by commentary: 'Bed of River

Mr Ryrie's House, now Yering Station, the centre point of Yarra Valley settlement. In Woiwurrung mapping (by memory, verbally) 'every spot has its name'. Tarrawarra is still familiar but sadly not whoever—or whatever—was 'all gone dead'.

10 feet rocks steep banks 2 feet of water in width'; and heading for 'Dead Trees Sapling Gums and Stringy bark upon Main Range.'

Finally: 'Deep gully deep gully 3 miles Main Range Head of Yarra River 3rd April terminated Survey'. The 'deep gully deep gully' are the headstreams of the Yarra Yarra River.

And at any rate, that was as far as the rations would take them. In the back of his fieldbook Hoddle has plenty to say about the trouble with rations. 'The man formerly a Convict upon being remonstrated with by consuming the Rations 3 days before due, said he would have Grub, whatever he could get.' Hoddle encamped in the Main Range for two days, where:

> it rained incessantly...On my return on 3rd Inst Beresford expressed his surprise at my return, and I told him, the cause was the men had eaten up the Rations—I never heard of such a thing was his reply, although I discovered he had abstracted 10 lb of Flour during my absence.

Hoddle told another of the men who had taken rations, 'If all have acted upon the same principle I should have starved.'

As soon as the survey was terminated, the trek back began as fast as they could go, four of the men sent on ahead with more rations than deserved. By the 9th of April Hoddle was 'encamped within 4½ miles of Stewarts Station...our old acquaintances Musquitoes and Leeches were distressingly busy'. It wasn't until the 16th of April that Hoddle was back at Ryries and able to obtain supplies—'Viz. 200 lbs flour. 126 Beef'. He reported later,

> I was under the necessity of returning from the survey of the Yarra Yarra, sooner than I intended, through misconduct of certain men of my party, consuming three weeks rations in a fortnight, and in our hasty retreat were obliged to leave several tools behind in the scrub.
>
> I therefore beg your Honor will approve of the extra rations, and the tools being charged to the men concerned.
>
> ...The river was full of rapids and in many places deep at

the commencement of the Survey at Stewart's Cattle Station the river was about 130 feet wide and near the Source the bed about ten feet containing but little water which was supplied by springs. The Tributaries were measured several over 20 feet wide running rapidly. I was obliged to erect two temporary bridges and to cut through a dense scrub for fifty miles and at its termination in the dividing range the scrub was equally thick and the timber both dead and alive was a constant cause of impediment the progress of the survey was continually slow.

...Black Wattle, Silver Wattle, tea tree, myrtle, musk tree, Sassefras, a tree which produces a pungent feed: resembling black Pepper, another tree like the coffee seed. The scrub is prickly willow, tea tree, tendrils, & vine creepers, and fern tree, many of them twenty feet high, the white gum* grows to an enormous size, many of them fifty feet in circumference upon the Dividing Range...

I lost one pack Bullock which received an injury and as I had only this...was a serious loss. I had a pack horse which caused me much trouble by constantly bogging...otherwise with the pack Bullocks who prefer some soft ground without difficulty.

I experienced much labour and was obliged to perform my journey on foot, the men had to carry their provisions and to dispense the luxury of a Tent at the latter part of the Survey.

I hope the Survey will meet with your approval upwards of 1300 bearings were taken on the track alone...Bearing and distance from Batman's Hill to Stewart's Cattle Station N72°15' 30¼ miles from do. to head of Yarra Yarra N80° E 40 miles the distance completed as a Bird flies.

...I succeeded in surveying to the Sources of that River...

---

* The white gum, the manna, grows along the waterways of the Yarra catchment. Wurundjeri were so-named the white gum, the *wurun* people.

The survey of the source of the Yarra didn't kill Hoddle: he lived another thirty-six years, until 1881. However it is perhaps not surprising that his fine 'country' house in Richmond (later to become Bethesda Hospital) was named after a different river: not Yarra Yarra but Millewa, the Murray.

~ ~ ~

Almost fifty years later, in 1891, there were still really only two ways into the 'wild, weird territory at the head of the Yarra Yarra' (as the area was described at the time). An excursion of the Field Naturalists Club of Victoria chose the back route of Marysville–Woods Point Road, part of the old goldminers' Yarra Track, continuing south down the Tanjil Track to walk in from above, or east.

The Tanjil Track ran roughly along the ridge separating the Thompson River watershed in the east from the Yarra watershed in the west. Rain falling on one side of the ridge ended up in the Gippsland lakes, on the east coast of Victoria; on the other side it rolled away to the Yarra River and Melbourne. The six men walking in were headed not for the nearby source of the river, but for one of its most spectacular and hidden sights: Yarra Falls, on one of the headwater creeks, that same 'large Water Fall' Hoddle had marked reaching the end of his expedition to the source of the Yarra Yarra.

In drenching rain, attacked by leeches, unable to proceed because of fallen timber, two—Dudley Best and James Searle—turned back. Their four companions continued and later cut down scrub to clear space for their tent. Torrential rain and a sea of mud kept them pinned there for several days. Hoddle would have found it familiar. It was November, the month in which he'd written, 'Wet to the skin from a violent thunderstorm, annoyed by leeches and musquitoes...confined to my tent.'

Eventually the weather lifted and the Field Naturalists went on, until, finally,

> ...before us there lie five more miles to the Falls, with only blazes to guide us. On the ridge we find ourselves in a forest of white gums. After a long, gradual ascent, during which it was rather difficult to follow the blazes, owing to the scrub and the heavy timber having fallen across the line, we pass

> down a steep descent...and cross the first tributary of the Yarra. Then comes a steep hillside covered with silver wattle, on which the track is difficult to follow, and a gradual descent through a wood with many sassafras trees to the small second tributary of the Yarra. For the most part scrub is absent and progress is only difficult and tiring on account of the ferns. Another ridge is crossed in a slanting direction, and then we come to the third and largest tributary, which is already a considerable-sized stream, though, doubtless, at the present time, swollen out by the recent heavy rains...The Falls lie some distance down the stream, and those of us with cameras hurry on to make the most of our time.

Baldwin Spencer, Melbourne University professor, later National Museum of Victoria director, and Charles Frost are the two with cameras—heavy wooden, metal and glass contraptions with equally heavy plates. George Lyell, who was behind, recalled later how they travelled by compass, blazing trees with their own tomahawks so they could get back out. He tells of Spencer and Frost climbing down over 600 feet from the top of the falls, where the noise of the white water was so loud they had to shout to be heard.

> ...We keep not far from the stream, which is bordered by a fringe of ferns and scrub, and in part tumbles along noisily over rocks. In the scrub the Lyre Birds are numerous, some playing on their mounds, but we are too anxious to make the Falls, which we can hear in the distance, to delay long to watch them...After two miles we find ourselves suddenly at the head of a deep gorge, cut out amongst the mountains and gradually broadening out in shape like the letter V from the point at which we stand. The descent beneath our feet, at the apex of the gorge, goes down abruptly for at least 1000 feet, with great granite rock masses projecting everywhere. Down this the water disappears in a series of great leaps. The scene is a fine one. Just as it comes to the edge of the gorge the stream is divided into two by a great block of granite. At the

> bottom of the first fall the two streams unite into a single one, which at once throws itself down in a white spray for at least 150 feet; then comes a series of small leaps, then another larger one, and so on until the bottom of the gorge is reached. From where we stand we can see the first few falls and hear the roaring of the water as it plunges from ledge to ledge, but cannot see the bottom of the gorge by reason of the dense vegetation clothing the mountain sides. Away in the distance the gorge opens out until it joins the main valley of the Yarra, hemmed in by range after range of hills—purple, blue, and grey, as they gradually fade away towards the horizon.
>
> It is no easy matter to clamber with our cameras down the almost precipitous side of the gorge close to the waterfall; both hands are really needed to hold on to the rocks and trees during the descent. It is quite impossible also to get anything like a comprehensive view of the falls without getting some distance away on to one of the far hillsides and cutting down a few trees and plenty of scrub. Two or three times we try to fix our cameras on projecting rock ledges, but the spray drenches ourselves and the cameras in half a minute, and we are forced to beat a retreat. At best any view we can get in the very limited time at our disposal can only give some idea of perhaps one of the many leaps which altogether make up the Yarra Falls, and can give no idea whatever of the grandeur of their surroundings...We cannot reach the bottom.

They made it back to their camp on the track, and their man, Kirby, at 4 a.m. They had taken the first ever photographs of Yarra Falls, the largest waterfall in the State of Victoria.*

~

---

* James Searle, one of the two who turned back, later became a city naturalist recording wildlife found in his Collins Street office: flies, mosquitoes, clothes moths, wasps, beetles, wood lice, butterflies and a Bogong moth.

The picture-perfect magazine version of the headwaters of the river, 1886. In reality much more 'wild and weird'.

A local guidebook relates a description of the Falls as a black hole only a handful of intrepid goldminers, bushmen and surveyors had ever entered. The density of the bush, the same impenetrable jungle Robert Hoddle had battled against, stopped anyone going in there. You could hear or smell but not see: you could not get near.

Mountain ash forest ground is covered in obstacles, literally tonnes of them.* Bark, say one and a half tonnes of it every year, fallen timber, branches, crowns, whole trees up to a hundred metres long—all of this chunked up thickly, with rot, lichen, moss, understorey myrtle, sassafras, silver wattle and other trees and plants compounding the chaos.

How typical of the Yarra, of Melbourne, that some of the greatest treasures and charms are practically hidden. And the Falls themselves are emblematic of the river in that they can't be taken in all at once; they have bends and diversions, and though they're there, not many people know much about them.

In the pre-motorcar era long bushwalks were a touristic pursuit. The young engineer John Monash, who was destined to spend many important periods of his life near the river, did several annual walks passing through the Upper Yarra region in the 1880s.

By the early twentieth century, Hoddle's route had developed into a very popular hiking track with Yarra Falls as its dramatic destination. From Walshs Creek—McVeighs Hotel to be precise—a bridle and walking track followed the river right up to and over the Tanjil Track to Baw Baw and Walhalla, coming at the Falls from the opposite direction to the Field Naturalists, downstream rather than upstream. There were stables for packhorses, huts with stretchers, spring mattresses and cooking facilities, guides, tourist maps, English trout in the water and signs indicating Views.

A 1928 bestseller offered the opinion that 'there is only one way of getting off the beaten track—take a swag. Victoria is full of possibilities for the walker willing to "waltz Matilda",' and went on to describe the track.

> For 16 miles it is a sidling pad winding just above and always within sight, or at least sound, of the Yarra, here a babbling stream running at the foot of a steadily deepening valley... The slopes above the river look primeval and untrodden...

---

* Eight new tonnes per year per hectare; maybe up to 550 tonnes in total per hectare of old growth forest: the largest amount per area of forest in the world, as David Lindenmayer has recorded.

> Some groves of beech through which the track winds, suggest a stage setting of Fairyland in their still beauty. The variety is endless, now a group of giant gums, now beech or wattle groves, now a young forest, here a marshy spot, there a sparkling stream with its sands aglitter with new chum gold.

Another guide described the journey as 'two days of river scenery' (to McVeighs), 'then three days of mountaineering the reaches and bends of the river, tumbling and foaming in its rapids...as pure a stream as ever mirrored the smiling face of nature...gloriously outlined with its fringes of golden wattle'. And of the Falls,

> Although these Yarra cataracts are clumped so close together, it takes some hours, and a fair amount of stiff climbing, even with all the conveniences that a clear track affords, to see them in detail...The beeches—old, gnarled, spreading, in something of the habit of English oaks—are thickly festooned on bole and branch with green moss. Underneath is a band of mimosa, below this a layer of fern fronds. Though dense, the forest is not dark, for through the light leafage of the beech and mimosa the sunlight sprinkles down upon the ferns. Towering over all, at intervals, is a giant mountain gum, the height of which is almost insensibly realised, on noting that the beech, with all its grandeur, is dwarfed by comparison into mere scrub.

Baldwin Spencer had also been greatly taken by the beech forests.

The Black Friday bushfires of 1939 burnt out nearly all the Great Dividing Range in Victoria. Construction of the Upper Yarra dam, which began in the 1940s, didn't destroy the Falls but did close the area for water catchment. The site of McVeighs, at the junction of Walshs Creek with the Yarra, is at the bottom of that dam. What the fires didn't take, water claimed.

~ ~ ~

The tracks are gone, the huts gone, the old maps a historical curiosity. It is illegal to enter the country, now locked up as part of our precious water catchments. Regrowth, scrub and fallen timber are dense. Around the head streams of the Yarra, around the Falls, the area seems as inaccessible to us as to Hoddle and the Field Naturalists, though the trees and plants are not the same. (Unlike the old eastern suburbs of Melbourne, where specific trees plotted by Hoddle now stand in green and manicured golf courses next to the river.)

Finally, the territory is for the water itself.

Melbourne is crowned with more than 140,000 hectares of forest set aside for water catchment, and that's where ninety percent of its supply comes from, some of the most beautiful water in the world. Most of the catchment areas are closed, and the remaining third is designated as State Forest—the inaccessibility is the most important factor in safe drinking water. There are less than half a dozen cities on earth with a comparable system. Most of the others have catchments that aren't protected, and therefore require a large amount of chemical treatment.* Only ten percent of Melbourne's water needs to be fully treated, it's generally so clean it doesn't need extra filtering.

Some of the catchment areas have been locked up for over a century and around half are mountain ash forest; they provide about eighty percent of the water. It's the areas with the tallest, oldest trees that yield the most water, and not just because they're better at 'cloud catching' or harvesting mist drip. Younger trees need more water to grow, and the ground beneath them absorbs more. Bushfire or logging can cut the volume of water by half. It can take up to 150 years to get back to the optimum forest.

The mountain ash is the Earth's tallest flowering plant, and its

* Consequences include the continued trend to the Coca-Colonisation of water as bottled product, that particular company's fastest-growing line.

tallest hardwood tree. Baron von Mueller, one-time director of Melbourne's Botanic Gardens, later Government Botanist, was one of those in the 1860s and '70s who searched for the record mountain ash. Giants taller than any other tree in the world were claimed, many on the Yarra's watershed: in the Dandenongs, on the Blacks Spur (supposedly 480 feet or 146 metres high: taller than the tallest redwood or sequoia), at Fernshawe and, it was rumoured, near the head of the river—probably the same ones Hoddle saw.

In 1872, Anthony Trollope, English novelist, was hugely impressed to hear about a fallen tree on the Watts River measuring 435 feet (listed as the tallest tree ever in *Guinness World Records*). The Inspector of State Forests reported that the area averaged 100 to 150 trees per acre, from 250 to 300 feet in height, all straight as an arrow, and he fully believed the tree in question had originally reached up five hundred feet. Melbourne's 1888 Centennial International Exhibition displayed a fifteen-foot diameter hollow butt from Menzies Creek labelled, 'Species *Eucalyptus Amygdalina* var. *Regnans* (White Gum)...seventy-two feet in circumference...four hundred feet in height.'

The searchers for the tallest tree then found one on a spur of Baw Baw that was 326'1". On Mount Horsfall in the Upper Yarra a tree measured 92 feet around the base. At Mt Monda was a giant 307 feet high. On the Blacks Spur one measured 295 feet and 53 feet around the trunk. Giants were defined thus: a minimum of 40 feet (around twelve metres) at five feet (or 150 cm) from the ground and 250 feet (77 metres) in height.

These trees were taller than any structure in Australia at the time, maybe four or five times the height of Melbourne's city buildings. Unfortunately, the biggest were the ones the timber splitters went for first. The true giants were probably gone by the mid-nineteenth century, used for roof shingles.

Before the Yarra or any of its tributary catchments was dammed and closed, Melbourne's drinking water came directly from the river itself in the middle of town: Robert Hoddle's fieldbooks show half a dozen Watering Places and Pumps between Swanston and Elizabeth streets. Garryowen described the stuff as 'frequently unfit for man or beast. In hot weather it was likened to a compounded dose of lukewarm water and Glauber salts and though it was physic one would hardly throw to the dogs, the people of Melbourne had to swallow it'.

In high tides the freshwater upstream of the Falls became contaminated with the salt. A convict work gang in 1839 was directed to raise the height of the saltwater barrier by applying stone, mud and mortar but the result didn't last long. The attempt was repeated in 1842, naturally destroyed, then rebuilt again. It was probably the first of many job creation schemes on the river. Men without work in the 1840s depression put in a stone wall that stayed there until Queens Bridge went up fifty years later; Lonsdale and Hoddle each came up with ideas for a dam.

The supply itself was in big barrels on cartwheels that were filled at the river above the Falls. They delivered one week's domestic supply at a time, emptied through a leather hose into a smaller household barrel. At the end of each week, recorded Garryowen, what remained might contain, apart from any innate 'qualities' of the water, 'an unsavoury sediment of mosquitoes, centipedes, spiders and cockroaches, dead, alive, and dying'.

Water was sold for extortionate prices at times, with the good stuff taken from higher upstream fetching a higher price. Reputedly, the further from the river you lived, the more dregs you got and the more likely it was that you would have to dilute the water with equally awful rum or brandy. Not surprisingly, some people collected rainwater in any container they could, or went down to the river themselves with buckets and casks in wheelbarrows.

At the Pumps, between Russell and Queen streets, there were a dozen private enterprise stations providing water for sale straight out of the river. Following the classical rules of supply and demand, the ever-more-prosperous water men would pump even when high tides pushed the saltwater over into the fresh.*

---

* It seems only one of the water men has been remembered as anything other than notorious. Thomas Watson, Waterloo veteran, 'was such an intense teetotaller, that, not satisfied with being an openly avowed water drinker…resolved to obtain a livelihood by vending the precious element'.

By 1849 Melbourne City Council had been formed, and a steam engine was erected on the river pumping water to a large filter near the north-east corner of Flinders and Elizabeth streets, where it was for public sale. Another steam engine of 1854, near Spring Street, pumped riverwater to a large cast-iron tank on Eastern Hill (the Eye & Ear Hospital site). The tank held 150,000 gallons and was forty feet square, fifteen feet deep, and raised a further fifteen feet off the ground on a bluestone stand. A beautiful piece of municipal architecture, it was relocated in 1892 to Cocoroc* at the Werribee Sewerage Farm (now Melbourne Water Western Treatment Plant) and still stands there.

The man largely responsible for the Elizabeth Street pumping station, the talented James Blackburn, later became City Surveyor and came up with a proposal for a gravity-fed water supply system for Melbourne. It included Victoria's first major dam, to be built at Yan Yean to harness the Plenty River watershed, its catchment rising to Mount Disappointment in the Great Divide. A Surveyor General's department field trip making a nineteenth-century feasibility study reportedly returned the verdict, 'The water in the gullies of Mount Disappointment was beautifully limpid and most refreshing as a beverage.' Charles La Trobe, Lieutenant-Governor, turned the first sod in December 1853. The system initially took in water from Plenty River through a two-mile aqueduct, and several decades later it was augmented to take in water from over the Divide via the Wallaby Creek aqueduct and Toorourong Reservoir.

When Yan Yean came into service in 1857, people reportedly were so utterly delighted at the spout of water not from the Yarra, they sang and danced sodden under the public standpipes. It did take some years, however, for Yan Yean water to become systematically efficient in its supply and purity. The head brewer of Foster's thought it was full of typhoid, and Trollope, in his tome on Australia, noted:

---

* Cocoroc (Wathawurrung for 'frog') was the Werribee Sewerage Farm company town, situated on one of the world's largest volcanic-plain grasslands.

> Melbourne is supplied from a distance of about twenty miles with millions of gallons of water...It is laid on to every house in the town and the suburbs, and is supposed to be the most perfect water supply ever produced for the use of man. Ancient Rome and modern New York have been less blessed in this respect than is Melbourne with its Yan Yean. I do believe that the supply is almost as inexhaustible as it is described to be. But the method of bringing it into the city is not as yet by any means perfect...I will also add that the Yan Yean water is not pleasant to drink;—a matter of comparatively small consideration in a town in which brandy is so plentiful.

Maroondah began with a small weir across the Watts River, which joins the Yarra at Healesville, in 1891, although its watershed upstream was reserved for catchment three years earlier. Within the catchment area there was a charming tourist destination called Fernshawe, formerly a stop on the goldminers' Yarra Track. 'One of the most picturesque villages in Victoria,' it was dubbed in the course of being popularised by photographers Nicholas Caire and J. W. Lindt and journalist The Vagabond. 'First glimpse,' he wrote, was:

> a clearing, a rustic boarding-house, some ladies in sun-bonnets carrying armfuls of woodland trophies; then a bridge over the laughing, gurgling Watts...The tallest fern-trees in the world shade the path. On each side there is the utmost luxuriance of vegetation—Nature run riot. The bush undergrowth, which elsewhere in Australia will be merely a few inches high, here attains many feet.

There were orchards, raspberry gardens, trout, native pheasants (lyrebirds) running round for beauty and recreation (that is, hunting), and a small town—just a collection of houses built from the surrounding forest, with bark or timber shingle roofs, picket fences, and gardens.

Caire wrote of:

> the rippling waters of the Watts River, with its overhanging ferns and deep shady glades, suggesting the homes of the fairies. The music of gentle zephyrs playing among the great giant gums, combined with the bird sonnets and the other multitudinous sounds of animal and insect life in the great forest, impressed one vividly with the feeling that they were in the precincts of fairyland.

He and Lindt sold thousands of photographs of Fernshawe.

For the sake of Melbourne's pristine water the whole township was bought and taken away in the late 1880s. The aim, as a 1915 Board of Works publication stated, was that 'In the whole area from which Melbourne's water is obtained there is not one habitation draining into the watershed, and horses, cattle, sheep, goats, and dogs are excluded from it.' Nothing now is left of old Fernshawe except some exotic trees, and a few pictures and stories.

The Yarra supplies more than two-thirds of Melbourne's water by giving up its catchment into huge dams built across the main river and on some of the smaller rivers and creeks that flow into it.* The Upper Yarra Reservoir, which wasn't finally completed until 1957, holds back the river above Reefton. When it was built it was the highest dam in Australia. The O'Shannassy River, which flows into the Yarra below the Upper Yarra dam, was held back in 1928, forming O'Shannassy Reservoir. An earlier weir had been constructed there in 1915. Upper Yarra began with a weir and aqueduct to O'Shannassy in 1939, before the much bigger dam, a huge postwar project, went in despite the shortages of steel and cement. To enable construction the whole river had to be diverted through a 2,700-foot-long tunnel.

Maroondah Reservoir, built over the Watts River, was completed in 1927. Silvan Reservoir, finished in 1932, is—like Cardinia, which

---

* As an example of the growing scale required: O'Shannassy holds about 3,000 megalitres, Maroondah 22,000 Ml, Upper Yarra 200,000 Ml and Thomson—out of the catchment—well over a million megalitres.

follows it on the pipeline—a storage dam of water collected elsewhere along the Yarra catchment and pumped in.

1967 was a year of severe drought and water restrictions in Melbourne, despite all the dams. Water was pumped out of the river at Yering Gorge below Yarra Glen, chlorinated, then added to the Maroondah Aqueduct which ran nearby, taking water in for Melbourne's supply. By the late twentieth century it had become necessary to locate a whole new storage reservoir, Sugarloaf, as well as a complete treatment plant, off-stream* there at Christmas Hills. Water has been pumped directly into it from the river since 1980, providing around ten percent of Melbourne's water supply.†

The source of the river is not an exact magical location, though several have been claimed. As one man who's spent his life working with the Upper Yarra's forest and water repeatedly says when asked: it's like the palm of your hand. Where does it start and where does it end?‡

There is no single spot. But west of Baw Baw, south of Mount Gregory...§

* The reservoir is not actually connected to the river or aqueduct, but is filled with water pumped from them.

† Some twentieth-century riverside homes in the middle and upper reaches got their own water supply from two sources: one tankwater and the other directly from the Yarra.

‡ Frank Lawless, Melbourne Water.

§ More than half a kilometre underneath the same spot south of Mount Gregory where the headwaters of the Yarra fall, where the Field Naturalists and Hoddle walked, is a near twenty-kilometre tunnel. It takes water that would have fallen into the sea on the east coast of Australia—from the Thomson River and Reservoir—into the Yarra and the Upper Yarra dam.

A rough biblical rollcall of those streams that begat the Yarra, from source to mouth, besides the many unnamed, runs:

Eighteen Mile Creek, Falls Creek, Nine Mile Creek, and Woods Creek, flow into the Yarra River;

Fehring Creek flows into Baker Creek, which flows into the Yarra River;

Contention Gully, Alderman Creek, Wombat Creek, and Victoria Gully, flow into the Yarra River;

Briton Creek and Bears Creek flow into Donovan Creek, and Snobs Creek, Theodore Creek, and Damper Creek which flows into Clear Creek, and Coolgardie Creek flow into Walshs Creek, which flows into the Yarra River;

Bumper Gully, Doctor Creek, Five Mile Creek, Bart Creek, Little Yankee Jim Creek, Armstrong Creek, Two Mile Creek, Big Bill Creek flow into the Yarra River;

Salvage Creek, Circle Creek, Tin Creek, Lowes Creek, Quarry Creek and Smoko Creek flow into McMahons Creek which flows into the Yarra River;

Muddy Creek flows into the Yarra River;

¶Red Creek, Federal Creek, Black Cat Creek, Richards Creek, White Creek, Orange Creek, Yellow Creek, Cassidy Creek, Flowerpot Creek, and Dead Man Creek, Geordie Creek, the Burn and Sooty Gully, the Little Flume, and the Big Flume which flows into Baker Creek, flow into Starvation Creek which flows into the Yarra River;

Crooked Creek flows into the Yarra River;

Bellel Creek, Deep Creek, and Smith Creek, flow into the O'Shannassy River, which flows into the Yarra River;

McDonald Creek, Braham Creek, Webster Creek which flows into Cement Creek, Anderson Creek, and Dead Horse Creek, flow into the Yarra River;

¶Strom Creek, and Wolfram Creek which flows into Muddy Creek, and Mortimore Creek, Inspiration Creek, and Crock Creek, Dwyer Gully, and Bluey Creek which flow into Smyth Creek, Collas Creek, Bride Creek, and Little Mick Creek, and Platts Creek, Johnson Creek, Charity Gully, Ahoy Creek, Hope Gully, Faith Gully which flow into Mississippi Creek, and Love Gully which flows into Lyrebird Creek, flow into Big Pats Creek which flows into the Yarra River;

Postman Creek flows into the

Yarra River;

Minah Creek flows into Starling Creek, which flows into the Yarra River;

Rocky Creek, and Pheasant Creek, flow into the Yarra River;

Calder Creek, and Ross Gully, flow into Four Mile Creek, which flows into the Yarra River;

Brisbane Creek flows into the Yarra River;

The Stratbraan, and Backstairs Creek flow into Scotchmans Creek, which flows into the Yarra River;

Ythan Creek, Dirty Gully Creek, Stockdales Creek, Walker Creek, Harrison Creek, and Dee River flow into the Yarra River;

¶Cemetery Creek flows into Mann Creek, and Ballarat Gully flows into Blue Nose Creek, which flow into Yankee Jims Creek, which flows into the Yarra River;

McKechnie Creek and Kennedy Creek flow into Frenchmans Creek, and with Platts Creek, and Don Creek, flow into the Yarra River;

¶Henty Creek, Fitzpatrick Creek, Mackley Creek, Moon Creek, Boys Camp Creek, Monnett Creek which flows into Tin Mine Creek, and Reid Gully, Don Gully and Jack Gully which flow into Blackwood Creek, Blake Creek, Learmonth Creek; Hoare Creek which flows into School Creek, Tharratt Creek which flows into Beer Creek, which flow into Saxton Creek, Adams Creek, Settlement Creek which flows into Golding Creek which flows into Hackett Creek, Kobecke Creek, Myrtle Creek, Taylor Creek, and Blackmore Creek which flow into Black Sand Creek, Ellis Creek which flows into Radar Gully, Fir Tree Creek, Condon Creek, Slaty Creek, Morgan Gully, Hearse Creek, Barrier Creek; and Tungsten Creek, Skull Creek, Sandys Creek, No. 3 Creek, King Creek, Two Bob Creek, Tugwell Creek, Tray Creek, Painters Creek, and Justices Gully which flow into Britannia Creek; all flow into Little Yarra River, which flows into the Yarra River;

Myrtle Creek flows into Don River which flows into the Yarra River;

Blackfeather Creek, Wombat Creek, Wet Lead Creek, and Speer Gully flow into Hoddle's Creek, which flows into the Yarra River;

Ure Creek, and Webers Creek, flow into the Yarra River;

¶Ti-tree Creek, and Perrins Creek which flows into Sassafras Creek, and Emerald Creek, Menzies Creek, Stoney Creek, Middle Creek, Boggy Creek; and Gembrook Creek, Wattle Creek; and Egg Rock Creek which flows into Tomahawk Creek, and Clark Creek which flow into Shepherd Creek; and Macclesfield Creek, and Hansen Creek which flows into Macraes Creek, which flow into Cockatoo Creek; and Lone Star Creek which flows into Sheep Station Creek, and Devils Creek and Wattle Creek; and Wild Cattle Creek which flows into Wandin Yallock Creek, flow into Woori Yallock Creek which flows into the Yarra River;

Slip Creek, Blue Jacket Creek, Punch Gully and Boggy Creek flow into Badger Creek, which flows into the Yarra River;

¶Morley Creek, Myrtle Creek which flows into Contentment Creek, Mosquito Creek, Ettersglen Creek, Mathinna Creek, Condon Creek, Sawpit Creek, Donnelly Creek, Mick Creek and Meyers Creek which flows into New Chum Creek, the Grace Burn, Picaninny Creek, flow into Watts River, which flows into the Yarra River;

Long Gully, Yeringberg Creek and Pauls Creek, flow into the Yarra River;

Full and Plenty Creek, and Stony Creek which flows into Dry Creek, and Lyrebird Gully and Pinchgut Creek which flow into Jehosaphat Creek, and Dixons Creek, flow into Steels Creek, which flows into the Yarra River;

¶Lilyponds Creek flows into the Yarra River;

Rich Creek, Myrtle Beech Gully, and Rifle Range Gully which flow into Lyrebird Creek, and Little Stringy Bark Creek which flows into Stringy Bark Creek, flow into Olinda Creek, which flows into the Yarra River;

Manna Gum Creek and Brushy Creek flow into the Yarra River;

¶Hunchback Creek, Reedy Creek, Five Mile Creek, Happy Valley Creek, and Boomers Gully, New Chum Gully, Chinamans Gully, and New Caledonia, which flow into Long Gully, and Sugarloaf Creek, Fryers Gully, and Stevenson Creek, flow into Watsons Creek, which flows into the Yarra River;

Pigeon Bank Gully, Break of Day Gully which flows into Jumping Creek, Parsons Gully, Thomsons Gully, Harris's Gully which flows into Andersons Creek, Stony Creek, and Mullum Mullum Creek, flow into the Yarra River;

¶Wild Dog Creek, Yow Yow Creek, Smiths Gully, Red Shirt Gully; and Chads Creek, Running Creek and Stewart Ponds, which flow into Arthurs Creek; and Watery Gully Greek, Scrubby Creek, and

Sawpit Creek, flow into Diamond Creek, which flows into the Yarra River;

Kestrel Creek, and Ruffeys Creek flow into the Yarra River;

¶Falls Creek and Russell Creek, which flow into Yellow Creek, and Joes Creek which flow into Jacks Creek, and Running Creek, and Cockpit Gully, Mill Gully, Yarra Creek, and White Elephant Gully and Wattle Gully which flow into Dry Creek, flow into Bruces Creek, and Scrubby Creek, and Barbers Creek, and Yallambie Creek flow into Plenty River, which flows into the Yarra River;

Banyule Creek and Salt Creek flow into the Yarra River;

Bushy Creek flows into Koonung Creek, which flows into the Yarra River;

Glass's Creek, and Donaldsons Creek which flows into Darebin Creek, and Connors Creek, flow into the Yarra River;

Malcolm Creek, Aitken Creek, Curly Sedge Creek, Central Creek, and Edgars Creek flow into Merri Creek, which flows into the Yarra River;

Blind Creek flows into the Yarra River;

Damper Creek flows into Scotchmans Creek which flows into Main Creek, and Back Creek, flow into Gardiners (or Kooyongkoot) Creek, which flows into the Yarra River;

Hawksburn Creek flows into the Yarra River;

Five Mile Creek flows into Moonee Ponds Creek, which flows into the Yarra River;

¶Dry Creek, Long Gully, and Slab Hut Creek which flows into Lintons Creek, and Number Three Creek flow into Boyd Creek, and Bolinda Creek which flows into Emu Creek, and Konagaderra Creek flow into Deep Creek; Distill Creek, Gisborne Creek, Slaty Creek, and Willimigongon Creek which flows into Turitable Creek which flows into Riddells Creek, and Longview Creek, and Kismet Creek which flows into Blind Creek, and Column Gully, and Lightwood Gully, flow into Jacksons Creek; and Taylors Creek, Steele or Rose Creek, flow into Maribyrnong River, which flows into the Yarra River;

¶Stony Creek flows into the Yarra River.

Melbourne is blessed with creeks, and rivers.

Bridging it I

In the beginning

The first bridges across the Yarra were built upstream by those now forgotten. There, you were close to the water; you could wade over in places, or cross only slightly above it. Rolf Boldrewood, visiting Yering in the 1840s, described a more elaborate crossing.

> We took a long ride, and, I well remember, crossed the river upon a primitive bridge, which enables me to say to this day that I have ridden across the river upon a single tree. It was even so. An enormous *Eucalyptus amygdalina*, growing upon the bank of the Yarra, had been felled or grubbed—I think the latter—so as to fall right across the stream. Afterwards it had been adzed level—a handrail had been supplied. A quiet horse could, therefore, be easily led or ridden across to the other side, the width being an average of between two and three feet.

Hubert de Castella wrote about the same bridge which originally formed the approach to his new property, Dalry, in *Les Squatters Australiens.*

> Wooden pegs had been put in on both sides [of the huge gumtree] to hold branches placed lengthwise to widen the bridge. The space between the trunk and these branches was filled with turf, and the whole thing made a track up in the air ten feet above the water, and a hundred odd feet in length, which brave souls went along without dismounting while the cautious led their horses across by the bridle.

Today you make that crossing to Healesville on the Maroondah Highway; but upstream in Warburton, where giant trees are still found metres from the river's edge, it would be physically possible to construct a bridge like this even now. It's the same way the river was crossed in Barak's story of the sun and the moon.

Hubert de Castella superseded the augmented single-log Ur-bridge by hiring local muscle, including bullock teams and ships' carpenters who'd missed out in the gold rush, as bridge-builders. A bridge named after De Castella, and situated further downstream where the Watts River flowed into the Yarra, later became the main crossing to Healesville. A rather handsome whitewashed wooden toll bridge known as Rourkes Bridge, constructed next to the original Dalry log site, found favour as the main route from the 1870s after tolls had been removed.

The Healesville crossing has been bridged again and again, more recently by bigger, rather undistinguished but eminently practical concrete bridges. The latest went up in 1963, with a long eastern causeway approach to avoid flooding. The previous bridge, which still stands on a diagonal angle downstream, was concrete formed with oregon, timber that landed on the Yarra way down at South Wharf after having travelled halfway round the world. Pieces of even earlier bridgework, left lying where they fell or were pushed, can be spotted underneath, and in the river itself.

~

The city of Melbourne had to wait ten years for its first bridge. Before that there were punts between Swanston and Russell streets and, earlier, rowboats. The first punt in Melbourne was built out of old ships' timbers and licensed in 1838 to Thomas Watt, who was replaced when he was found to be getting the punters drunk. John Hodgson ran the next conveyance upstream in the early 1840s, and propelled it with ropes wrapped around riverside trees, which passengers sometimes hauled. A government punt ran slightly further upstream, in line with Stephen (Exhibition) Street. The punts carried people, horses, bullock teams, dairy herds. Aborigines and city councillors rode for free.

The private enterprise punts ran until the first bridge went up in 1845: Balbirnie's wooden toll bridge. Small, low to the water, crossing the river on an angle, it was replaced in 1850 by the first Princes Bridge. A single stone arch of bluestone and granite, its span was the largest in the colonies—150 feet (not quite 50 metres) long, 30 feet wide—and indeed in the entire empire, except for the famous London Bridge itself. The builder believed it had 'the finest appearance of any in the British Dominions'; a later mayor described it as being of very light, graceful, and artistic appearance. It joined Swanston Street to the St Kilda Road, as its successor still does, and carried such heavy traffic that by the time it was replaced, restrictions had been imposed.

That new bridge was long overdue. Alfred Deakin said that one of the

> chief obstacles to the construction of a bridge sufficiently magnificent to meet the demands of modern Melbourne was the fact that the existing structure was a beautiful, and in its way, a splendid structure...It was felt that as long as the old bridge stood before the eyes and in the hearts of the people of Melbourne there would be no chance of getting a new bridge.

So the government demolished it in 1884 and put up a very temporary wooden structure. Apart from the huge rise in traffic due to the population explosion fuelled by the gold rush, there were several other structural reasons for a new and larger bridge. One was the introduction of cabletrams—by the 1890s Melbourne's system was the world's biggest. Another reason was the scheme which proposed to double or triple the city width of the Yarra, therefore also the bridge, and take thousands of tonnes of rock from the riverbed and the south bank.

The new (and current) Princes Bridge opened in 1888. It was built by David Munro and designed by D'Ebro & Grainger (father of composer Percy Grainger); Carlo Catani* was Assistant Engineer,

* St Kilda's Lower Esplanade Gardens are named after him.

and the young John Monash, who became Australia's greatest general of World War One, drew up the stone masonry specs.

The design was based on Blackfriars Bridge, London; the bluestone came from Footscray and Malmsbury, with granite from Harcourt, concrete, two thousand tons of cast iron and a thousand of wrought. It was described in an illustrated periodical as 'a structure not unworthy to span the Thames, the Tiber or the Tagus', about the highest praise that could be given at the time. With not one but three spans of a hundred feet each and about the same breadth, it was claimed as the widest bridge in the world. Two tramlines ran alongside four carriage lanes, all laid with redgum blocks, plus two very wide foot pavements.*

The redgum has disappeared, but the underside of the bridge remains much the same. Multiple red-leaded arches sit bolted onto strong bluestone. Set in the dozen decorative spandrels along its sides are coats of arms slightly corroded belonging to the people who put up the money: the State Government of Victoria and the cities of Melbourne, South Melbourne, Prahran, St Kilda, Malvern, Brighton, Caulfield and Moorabbin—mostly bodies that no longer exist.

~

The rebuilding of Queens Bridge in the 1880s was part of the destruction of Melbourne's historical fulcrum. The Falls—the low, rocky, natural barrier there between saltwater coming in from the Bay and freshwater flowing downstream—were blasted away. A previous wooden bridge, actually named Falls Bridge, had been built in 1860 where the Kulin originally crossed the Yarra, wading over the rock Falls. The design of the new bridge—as elegant beneath as above, with its silver painted curves and rivets—was partly the work of Carlo Catani and it too was built by David Munro & Co. (again with masonry specs by John Monash) around the same time they were doing the Sandridge/Port Melbourne & St Kilda rail bridge slightly upstream. The Premier of Victoria then, Tommy Bent—also

---

* David Munro & Co. also supplied several million redgum paving blocks for Melbourne's entire cabletram system.

Queens Bridge in the early 1900s—with a live dock below it, before Spencer Street Bridge stopped the ships coming up. Blokes and bales, cargo; a ship's hawser strains against the outgoing tide; Flinders Street Station upper right.

chairman of directors of David Munro & Co.—was sometimes described as 'by name by nature'.

~

Johnston Street Bridge is just downstream from another one of the Yarra's natural fords, called Dights Ford in the 1840s. (The others, apart from those in what is now known as the Yarra Valley, were near Newport early on, upstream of Banksia Street Bridge and of course the Falls at Queens Bridge). John Hodgson ran a punt between St Heliers House and Abbotsford towards his home, Studley House. At first it was for people only, then from 1846 a larger operation started from Clarke Street carrying men on horseback as well.

The first bridge went up in the late 1850s, when the approach was cut into the hillside down from Studley Park, still there today. Big stone abutments supported a wooden arched bridge which dry-rotted out in only a few years. An extra timber framework had to be built in below, from the river up, to hold it. Incredibly, it withstood the 1863 flood, and stood indeed until replaced by iron girders installed on the same abutments in the late 1870s. This was the bridge Fitzroy's night soil was dumped from.

The second, iron, bridge was adequate until the speed and weight of hitherto-unimagined cars and trucks tested it. A reinforced concrete bridge was built in the 1950s, crossing the river diagonally and therefore making the road approaches sweep straight through, as opposed to the earlier crossing, at right angles, which forced the traffic to turn sharply.

The Flow

And his Ghost may be heard, as you pass by that Billabong…

If you're in Melbourne and not too far from the Yarra River you could easily be passing by a billabong yourself, or at least the site of one. Within an old swaggie's spit of the Eastern Freeway are several of the most beautiful extant billabongs of the Yarra River. And there are more, further upstream.

Billabongs are not some weird, nostalgic theme-park idea of the Outback, visited on that once-in-a-lifetime trip around the continent; they are part of the poetic drought-and-flooding-rain cycle of our natural landscape. It's just that in the past we've generally tried to hide or destroy them, mostly successfully: since settlement of Victoria, about a third of river wetlands have completely disappeared and almost another third have been partly ruined.

The flows of Australian rivers are generally three times more variable, or extreme, than those of the rest of the world, as well as being lower. A 'once in a hundred year' Australian flood (like, say, the 1934 Yarra flood) is on average five times, but sometimes twenty or thirty times, the size of an annual flood; whereas in the rest of the world a hundred-year flood is usually only two to three times the annual average size. Droughts can be similarly extreme.

Like Melbourne's climate, with its 'four seasons in one day' weather (actually at least six*), the Yarra River is also an extremely dynamic system. It operates on a much longer chronological scale than ours, but nonetheless it only stays the same if we make it. A time-lapsed, Bunjil-eyed view of the river over tens, hundreds, thousands of years would show a living thing expanding (flood) and contracting (drought), changing beds, looping cutoffs and billabongs, running faster or slower, in different unpredictable patterns.

In the past century, the Yarra has changed and shifted enough in one upstream region to blur the legal boundaries and reservations once plotted along its course. Legal frontage may alter because its original definition was expressed in terms of a set distance to the river (which may have moved), or to another boundary (which hasn't).

The river's shape is created by its flow, and that is the result of a matrix of factors.

Billabongs† are made gradually and periodically along flood plains. In a meandering, curvy alluvial river like the Yarra, the outside of each bend is the fastest, deepest and most cut-into or naturally eroded part. The opposite bank, the inside curve, slows the flow and collects sediment, sometimes to the extent of forming a little beach. In high flow the river can break through a different route, perhaps weakened or opened by erosion, bypassing a loop or curve. Eventually, after repeated floods and erosion, the river may keep going on its newly formed course, bypassing the old silted-up bend altogether, which becomes a billabong. The new course or shape alters the flow, which will change again downstream, creating another meander…and so on. The cut-off curve naturally fills with sediment over time, its changing depth and distance determining

---

* Melbourne's seasons have been identified as true spring, high summer, late summer, early winter, deep winter, early spring.

† Known in other parts of the world as ox-bow lakes.

Cleared, grazed billabongs fat with flood alongside the river, Yarra Valley.

when and how often it reconnects with the river's water. In the flood plains between Yering and Yarra Junction, billabongs are formed about once every eighty years.

The natural river also has islands, nowhere more so than in the aptly named Bend of Isles reach. Lushly seen through stringybark from the rocky ridge above, they appear as a contemplative scroll of flow and reflections that happen also to be of particular biological and geomorphological interest. Hoddle noted islands far upstream in his fieldbook of the Expedition to the Source of the Yarra Yarra.

Dights Falls originally had several islands, large enough to be treed, but like snags and billabongs, islands were once thought of as obstructions and so removed.

River islands, not always water-surrounded but large enough to appear so on maps, can be found at Warrandyte and Templestowe; there's also man-made Herring Island in South Yarra. Some islands were created by goldmining excavations (such as The Island at Warrandyte near Parsons Gully) or flood diversions, others by billabongs. The patchwork of islands in the middle and upper reaches of the river, some with vegetation thick enough for a man to battle through, are mostly small islands measured in square metres, based on rocky shale and silt that plants have caught hold of: low enough to flood in high water, just big enough for the dreams of wet-ankled children.

The formation and dissolution of natural islands is part of the natural river's dynamic, like that of billabongs.* Silt and debris may catch on rock formations, accumulate, and allow vegetation to take hold. This obstruction moves the river's current to a new course, depth and speed. The island may, over time and further accumulation of large wooden debris, increase in size, join with the bank and persuade the river to divert. Alternatively a deeper, faster current caused by the island's formation may end up (after reaching a base level of erosion) cutting into the original foundations of the enlarged island. Flow, diversion, equilibrium altered: Bunjil-scale processes.

Billabongs are shadows and echoes of the river, fat or thin according to season. Waterholes in a chain, whole cut-off loops, bends or meanders of the river with their own separate, higher water level; within days, months, seasons and years the river's flow will vary, and they wax and wane with it. In drought, being separated from the main flow, billabongs can dry up completely. In flood, the river overflows into them and they join once again with the moving stream they were formed from, taking in fresh water and flushing out a soup of micronutrients and zooplankton—the first links in the food chain—to spark an explosion of biological activity. For they function, crucially, as hatcheries and feeding grounds, arks of the uncharismatic microfauna that sustain the ecological health of the whole river.

There were billabongs all along the Yarra. The older the directory or map, the more billabongs, wetlands, waterholes and creeks you will

* The 'island' just south of Banksia Street, Bulleen was formed in the 1950s.

find marked. At settlement, the river flats were punctuated by billabongs on the approximate sites of (among other places):

- Alexandra Gardens—a large wetland roughly the size of two city blocks, big enough to be formed into the Domain Lagoon and have many islands;
- a swathe of 'lagoon' stretching from there to the Botanic Gardens;
- where the railyards are now, stretching from Federation Square to the Melbourne Tennis Centre and as wide as the block between Exhibition and Spring Streets—again, big enough for an islanded section;
- the Botanic Gardens (also islanded, later becoming ornamental lakes);
- the old Rosella factory, Cremorne (next to the Nylex clock)—a billabong known as Wrights Swamp, west of the Sandringham line rail bridge (described by a contemporary observer as the beginning of 'a string of seepage lakes…along the northern bank from Church Street to the Morgue')…

…and also Olympic Park and Domain Tunnel; Alexandra Avenue west of Punt Road; Goschs Paddock; Monash Freeway east of Punt Road; Melbourne High School oval; Como Park; Yarra Boulevard, and Kevin Bartlett Reserve, Burnley; west of Denham Street, Hawthorn, north of the Burwood Road Bridge; Abbotsford Convent farmlands; Fairfield, near the hospital; west of Burke Road; Veneto Club, Bulleen Park; Camberwell Public Golf Course; Trinity Playing Fields (between Bolin-Bolin and Koonung Creek confluence).*

West of St Kilda Road, around the back of Victoria Barracks, there was a huge swamp spreading out from that much earlier river delta course north to City Road, south to Albert Road, and diagonally slicing Moray Street.

---

* One observer, Christopher Bailey, estimated that in his own neighbourhood, between Darebin Creek and Burke Road, there were more than fifty billabongs.

Bunjil-eye view of what's left of the great Bolin-Bolin billabong system. Yarra River upper left and right, Bulleen Road at bottom.

There are billabongs, or what remains of them, still to be seen at Bulleen (once Lake Bulleen or Bolin-Bolin, the great Wurundjeri food source and ceremonial ground), Kew (formerly known as Willsmere Lagoon), Alphington, East Kew, Ivanhoe, Heidelberg, Eltham and Templestowe. There are small, mostly drained, billabongs in grazing land (both former and current) in Heidelberg, and from Coldstream upriver to Woori Yallock. Most of the lower Yarra billabongs join with the river on average once a year; upstream it's perhaps only once in five years, thanks to control of flood waters by upstream damming.

What we know as wetlands or billabongs also used to be described as swamps, lagoons or backwaters; the terms have been interchangeable. In the 1840s, Charles La Trobe, Superintendent of the Port Phillip District, described the river in general as 'a chain and a half to two chains in breadth, and eight or ten feet in depth'. (The surveyors did literally use chains, with a standard length of 66 feet or just over 20 metres. Hoddle marked the river's width in town as 160 feet.) La Trobe also described, in connection with evidence of floods, 'the frequent occurrence of ponds or lagoons lying in hollows behind the natural bank, and evidently fed from time to time, from a break at the lower extremity, by some strong back current'.

Not that they were necessarily threatening or unattractive: he called the site of the future Botanic Gardens, with its lagoon/ billabong, 'a veritable Garden of Eden'. An earlier visitor noted the river there was deep, and 'difficult to navigate on account of the quantity of sunken timber...about sixty feet wide, and margined with trees and shrubs'.

Part of the large Docklands area was originally Batman's (or West Melbourne) Swamp, also known as a 'lagoon'. Robert Russell drew it as a 'Salt Lake'—'at times quite dry' and George McCrae recalled that it was 'termed indifferently "The Blue Lake"'. Situated between the city and Footscray, east of the Maribyrnong and north of the Yarra, it was as big as the grid of Melbourne city itself. Grimes' expedition of 1803 noted 'a large swamp between two rivers; fine grass, fit to mow; not a bush in it'. John Batman, in the diary of his first visit to Melbourne, recorded,

> I crossed on the banks of the river a large marsh about one mile and a half wide, by three or four miles long, of the richest description of soil—not a tree. When we got on the marsh, the quails began to fly, and I think, at one time, I can safely say I saw a thousand quail flying at one time—quite a cloud. I never saw anything like it before...At the upper end of the marsh is a large lagoon. I should think from the distance I saw that it was upwards of a mile across, and full of swans, ducks, and geese.

The Moonee Ponds (Creek)—or Monee Monee waterholes, as Hoddle first surveyed them—billabonged around Flemington and North Melbourne, terminating before the huge Lagoon, itself quite distinct from the Yarra. Various other small creeks upstream also originally ended in wetlands or billabongs rather than in the main river. The 'chain of ponds' style of waterway was not uncommon. Within tidal reach in the old river delta area, there were a number of much smaller saltwater lagoons, mostly south of the river. Land south and west of the town site was labelled on first maps as a marshy plain with even a 'morass' (Southbank), or simply low swamp with the occasional saltlake or lagoon.

The West Melbourne lagoon was partly filled in with the debris from the levelling of Batmans Hill, surveyed centre point of the entire colony of Port Phillip, and destined to become the site of the Spencer Street railyards. Much later, in 1912, George McCrae wrote,

> You may search for it in vain today among the mud, scrap-iron, broken bottles, and all sorts of red-rusty railway debris...yet, once, it was there; a real lake, intensely blue, nearly oval, and full of the clearest salt water...fringed gaily all round by...pigface...in full bloom, it seemed in the broad sunshine as though girdled about with a belt of magenta fire...the whole air heavy with the...odours of the golden myrniong flowers...

~ ~ ~

By the second half of the nineteenth century, that beautiful blue salt lagoon in Batman's Swamp had become 'Lake Lonsdale', a large, shallow cesspool for the city's waste, commented upon for its stench rather than, as once had been the case, the perfume of the surrounding flowers.

At that time, people believed that 'miasma'—noxious gases and odours, or simply bad air—was the cause of fatal and dangerous disease. Some even wondered whether clearing so many gum trees caused such illness, because eucalyptus vapour was known to protect against and nullify the evil miasma. As early as 1840 Robert Hoddle described 'Melbourne, on the river side…surrounded with a marshy plain, which is frequently inundated; the miasma arising is injurious to the health'. Only later in the nineteenth century did the concepts of germs, micro-organisms, bacteria—infection and its prevention—come to be understood.

In some ways the theories coincided: bacteria in waste could contaminate water and transmit disease; the smell and vapours were a clue to their presence. The government itself explained officially how the high death rate in Collingwood was caused by low-lying miasma or vapours (rather than low-lying sewage, general lack of hygiene and overcrowding).

'Nothing can be more…repulsive,' ranted the *Picturesque Atlas of Australasia* at the height of the 1880s boom,

> than the approach to Melbourne by the river Yarra…polluted by the drainage and sewage of the city and of half a dozen suburbs, [it] is as offensive to the eye as to the sense of smell; while the malodorousness of the atmosphere is aggravated by the fumes from various noxious industries that have been established on its banks.

That was the view during the good times. What had been christened Marvellous Melbourne was known concurrently as Marvellous Smellbourne. The Yarra was one of the filthiest rivers in the world.* Thousands of tonnes of blood and guts were dumped annually to float, putrefying, in the river along with dead cattle and the outpourings of live ones; plus what were politely listed as 'numerous animal carcasses...and decaying vegetable matter from manufactories'—dead sheep, pigs, horses, chooks, fish, dogs, cats and rats, as well as factory by-products.

During the 1840s depression there was more money in turning sheep into tallow for candles and soap than in using them for meat, and when the first boiling-down plants went in they created such big business that tallow was exported. Not all of it, however—surplus globs would find their way into the river and bob around endlessly. There were slaughterhouses or abattoirs, along with every conceivable sidebar business, up to Dights Falls: fellmongers to prepare the animals' fresh, bloody skins for tanneries to make leather on the open ground; wool scourers to wash the fleece (in the 'fresh' water on the riverbanks); starch and glue factories and bone mills, to process hooves and horns; candle and soap factories. And all the unusable waste—heads, legs, megalitres of gross liquid—emptied into the flow.

In 1847, despite this, garrison soldiers reportedly still found the river above the city Falls clean enough to do their washing in, although it was a pity the soap and other liquid from their undergarments ran back into the town's drinking water stations.

Water taken from the Pumps at one point was described as having the consistency of very weak gelatine. In its lower reaches, the Yarra was a vomit-inducing open sewer, or, as Garryowen put it, 'a *cloaca maxima* of festering impurities'.†

---

* Even in 1970 Prince Charles, a well-travelled visitor from Britain, asked when meeting the Upper Yarra shire secretary, 'Is the Yarra any cleaner at Warburton than at South Wharf? Down by the *Britannia* it is one of the dirtiest streams I have ever seen.'

† He was probably alluding to the main sewer of ancient Rome, but a literal translation of the Latin might be 'biggest shithole'.

In a town of hundreds of thousands of people with no sewerage system, before the advent of the night or pan man every building had a pit toilet dug into the ground out the back, or else people (or their servants) emptied their pans and buckets into communal cesspools. If they were extra slack or disgusting, it might be a nearby vacant allotment.

There was no stormwater drainage either, just open gutters that ran like tiny creeks of nightmare, picking up dunny overflows including infected matter; dirtied kitchen, laundry and bath water; guts dropped out of backyard-slaughtered sheep; tonnes of horse dung and tonnes more silt from the notoriously unmade roads of Melbourne. All of it went swirling and blobbing into the river. The open street drains in the city grid were so deep they had little bridges.

Clayey, flat, low areas round the city or inner suburbs were worse—sometimes liquid didn't fall away to the river, but sludged under houses. A parliamentary report in 1852 detailed,

> In the backyards and enclosures, more astounding accumulations of putrescent substances and rubbish of all kinds, than...in the very worst parts of the dirtiest English or Continental towns...[On the present site of Myers main city store] there is a space of upwards of a hundred square yards hitherto occupied by a green putrid and semi-liquid mass, partly formed by the outpourings of surrounding privies.

When the stuff got through to the fresh water supply—as, with seepage, floods and runoffs it inevitably did—it spread diphtheria, typhoid and dysentery. Your chances of dying while living in Collingwood were greater than anywhere else: if you hadn't had your sixth birthday the odds were ten to one.

And it wasn't just Collingwood. Wherever you were, it was the luck of the draw. Nicholas Caire, who photographed the pristine beauty of the water catchments, had a twenty-year-old son, just beginning to follow in his artistic footsteps, who died of typhoid. The first head of the Botanic Gardens, that Garden of Eden, reputedly died from drinking bad water. The young Mac Robertson's brother's death was due to typhoid. And James Blackburn, saviour of Melbourne's water supply and planner of Yan Yean, also died of typhoid before his vision became reality.

The councils finally stopped household cesspools and pits being used, and the whole takeaway dilemma began. 'Night soil',* one of the great euphemisms of history, was discreetly removed—then dumped in Fitzroy Gardens, Princes and Fawkner Parks, Fishermans Bend, into the nearest waterway and onto commercial orchards, market gardens and municipal depots. A suburb's worth went into the Yarra over the side of the Johnston Street Bridge, or next to it, every night for years.†

The manuring of public gardens, however, was officially sanctioned and intended to improve soil quality as well as getting rid of the malodorous mountains. The night trenching must have worked, because in the 1880s the *Picturesque Atlas* approvingly commented of Fitzroy Gardens, 'The natural sterility of the soil was overcome by artificial means...A stranger from Europe finds considerable difficulty in believing that the lofty and umbrageous trees of exotic origin which now adorn the gardens are little more than twenty years old.'

It was night soil that created inner-suburban Melbourne's network of laneways. The sanitary closet (toilet or dunny) stood in solitude up against the back fence. It had a creosoted galvanised iron pan, about the size of a small, broad, rubbish tin, sited below a wooden seat, and a little door below, giving on to the lane. The night man would open the door—one would hope not to be in there at the time—remove the full pan, empty it into his much larger tank and

---

* The 'night men' were at first only allowed to work under cover of darkness.

† Disposal of night soil into the nearest wetland occurred in newer suburbs well into the 1960s. Sewerage overflow outfalls into the river were reported by the score from the 1950s to 1970s. In the mid-1960s more than forty million gallons of raw sewage were flowing into the Yarra in one year; there are still occurrences caused by floodwater entering the system. Until comprehensive sewerage reaches suburbs, septic tank seepage also continues to end up in the waterways. In the Shire of Yarra Ranges there are reportedly 23,000 septic tanks of which 15,000 are thought to be failing. Grey water was legally plumbed to the stormwater system—our creeks and rivers—only a few decades ago.

cart and replace it, with maybe a few slops remaining. Initially you had to pay extra for him to replace the full pan with a clean one.

Gentlemen of privilege might place their posteriors on superior WCs. Before Melbourne was sewered, water closets such as those at Parliament House, the Treasury and Government House flushed straight into the Yarra, creating a stench even for those who were believed (due to their social position or self regard) to be unable to smell it.

James Blackburn, as well as devising the Yan Yean water supply for Melbourne, suggested a sewerage system fifty years before one finally went in. It was the big depression of the early 1890s, along with a Royal Commission into the scandalous stench and the fatal sicknesses, that finally encouraged its development.

A massive work program began in 1892; the system first became operational in 1897. Pipes were laid from every house, shop, factory and office, mapped and calculated across the entire metropolis to fall by gravity to a point in Spotswood near the mouth of the Yarra. There, a pumping station pushed the dark, liquid underworld river carried by the main sewer up and into an open channel, down which it fell another sixteen miles to Werribee Sewerage Farm. Then seen as barren flatland edging Australia Felix (although today it's the second-largest bird sanctuary in Australia, after Kakadu), the Farm was big enough to require its own company town. They ran championship beef, and processed tonnes and tonnes of Melbourne's sewage. It was uncalled for, the expression of derision: 'He couldn't get a job shovelling shit.'

~ ~ ~

As the first mapping of the Yarra was being done in 1803, James Flemming observed that 'wreck on the trees' showed the river could rise metres on occasion, but that 'the greatest part of the land is above the floods'. The first big river flood after settlement peaked in Melbourne on Christmas Eve 1839. Kulin forecast it a week or two beforehand (in reference to Barak's tale: the sky did fall and burst; people—drunk people—did drown).

After a hot and windy first three weeks of December there were three days and nights of rain. Snow fell on the Upper Yarra and melted quickly. What is now Southbank was quickly submerged under two metres of water, washing away the brickmakers set up there. An old colonial later reported rowing from the Customs House in Flinders Street across South and Port Melbourne to the beach. Batmans Hill (now, flattened, the Spencer Street Station site) was an island; Collingwood and Richmond became one huge circular lake. The flour mill at Dights Falls was under water to the second storey.

The next major flood was in winter, at the end of July 1842. Again, the south bank was inundated and Melbourne reduced to a string of islands. This is when Michael Cashmore undertook his most famous journey: overland by open boat from Footscray to Flinders Street (the Royal Highlander Hotel to be exact) where he and his mates tied up at the bar.

In October of that year came the next big flood, the Yarra rising fifteen metres at Heidelberg. Crops planted along the river and its tributaries Merri, Darebin and Moonee Ponds creeks were washed away, and the same low-lying areas as the last time were covered by the waters.

Two years later the suffering began again, this time the brickmakers evacuating ahead of the flood and making fast along with other riverbank inhabitants, whether fellmongers or householders. Boating in the town's streets seemed to be seasonal. At Dights Falls, where the river rose about twelve metres, people had to be rescued from being swept away and drowning in the streets.

There were half a dozen floods in the first ten years of settlement. A 1960s Board of Works table lists the magnitude of the Yarra's floods from settlement: the 1839 flood is the largest at 58,000 cusecs.* The 1863 flood was as big, other 1840s floods still in the fifty thousands. In 1863 38,000 cusecs were passing the Botanic Gardens, with a quarter of the total flow not making it under Princes Bridge (then single-arched), but rather flooding across the old river delta through Albert Park to the sea—which itself had risen tidally an extra metre. As well as this and the torrential rain, a south-west gale pushing water back up the river may have been another factor in the inundation. The 1934 flood magnitude was 40,500 cusecs, peaking at Warrandyte with about two years' worth of flow passing in a single moment.

Early on, Elizabeth Street, located between the two hills of Melbourne's street grid, was 'a jungly chasm—an irregular broken-up ravine, through which the winter flood-waters thundered along over shattered tree-trunks, displaced rocks, roots and ruts' or at its best 'a shallow gully'. It couldn't be crossed below Lonsdale Street in heavy rain, and was still recalled in the 1920s as 'within the memory of our grandfathers...a brawling impassable torrent in winter and a snake-haunted gully in summer'.

Swanston Street was described as a shallow gully, Flinders Street a 'swamp', and Collins Street 'slushy and sticky'. Holes in city streets were described as big enough for a child to drown in. Facetiously, two unusual Yarra tributaries were named: River Townend, running from the corner of Collins and Elizabeth streets (after the 'fat, comfortable-looking grocer' on the south-west corner); and River Enscoe, from the north-west corner of William and Flinders streets (after a business countinghouse there).

Garryowen mentions discussion of 'putting on a punt' to cross Elizabeth Street during winter, and the advertised sale of stilts so that

---

* 58,000 cubic feet of water rushing past per second.

the population of Melbourne could get around. A man was reported to have drowned with his horse in Elizabeth Street in the 1850s. Another experienced:

> a current…so impetuous that it made one giddy to gaze at it as it roared past, empty cases, coffee tins, old hats, sardine boxes, discarded clothes, tattered mats, butchers' offal, and all the varieties of household filth and warehouse abomination hoarded since the previous flood, careering frantically on its bosom. I saw a fine horse…drowned…at the crossing in front of the Post-office.

True, the roadway was drained by deep culverts on either side, but the footbridges over them would wash away past the barricaded shops. In the 1880s, 'In one heavy storm, indeed, a sober strong man was carried off his legs by the force of the stream, and ignominiously drowned in a gutter.'

Looking towards the Melbourne GPO in the 1972 flood. A fair bit of chop on Elizabeth Street as it reverts to what it once was, a waterway.

Elizabeth Street was a creek first, and in times of heavy rain—in that case, the heaviest rain ever recorded—it reverted. This tributary became one of the first huge stormwater drains constructed, in the 1880s, and is now known to the illicit underground explorers the Cave Clan as the City Drain. Even by 1972, after the watercourse had been contained underground for decades, a violent storm recreated River Townend above ground to a depth of metres in one afternoon. (In another 1970s flood, you could row along the riverine sea covering Melba Highway outside Yarra Glen, using cat's-eyed mile posts as markers; part of the South-Eastern Freeway also temporarily became a waterway.)

By the 1848 flood, the Royal Highlander pub, islanded again, was running ferry boats as a customer service. The town's open street drains were described as impassable reservoirs or whirlpools. South Melbourne's lowlands were under a metre of water and Richmond was isolated: Fitzroy Gardens and Richmond and Collingwood Flats were all under. Bernard Barrett has said, 'By the mid-1850s an hour's thunderstorm could create a lake covering two square miles on the Flat, rising two feet to the floors of the houses.'*

A destructive hurricane was reported over Melbourne one night in November 1849. By the next day there was the same old huge flood, with Batman's Swamp described as 'a new *Curiosity Shop*' containing a swirling mass of 'furniture, wood, bacon, pork, and poultry etc.', washing through from the slaughterhouses, and houses, upstream. The water went south for a kilometre down the St Kilda Road. This flood, like the one two years earlier, was put down to a large snow-melt.

In 1863, during severe flooding, a hansom cab complete with driver and horse was swept down Swanston Street and into the river. (The cabbie was rescued, the horse not.) At Warrandyte and Templestowe, bridges washed away; from there downstream to Alphington, crops and fences were gouged out, cattle drowned. A

* 'Richmond and Collingwood Flats' was then a topographical description; by the last quarter of the twentieth century it would refer to high-rise public housing in the same locations.

thousand-hectare lake was created. The decorative new Burnley gardens of the Horticultural Society disappeared down the river (later to be replanted with more than a thousand varieties of fruit and trees within their fifteen hectares).

Six months later the newspapers were reporting the river flooding again, and 'St Kilda cut off from communication with Melbourne; Emerald Hill is an island of Port Phillip Bay; Richmond is half under water; and Sandridge is no one knows where.' Goldfields on the Upper Yarra were in complete disarray.

The 1891 flood was another big one, with a metre of water in parts of Richmond and South Melbourne. In Trennery Crescent (site of Yarra Falls woollen mills, close to the original Victoria Park home of Collingwood Football Club), waters reached the second-floor balconies of terrace houses. In South Yarra, more than a thousand people were made homeless. Three people died.

Though not the largest flood, 1934 probably had the greatest impact because of the number of people and buildings affected. Every creek and river in Melbourne broke its bank, and the Yarra recorded its highest flow, nearly 97,000 million litres in one day.* The cause was the highest amount of Yarra catchment rainfall recorded within a three-day period: cyclonic weather had swept the state. This flood is also the one most recorded in our communal visual memories. The old Burke Road bridge at Ivanhoe and paddocks for half a kilometre around were completely under water. Kanes Bridge in Studley Park washed away; houses near the river in Kew were flooded up to their chimneys or second storeys; Kooyong Stadium was under water. At Johnston Street the river was more than twelve metres higher than usual. Boatsheds, landings and watercraft washed away. Como (Herring) Island was completely under water, its vegetation destroyed.

The river reached as far as Toorak Road, near Chapel Street, and at the other end, carried away the Gardiners Creek road bridge.

---

* The lowest recorded flow is 17 million litres in one day, which gives some indication of the variation and dynamics of the river.

More than half a dozen people died and 1,500 were made homeless. Factories in Richmond and Collingwood were flooded and jobs were lost; thousands of houses in Abbotsford, Richmond, Kew and Heidelberg were damaged.

Upstream was just as severe. At Warrandyte a mob of sheep, a haystack and a number of huge trees were reported to have swept by in the raging torrent. It washed away three bridges in Warburton, as well as many stacks of logged and milled timber (in the process destroying further property downstream), and flooded the Seventh Day Adventists' Sanitarium and Signs Publishing factories, later rebuilt in a safer location. (More than fifty years later, Signs staff wrote that they were still finding pieces of movable type revealing themselves in the riverbanks.)

Sections of the Yarra can even flow backwards. Big spring or king tides flooding in, aided by strong south-westerly winds, can push up against the downstream flow. These circumstances, along with several days' heavy rain or snow-melt in overflowing catchments or a full moon's extra tidal effect, can all be factors in high water or floods on the Yarra, and that seemingly unnatural once-in-a-lifetime occurrence.

Two large natural flood storage basins exist on the river: Chandler Storage, which runs fifteen kilometres from Chandler Highway bridge up to Plenty River; and Yering Storage, which runs forty kilometres up from Yering Gorge to Yarra Junction. Because of the amount of water they can hold, a flood going downstream to the city of Melbourne can be reduced in volume by a quarter and delayed by about twelve to eighteen hours. That delay lessens downstream peak flood levels, because water from the middle and lower tributaries can get through the river and out to the Bay before the deluge from the Upper Yarra hits.*

These flood storage basins are the ghosts of the lakes Billibellary spoke about in the Yarra creation story: the lakes filled with the

* Water from the upper reaches takes about three days to come down.

water dammed by lava flows downstream, on raised flood plains formed by metres of alluvial or river soil.

Around the suburbs there are much smaller retarding basins (disguised as green open space near waterways) designed to serve the same function in times of severe flood, and based on where original creeks or wetlands may have been. They are built into new developments—sometimes as new waterways or wetlands—and serve to naturally filter stormwater before it hits the creek and river systems as well as taking in floodwaters and lowering the surge.

~ ~ ~

When, in the middle of the nineteenth century, Rolf Boldrewood* (and Robert Hoddle similarly) described the Yarra, upstream at Yering, as 'not much less wide or rapid' than the river in the centre of the city, they were not using poetic licence. In fact, the original cityside Yarra was much closer in appearance to those upstream, unengineered reaches. From its mouth as far up as Cremorne Rail Bridge, the modern Yarra is a constructed environment unrecognisable from its earlier natural state.

And this is because the river, in its lazy way, is implacable. It meanders and spreads around obstacles, changing with its own dynamics: the obstacles are part of it. The old river was recalcitrant, and unfortunately that messes with the infrastructure of a big city. It had to be controlled—with 'realignments', levees and retarding basins. The river was cleaned up and made as un-Australian as possible, that is, as regular and European as it could be. Notions of a 'meandering sluggish river' were opposed by those of a 'safe navigable urban river'; a tidy sense of beauty was imposed.

In the decades after settlement it could take days by sail to pass the lower reach of the river, from Queens Wharf in the centre of Melbourne across Hobsons Bay to Williamstown. You might get stuck on a mudbank waiting in deep tedium for the tide near one of the stinking boiling-down plants, watching pigs feeding on hills of discarded sheep's heads; or be becalmed and wait for wind in Humbug Reach, where the Yarra did one of its 200-degree turns, picking up the Maribyrnong River on the way.

Garryowen described the banks of the Yarra Yarra down to the

* The Boldrewood family's 130-hectare riverfront property, Hartlands, exactly opposite Bolin-Bolin Billabong, would become prime Heidelberg School landscape.

'Saltwater confluence' as originally 'low marshy flats, densely garbed with teatree, reeds, sedge and scrub. Large trees, like lines of foliaged sentinels, guarded both sides, and their branches protruded so far riverwise as to more than half shadow the stream'. Rolf Boldrewood wrote of 'the tortuous but necessary navigation of the Yarra Yarra...which noble stream, moving calmly through walls of ti-tree'.

The banks were crumbly, irregular. A mud bar at the entrance stopped any ship with a draught of more than a couple of metres from entering and the river itself was barely wide enough for two vessels to pass each other. Even by the late 1870s, despite dredging, only ships with a draught of less than four metres could enter Melbourne without running aground.

The river's mouth was altered and shifted slightly in the 1860s—moved about three hundred metres east, widened to approximately sixty metres, and straightened in the direction of Newport. However the biggest changes wrought on the river were devised in the late 1870s by Sir John Coode, an English engineer brought out by the new Melbourne Harbor Trust. His scheme was: to widen and

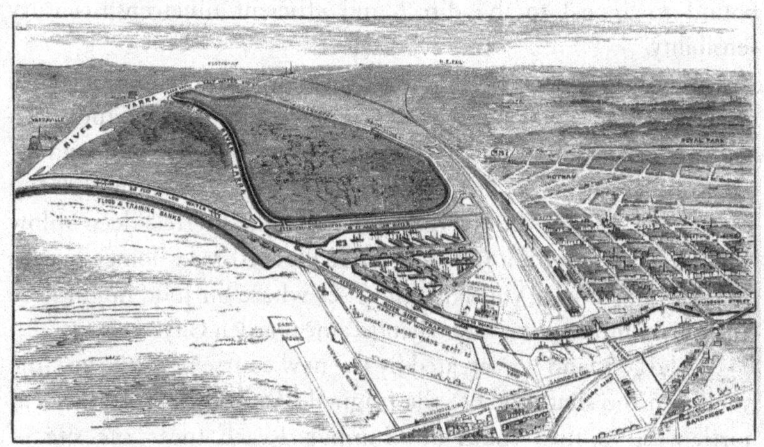

THE NEW CHANNEL FOR THE YARRA.

Detail of the soon-to-disappear section of Yarra and the river channel that replaced it.

deepen the river from its city reaches down; to cut a new regularly curved channel bypassing Humbug Reach and the old Fishermans Bend (actually an opposite bend to the area that now bears the name); to drain West Melbourne Swamp and put in a huge dock; to blast away any rocky reefs and to embank the lower reaches. The river was to be shortened by more than a kilometre.

The scheme would enable deepwater shipping to get in and out faster and to dock right in Melbourne, close to a rail terminal. Not only that, floodwaters would be able to sweep away unhindered, straight through to the Bay, while confining and concentrating the current would sweep sediment along and lessen the need for dredging. As a bonus, the millions of tonnes of earth excavated could be used as fill for the swampland, reclaiming it for further industrial development.

Given that the havoc wrought by the serial floods of the preceding decades had provoked all sorts of administrative hand-wringing, including government inquiries and royal commissions, a plan that would control flooding by 'getting water away quicker', as well as deepening the harbour, getting more ships in and so on, was bound to appeal to the direct and efficient nineteenth-century sensibility.

The centrepiece of this grand plan was the relocation of an entire section of river south of its original course through the artificially constructed Coode Canal. Dug by steam shovel and hand for over a mile, it was 266 feet (80 metres) wide at water level, 100 feet (30 metres) wide at the riverbed and 20 feet (6 metres) deep at low tide, on a curve with a radius of 10,000 feet (three kilometres). It's such a regular curve you can almost see where Sir John might have stuck his compass point into what became Garden City.

A large island was created by the new course of the river—the canal—in the south, where the original bend of the Yarra headed north-west to turn south at Humbug Reach (near the site of Footscray Road, now Harbour Esplanade) and Maribyrnong River in the west (south of Parker Street, Footscray). The original section of the Yarra from that historic confluence down to the canal became the lowest reach of the Maribyrnong River. What we know now as the confluence of the two rivers (at Holden Swinging Basin, between Lorimer Street, Fishermans Bend and Yarraville Wharves) is actually the old Yarra meeting the new Yarra.

The bypassed curve of the river not now part of the Maribyrnong has disappeared (imagine the angle of its direction as extending from Ingles Street, Port Melbourne, and touching the furthest berths of Swanston and Appleton docks). Dredged river silt filled it, mostly from the excavation for Appleton Dock, and there was Coode Island: finally a geographical location rather than a description. Hundreds of shipping containers are now stacked high over what was Humbug Reach. (It was this sharp bend that had to go, as well as the shallowness—big ships were unable to turn around such a constricted area.)

At the Coode Scheme's completion in 1886, when the sluice gates were lifted, it took a week for the river to fill the new channel. The cut had taken nearly seven years to construct. It was months before the earthworks and construction holding the water back were removed and the river embanked ready for business.

Then work began on the eastern fringes of West Melbourne swamp, site of the former Blue Lake, to create the huge new Victoria

Water starts flowing into the new section of the Yarra River, 1886, close to the current site of the Bolte Bridge.

Dock, largest dock in Australia and second largest single dock in the world, not to mention the Empire. The river within covered about fifty hectares, by 1919 to a depth of about ten metres, approximately three million cubic metres. Canals were built to drain West Melbourne swamp; a couple of million tonnes of earth excavated from Coode Canal and the dock filled it, and the continuation of the Moonee Ponds Creek emerged, as the Railway Coal Canal, into the river at Victoria Dock.

The river's depth and width along its southern bank were doubled and tripled, respectively, by excavation, dredging or blasting* and embanking. Eventually the riverworks reached upstream to the Botanic Gardens, with the banks themselves raised in places. The rocky reefs in the city section of the river—at Spencer Street and at the Falls at Queen Street—were dynamited away; the rock was used to line Coode Canal and embank the river all the way down to the Bay, with 'training walls' put in along the sloppy, sandy, natural bits, laying out where the defined banks should be. Saltwater now had tidal reach all the way up to Dights Falls and the fresh-water/saltwater separation of the Falls, the original reason for Melbourne's siting, was gone.

River dredging started in the late 1840s and has gone on ever since, keeping channels clear for shipping and providing fill for the 'snaky, swampy' lower reaches (the surplus was dumped in the Bay). Silt—the cause of the notorious turbidity—is a perennial problem. As the river slows closer to its mouth and the level of the sea, sediment (carried from upstream and held suspended by the flow) drops, a process aided by reaction with the saltwater making it clump.

Ever since settlement, with its land clearing and cultivation, more silt has been coming down.† One of the reasons Coode recommended the channelising of the lower Yarra and Maribyrnong

---

* As late as the 1930s, on Sir John's recommendation of many years before, thousands of tonnes of rock were blown out of the riverbed just upstream of Princes Bridge.

† It has also carried 170-odd years of contamination with it—it's this area that critics of port channel deepening are concerned about disturbing and letting loose in the waters of the Bay and River.

was to contain and concentrate the power of the outflowing tide and current in clearing the inevitable silt. By the 1880s, about half a million cubic metres of the stuff were dredged from the river each year (the dredger *Bunyip* could lift 175 tonnes in half an hour). Though part of that was excavation for river widening, river depth was also increased each year.

Except, that is—before the Board of Works sewerage system became fully operational in the twentieth century—where the town's sewage was flowing out to settle on the bottom of the river. In 1896 and '97, more than a hundred thousand cubic metres of silt were dredged out of the river between Queens Bridge and Spencer Street alone, yet, after all that, the river was shallower there than it had been in 1895. The *Jubilee History of the Melbourne Harbor Trust* ascribed it to the quantity of sewage coming down: 'The foulness of the River Yarra,' it said, '...was a byword of jest and disgust.'

By the end of the nineteenth century, the amount of silt deposited annually in the lower reaches of the river was estimated at 1,400,000 cubic yards. Prior to World War One, day and night dredging* maintained the river at standard depths: 37 feet (11.28 metres) from the river mouth up to Spotswood, 32 feet in Coode Canal up to Johnson Street, and then 27 feet up to Spencer Street in the city. By the early 1900s Coode Canal had already been widened and deepened again several times. In the 1920s, hundreds of people were employed in dredging operations on the river and out through the shipping channels.

The port section of the river was 40 feet deep by the 1970s, and the channel to Swanson Dock more than 400 feet wide. Ships kept—keep—getting wider and deeper; channels have to match them.

The Coode canalisation and channelising continued up the river. The next big scheme was the Botanic Gardens or New Cut, put in train by the 1891 flood. Carlo Catani, Public Works man in charge of the whole scheme, described Batman Avenue (the earlier Yarra Bank

---

* The only reason it eased up then was that the Royal Australian Navy had another use for some of the floating hardware.

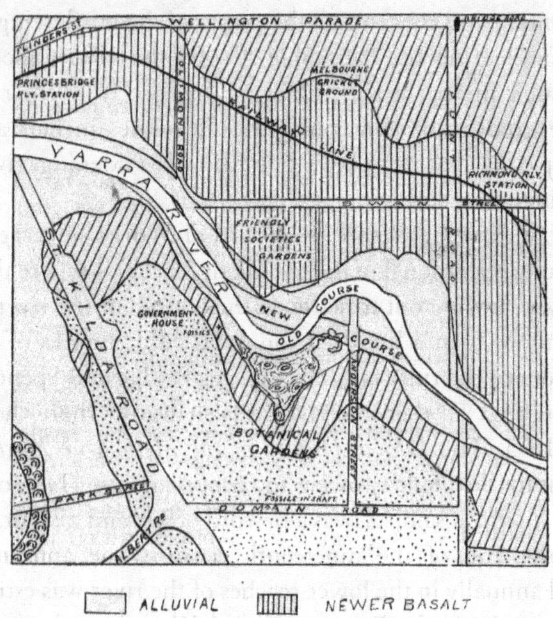

A geological map of 1910 shows where the river was shifted near the Botanic Gardens, and Morell (Anderson Street) Bridge built over dry land.

Road) and Alexandra Avenue as 'ornamental drives where people go to see and be seen'. His intention was,

> besides the principle of reducing the flood-level, the other equally important one of improving and straightening the bed of the river for navigation and recreation purposes, and also that very important factor of forming a beautiful promenade, worthy of Melbourne, on the bank of the river, where all classes could meet.

He loved the scheme so much that when his departmental budget became a casualty of the 1890s economic crash he is said to have planted a lot of the oaks, elms and poplars himself.

The 'major realignments' or channelising went up to Church Street Bridge. The river was deepened, widened on the south side near the Domain to about one hundred metres and embanked from Princes Bridge up to Punt Road. An entire northward and southward bend was taken out, making the stretch one smooth curve. The cut-off southward bend became an auxiliary part of the Ornamental Lake (formerly lagoon, formerly billabong) in the Botanic Gardens, with ornamental islands and promontories landscaped and built up.

The created Long Island is the original riverbank, and it shows how narrow a strip of land could separate the billabong/lagoon/lakes from the Yarra. Rustic bridges over the lake were built from trees along the riverbank. Baron von Mueller's riverside cottage (the Plant Craft Cottage, near Gate H) now overlooked a lake some distance away instead.

The next northward bend upstream, towards Swan Street, was filled (the tip became Goschs Paddock, now a low-lying area of green between Punt Road and Olympic Park), and the river was cut a whole new bed to its south. Morell Bridge was built over the dry and empty excavation in 1899, before the river was rerouted back in. The new riverbed cut to the north of the modern Botanic Gardens stretch, taking in part of what had been the large billabong on the Richmond side of the river.*

Fill from the cut and the widening was used to bury the rest of it, and build up what became the causeway of Alexandra Avenue, from Anderson Street to St Kilda Road. This was the new northern boundary of the Botanic Gardens, rather than the river's banks. The ornamental lake created from the Domain Lagoon, another old billabong, was also filled and became Alexandra Gardens.

Further up, to Johnston Street Bridge, the river has also been considerably 'modified'. Between 1902 and 1905 the Board of Works took out a lot of trees and snags along the river in the section from Cremorne up to Johnston Street Bridge: in fact, 1,072 snags, 1,100 stumps, 1,209 willows, twelve piles and several sunken boats. By the late 1920s the Board of Works had control of the river, and removed

* The site was originally used for Melbourne's first Zoological Garden in the late 1850s.

almost 25,000 snags from its course up to Templestowe, inventing or adapting several new tools to grapple with the problem.*

The Board's purpose was to clear the river's flow for flood and navigation, safety and beauty. They pursued it vigorously until even the golf clubs were concerned about the number of trees they were removing from the river banks, fearing it would cause more flooding rather than less, and local papers reported erosion occurring at three times the normal rate.†

The stretch between Punt Road and Gardiners Creek was 'beautified'—the river widened, and crumbly irregular natural banks graded, beached and grassed—a process that continued upstream as far as Bridge Road over the next decade. Banks upstream from Princes Bridge that had been artificially sloped were beached with bluestone from the Quarry Cut at Richmond after it was taken over by the Board of Works in the 1920s. (The river immediately above Princes Bridge had been doubled in width from the south side when the new bridge went in during the 1880s.)

In Burnley, the Yarra snaked around some large dug-out quarries on the Richmond side, with only narrow ridges of stone left separating them from the river. To give floodwaters a more direct exit path, a new channel was cut through, joining with the water already filling the old quarries and bypassing the old loop, although the river was still allowed to flow there. The new cut was 10 feet (3 metres) deep and 75 feet (23 metres) wide.

Together with the old loop, it created Como (Herring) Island, which was then built up with earth taken out of the cut. It took a few years to establish the island, dumping river silt dredged from between Queen Street and Cremorne Rail Bridge onto the island's basalt base and building up levee banks to fill the quarried area.

The river was also dug out and widened on the Richmond side from Church Street upstream to the Quarry Cut. The Board, and

---

* It's perhaps an indication of the mentality involved that the MMBW's corporate history was able to report an exact quantity of snags: 24,413.

† As noted by T. S. Hall commenting as early as 1911 on the loss of original bush surrounding Melbourne waterways, 'The cutting down of forests over large areas increases the danger of floods by pouring into the river water that should have taken weeks or months to find a way into them.'

later the Water Police, used part of the flooded quarry for a boat harbour and slipway.

Melbourne & Metropolitan Board of Works became responsible, in due course, for freeways as well as the river. So by 1969 they could do things like reroute the Yarra at Heyington/Burnley by cutting a loop out (the site is now the E. J. Bastow Oval), because it was cheaper than building three bridges for the South-Eastern Freeway* to cross it. Originally, Burnley Gardens just about backed onto the river. (To view some spectacular ugliness in a beautiful location, take a walk under the freeway just up from this Heyington 'diversion', where the feet of the freeway are sunk in the guts of Gardiners Creek at its confluence with the Yarra. This saved the cost of paying for privately owned land alongside it.)

Waterways such as the Yarra and its creeks were seen merely as drains, annoyingly unpredictable in their overflow—the Yarra was actually known as No. 1 Drain—and the green flood-plain corridors were the most obvious, simplest and cheapest sites for freeways. Moonee Ponds Creek and the Tullamarine Freeway are another great example.

In the 1970s, with the eight to ten lanes and thousands of tonnes of the Eastern Freeway going through, there were more earthworks: whole loops or bends of the Yarra were filled or shortened, such as Deep Rock swimming basin located near where the Merri Creek joins the river just above Dights Falls. Originally, the confluence formed a pincer promontory on the Yarra's northern bank east of Merri Creek, ending in a couple of islands in the bend toward the Falls, although these were already gone by 1900, and the northern loop was filled later.

Bebejern, Barak's father, and Billibellary, Barak's uncle, both Wurundjeri headmen and 'signatories' to Batman's treaty, were buried in Aboriginal ground there, but by the latter twentieth century the exact location of the burial sites was unknown. The unmarked earth was moved, cut or filled; the river and creek 'realigned' for the freeway.

---

* Now the Monash Freeway.

It would now be impossible to trace what was before. We have lost not only names, words, knowledge, waterways and bush, but the graves of great men.

The other 'diversion' created for the Eastern Freeway was to obliterate a natural loop downstream of Kew Billabong—like Deep Rock, a stretch of the river with a constructed community swimming area—and bypass it with a much shorter channel, half a kilometre long and straight as a ruler. The main cut-and-filled river loop is buried under a golf course on the other bank. Its two southernmost bends lie under the Eastern Freeway, about three-quarters of a kilometre outbound from Chandler Highway overpass.

The process of ruination and annihilation of the Yarra's billabongs, lagoons, waterholes and creeks has been repeated over and over for more than a century. The stages can take decades: a waterway or wetlands becomes a receptacle for human sewage and rubbish, is rightly pronounced a disgusting health hazard, and the problem is solved by either filling it in, concreting it or putting it underground.

At first this process, like the dumping sites, was informal or illegal; after the establishment of municipal and sanitary rubbish collections the sequence was managed officially. In the late 1960s 'sanitary landfill' was still being tipped into natural billabongs in the middle Yarra area and covered with soil cut from the surrounds. Billabongs and river beaches were destroyed.

Every time you see a sward of municipal green, take a moment to wonder where the creek is, or the billabong, the waterhole, or the river's edges (now, with cut and fill, a golf course, freeway, tennis court, carpark, scout hall, playing field...).

Every community's history can tell the story. In the nineteenth century, Fitzroy and Treasury Gardens were praised for the fact that an 'unsightly gully'—that's a little creek that naturally flowed through there—had been 'completely masked by trees and shrubs'. But actually it was more than unsightly, it was running with raw sewage from salubrious East Melbourne and Fitzroy and surrounded by dumped garbage; so the out-of-sight-out-of-mind position was understandable. A local history of 1912 describes a former creek of

Dredging silt and building up the river banks, 1882: what is now known as Southbank Docklands area.

(South) Yarra: 'The main drain, useful, but ugly…was once the bed of the stream that flowed through the useless but picturesque swamp.'*

As late as the 1970s historians could write of a spot in Yarra-tributary suburbia, 'Eventually all this land has been reclaimed, and no one strolling on this green expanse today would even suspect the existence of the creek.' (This particular creek had been large enough to appear as a major waterway on 1880s maps.†)

The attitude that, up until relatively recently, insisted on endraining and de-naming messy flora- and fauna-banked creeks or 'unwholesome and useless swamps', and mocked public opposition to embanking or channelising of the river, has had to be re-examined. That model, developed to deal with rampant human and industrial waste, persisted even when the causes were gone. The habits and attitude continued long after the practices were rendered unnecessary by a functioning sewerage system and organised waste management.

---

* The place where this drain empties into the Yarra was reported in 2005 as the most polluted of all river sites tested.

† Connors Creek, flowing north-west through Kew and entering the river under the Eastern Freeway near Kew Billabong.

Attempting flood control by smoothing and straightening riverbanks makes flow a lot faster, but it destroys the river as a living environment, increases silt and turbidity and may even increase flooding downstream. Less vegetation and more hard surfaces in areas leading to the river also speed up stormwater flow, increase erosion and shift more silt. Desnagging has been proven to be of little value; rock beaching is useful only when 'soft engineering'—that is, a planted bank (with 'root armouring')—cannot survive.

Today, public corporations, private companies and community organisations replant all along the river. We know now that removal of vegetation leads to destruction of wildlife habitat, negative biodiversity and general river ill-health. Banks erode and the higher turbidity creates poorer water quality, accelerated when there is insufficient natural debris in the water or on the banks to filter sediment and pollution. A six-metre strip of natural vegetation can trap up to 90 percent of sediment and phosphorus heading down for the river.

Desnagging, in fact, has come to be officially listed as a Potentially Threatening Process under the *Victorian Flora and Fauna Guarantee Act*. Nonetheless, desnagging and bulldozing of the riverside were still being carried out by government bodies and contractors in the middle and upper reaches of the river in the early 1980s. It's only since the 1990s that Melbourne Water, the economically rationalised reincarnation of the Board of Works, has been 'resnagging': putting snags back in parts of the Yarra—or at least allowing them back; and even then, private clearing has persisted.

When Garryowen described the early settlement Yarra as 'half-choked with the trunks and branches of fallen trees and other impedimenta' he was talking about its natural state. This large wooden debris, supplied by trees along the riverbanks (and now known as LWD) is going back in, too. In the twenty-first century, waterways planners and real estate developers look for 'off-stream stormwater storage areas'—billabongs and wetlands—for beauty, biodiversity, flora and fauna habitat, and better water quality through sediment clarification and removal of phosphorus and nitrogen.

If these areas aren't there they're designing them back in. The government's aim in its Victorian River Health Strategy is for rivers to have 'flows that rise and fall with the seasons, inundating flood plains, filling billabongs and providing a flush of growth and return of essential nutrients back to the river'. Billabongs have been artificially created, whether from remnants of agricultural dams, or landscaped into new public projects. More billabongs, wetlands and waterways will hopefully be preserved, or reinstated. Even the old Turning Basin—site of Melbourne's founding—was re-established and reopened by the City of Melbourne in 1997 as an award-winning piece of urban design, rather than the filled-in carpark it had become. Ironically, the English-garden-style European rivers we attempted to recreate for so many years are now having their own 'billabongs' or cut-off meanders recreated, too, where possible, because it's better waterway management.

Christopher Bailey was a suburban amateur naturalist born in the late nineteenth century whose focus was the Yarra. His mother had grown up on the river in Hawthorn, and as an adult he brought up his own family alongside it in Ivanhoe. For several decades till the 1970s he kept a scrapbook record of what was happening to his river. Pasted into the frontispiece of the first half-metre-high volume was the handwritten inscription:

> My duty as a Historian is:—
>
> To search and record all the events that have changed, are changing, or are likely to change the Yarra Valley from a rural nature.
>
> To collate these facts, and suggest ways that will keep the valley as close as possible to an environment that will give rest, healing, and stimulation to all who enter its portals.

He fought many battles. Towards the end of his long life, recollecting the filling with garbage of a maze of billabongs, he wrote, 'If the billabongs had been kept in their natural state, what a city of world fame Melbourne would have become.'

Bring back the billabongs. Give us back our real river.

DISASTER

32 DEAD
19 HURT
4 STILL MISSING

Moment of impact

BUREAU SAYS. — City: Mostly fine, brief morning shower. Expected top temp., 66 deg. Yesterday's top, 64 deg. ●Details, Page 42.

The Sun NEWS-PICTORIAL
DAILY AT DAWN
44 FLINDERS ST. PHONE 63-0211 BY AIR 6c 5c
Melbourne, Friday, October 16, 1970 60 Pages

THIS is the moment of impact as a 384ft. span of the Westgate Bridge collapses yesterday.

Clouds of black smoke billow from the 2000-ton tangle of steel and concrete.

The dramatic picture was taken by a boy, 10, using his father's 35 mm camera for only the second time.

Udo Rockman, of [illegible] Rd., Carnegie, was on an outing with 40 other pupils from Grades 5 and 6 of the local State school.

Their two buses, on a tour of city buildings, had stopped to let them look at the bridge.

"I took the picture of the bridge and then we heard an explosion," Udo said last night.

"So I put my camera up again and took another.

"At first I thought they were blowing something up.

"Then we realised the bridge was falling. I didn't see any men, but some of the other boys and girls said men were jumping and falling from it.

"When the bridge hit, it caught fire."

Other pictures of the crash were taken by **Karen Russell**, 11. They are on Page 2.

● UDO ROCKMAN, 10, who took the picture above with his father's camera.

By ALISTAIR SMITH

THE official toll in the Westgate Bridge disaster is 32 dead, with four men still missing last night.

Nineteen men were injured, many seriously.

Sixty men worked on late into the night under floodlights looking for bodies in the twisted metal and debris.

The collapse of the $42 million bridge over the Lower Yarra was the worst industrial accident in Victoria.

Sixty-eight men were in the area, some at lunch, when the disaster occurred at 11.50 a.m. yesterday.

Some of the men were in huts on top of a span which collapsed on to huts below.

Others were working inside the span and went with it to their deaths.

A Royal Commission will be held to find the cause of the collapse, the Premier, Sir Henry Bolte, announced.

The chairman of the Lower Yarra Crossing Authority, Mr O. G. Meyer, said last night the mid-span — 384 ft. long and weighing 2000 tons — collapsed first.

"This caused the pylon to collapse," he said.

"The span fell more than 150 ft."

The resident engineer on the site for the London design architects Freeman and Fox and Partners, Mr Jack Hindshaw, was killed.

Only six weeks ago he had assured a meeting of bridge workers that the bridge was safe.

Also killed was **Mr Ian Miller, 30**, the project manager of the concrete sections for the bridge constructors, John Holland (Constructions) Pty. Ltd.

Eyewitnesses of the bridge collapse described how there was first a sound like an explosion.

Then the span fell — slowly.

● CONTINUED PAGE TWO.

● *More pictures, reports — Pages 2, 3, 4, 5, 6, 17, Middle Pages, Back Page.*

Bridging it II

From the ruins

There are Yarra bridges, once well known, that no longer exist: the Studley Park, from the northern end of Church Street; the Botanical, from the Gardens to its own railway station; the original Chapel Street, built out of Crimean War army disposals; and the meeting of (damaged) minds—between the two lunatic asylums of Yarra Bend and Kew.

There was also a bridge that disappeared beneath the very feet of men, out of the blue into the Yarra mud below.

~

West Gate was going to be the biggest bridge in Australia, its length the same as the entire east–west axis of Melbourne's famous city grid as laid out by Robert Hoddle all those years ago. The furthest downstream of all Yarra crossings, it was also the only one designed to permit shipping to pass underneath. It was begun in the boom of the late 1960s to replace the Williamstown ferry, which had run in one form or another for more than a hundred and twenty years.

John Spottiswoode, lag, ran the first regular ferry service in the 1840s. Though there were reports of trouble with bad language, he scrubbed up to become Mr Spotswood and respectable, as did (eventually) the suburb named after him. The car ferry that the West Gate was to replace started up in 1931, running its chains from outside the old Newport power station across the river to Williamstown Road in Port Melbourne.

By late 1970, several years of construction had taken the West Gate Bridge a fair way towards completion. It was to be one of the longest cable-stayed box girder bridges in the world, two and a half kilometres long, with a middle span of a third of a kilometre and eight traffic lanes with two outside spares, standing 52 metres above the Yarra's high water. At this point the concrete piers and approaches were in place, with erection beginning of the five steel centre spans.

It all looked very impressive but in fact, according to the subsequent Royal Commission, the course of the construction comprised several years of incompetence, arrogance, backbiting, fear and general negligence by the professional parties involved, culminating in disaster. The first steel span on the eastern side was up, but the engineers and construction managers had had problems with buckling, and consequent corrections. The next steel span to go up was the first on the western side, and similar problems occurred.

On Thursday 15 October 1970, at 11.50 a.m., the first steel span on the western side collapsed, taking a pier support, several thousand tonnes of bridge and the lives of 35 workers with it. It was Australia's worst industrial accident. Any bodies that were recognisable as such, and not completely crushed or burnt in oxy fires, were coated in Yarra mud. It took a week to get them all out.

A group of school children on an excursion happened to be the ones watching at the moment of collapse. They reported seeing men jumping away, as well as falling helplessly into that twelve-storey drop. Some survived; rode the thing down.

No one simple design fault was identified; nonetheless the English firm responsible was given the largest part of the blame in the mesh of incompetence found to have caused the tragedy. Construction was halted, the fallen sections had to be removed, and it took a long time for the bridge to get up again. Redesigned and strengthened with altered construction methods, it was finished and finally opened in 1978.

A memorial sits at the base of the western pier. The concrete piers, described in the seventies as 'big enough to fit their own drive-in movie screens' form the massive curves of the bridge approaches. Seen from the ground, they have a brutal elegance: as with all Yarra bridges, West Gate can also be seen as sculptural form, and appreciated as such.

~

The first Sandridge Rail Bridge was built only a few years after the first Princes Bridge, and carried the first rail line in Australia, from Hobsons Bay/Sandridge/Port Melbourne, where the big ships tied up, to the city. Four steam locos (one called *Yarra*) ran on the line. The first bridge was of timber, with the line crossing the river at a right angle towards Flinders Street. The third bridge in the same spot, several decades on in the late 1880s, crossed the river on a 33 degree angle, the line eventually sliding into the last platform riverside of Flinders Street Station (once upon a time the busiest railway station in the world).

It was another David Munro bridge, of stone, steel, iron and concrete; solid and decorative. A basalt pilastered and pedimented niche stands empty above each pier. Beneath, the heavily riveted gunmetal grey arches and these supports form a wonderfully long water loggia in the diagonal stretch across the Yarra, corroding steel and concrete carried in its innards, and ending in beautiful abutments of finely detailed heavy stonework.

This last bridge was closed in 1987, a century after it was built, when the rail line disappeared and became 'light rail', actually a heavy tram system running elsewhere in the city. It is now flanked upstream by Southgate Footbridge, and looks downstream to Queensbridge.

~

The Chandler Highway Bridge was originally the Outer Circle Rail Bridge, and the Outer Circle was the fruit of a scam rail scheme supported by state politicians including Tommy 'by name by nature' Bent who—funnily enough—made money out of associated land speculation. John Monash engineered the bridge on the northern part of the line in 1890, and recorded seeing his life flash before his eyes there as he narrowly escaped being crushed by falling stone.

Last stop was Fulham Grange, just north of the Yarra (now the Amcor site), and this survived as a factory spur between the river and bridgeside papermill and Fairfield Station. The line closed within a few years of its opening, but nearly four decades went by between the depressions of the 1890s and the 1930s before the rail lines were ripped up and a road laid over the bridge and along the reservation to Princess Street, Kew.

~

At Yarra Glen—the township drawn from Burgoyne and Yarra Flats and so named when the railway arrived—the rail bridge was a claim to fame. Eight hundred men worked putting the line through in the late 1880s, with twenty bullock and a dozen horse teams. For nearly fifty years it was said to be the longest bridge in Australia: more than two kilometres of redgum piles crossing the bottom of the Yering flood basin, Billibellary's lake, and bearing 502 wooden trestle spans, two-thirds of which were were filled with earthen embankments in the 1930s.

~

There are fewer bridges than there might be arising from the construction in the late 1960s of Melbourne's first freeway, the South-Eastern. The river was rerouted to save on bridge building, but Heyington Rail Bridge, first constructed in the 1890s, did have to be relocated and built anew. The freeway, formerly known with fondness as the South-Eastern Carpark, was enlarged in the 1990s, becoming part of a private tollway named after John Monash—a fitting honour for the engineer, given that it also leads towards the university named after him. The freeway bridges appear to the driver as unremarkable but the bridge that carries the freeway over the Yarra was the second longest in Victoria. (It's the one with its feet sunk into Gardiners Creek.)

~

Working the river with private enterprise tollways has a long history, which didn't just start when Citylink built the Bolte Bridge. Its 140-metre-high multimillion-dollar twin towers are probably the largest, most expensive decoration to be found on any Yarra crossing. Not actually attached to the bridge, they are more like a visual reminder of what one should look like, markers in a flat landscape, although this award winning project (by DCM architects) is not some mere sketch. Steel piles 48 metres tall (the one in the middle took a 24-hour concrete pour to fill) sit in the notorious Coode Island silt, carrying half a kilometre of six-laned dual bridge. Five land-based piers hold the bridge up; the central one sits islanded at what was the end of North Wharf, and the opening to Victoria Dock or Harbour.

~

The first Eltham–Templestowe bridge went up as a tollway in 1855 but only lasted, probably unprofitably, till the 1863 flood. It was serendipitously replaced by what had been the old Warrandyte punt, washed downstream from its moorings in those same floods. In 1861 the first Warrandyte Bridge had superseded the 1850s gold rush punt, but it too, was washed away in the 1863 flood.

The old punt, though now down in Eltham, outlasted both bridges; at Warrandyte a pulley boat system was used until the second Warrandyte Bridge was built in 1875. This bridge was designed and constructed out of local yellowbox by the multi-talented Mr Wingrove, Eltham's Shire Clerk, Engineer and Surveyor for nearly fifty years. It survived going under the biggest floods of 1934 and at its demise, demolished for a new concrete bridge in 1955, it was the oldest surviving Yarra bridge.

~

Studley Park Bridge, a wooden penny toll bridge of the 1850s, ran from the end of Church Street, Abbotsford just north of Victoria Street, and led via another roadway to Nolan Avenue, on the ridge where John Hodgson had his home Studley House (later Wren House, Xavier Prep School). The bridge was built privately, with investors including Hodgson, whose punt had operated just round the bend.

Reportedly, the contractor was the man who put a bridge over Niagara, although one may wonder. The heavy wooden trestle was approximately seven metres wide. The timber for the piers was cut in the Dandenongs, the piles were redgum and the laminated arches were Baltic pine. It was once depicted as modern and elegant but its decades of decay were graphic, beams pitching and yawing at all angles.

The 1891 flood went full bore through the bridge, and it was finally demolished some time later, but its true decline dated from the late 1870s, when the government abolished tolls on their own bridges—such as Johnston Street, the next bridge down. The company owners wanted to demolish Studley Park Bridge then: with no tolls coming in, there was no commercial gain to be had from it, merely continued expenditure on maintenance. Ten years later Kew and Collingwood Councils and the Board of Works had to fight about who would take the rotten old thing away. Gone before the advent of the motor vehicle, it left a core of users pressuring the government (successfully) to build another bridge at Victoria Street.

~

The bridges of Hawthorn date from the early 1850s. Palmers Punt transported customers from Richmond to (the bottom of Denham Street) Glenferrie, and in 1842 was in great demand. Huge quantities of firewood for Melbourne crossed the river at this point. The second bridge over the Yarra, after Princes, was built out of wood here in 1851 and operated through a tollhouse on Bridge Road. Free passage, as Geoffrey Blainey notes, was given to men of the cloth, politicians, men in uniform (soldiers and police), churchgoers, funeralgoers and men carting manure—an interesting list for set theory.

Secure only in comparison to the punt, the low bridge, which stood upstream of the current bridge, had to be chained to large trees to stop it being swept away by flood. What replaced it in 1861 was a higher iron bridge of lattice girders resting on massive stone piers, with internal archways. It is now the oldest existing metal truss bridge in Australia.

Working the River

Australia's breakfast, and Australia's beer, came from the banks of the Yarra. There wasn't always a distinction between the two notions, particularly for some waterside workers coming off nightshift and settling in at the early openers. Various icons of Australian manufactory can be sourced to sites along the river. The yeast leftovers after CUB has been brewing go to Kraft—down the road from GM Holden in Port Melbourne—later emerging as Vegemite.

Foster's Lager is made next to the Yarra, and based on the profile of water drawn from its upstream catchments. Melbourne beer was once hopped from vines that grew upstream at Kew, Coranderrk and Heidelberg, and shipped downriver by barge to the port where waterside workers sent it out into the world. It's now bottled in glass from the former Australian Glass Manufacturers or ACI, downriver next to Scienceworks Museum at the old Spotswood Pumping Station. This factory has provided Melbourne with beer bottles since 1872. Once they were shipped in straw envelopes cut and manufactured in upstream riverside paddocks. Later, cardboard packaging was milled using riverwater on the banks at Fairfield, several kilometres away. The Weet-Bix Australian workers ate for breakfast were made using power from the river's flow way upstream in Warburton. The sauce on their lunchtime pies, the tanned leather of their boots, the apples they snacked on, the knitted wool of their socks and jumpers, could all have come from along the river's banks. At one time there were geographical reasons for all of this.

Some were on the river for what was beside it, some for what was underneath it, some for what it would take away. Some just wanted the power, the cool or the wet of it.

The boats might have gone, a lot of the ships too; the workers, woollens and Weet-bix. But in the early 2000s, the beer was still there.

Various breweries have been sited near the river. In 1840s Melbourne an ancestor of the artistic Boyd family, John Mills, wanted to build a conduit direct from the Yarra just above the Falls to his Flinders Street brewery. In the 1850s George Coppin had a small brewery in Abbotsford (downstream of the current megasite) at around the same time he ran Cremorne Gardens even further downstream. The ex-Shamrock Brewery on the next block from Coppin's later carried more fame by hosting the 1930s Skipping Girl vinegar sign atop its old roof, the first sequenced rooftop neon in Victoria. In Richmond, Tiger Beer was brewed out the back of Church Street riverside from 1929 to 1962.

But no Yarraside brewery is older, larger nor more influential than the Abbotsford brewery, ultimately producer of Australia's most famous beer, Foster's Lager. Beginning as the Melbourne Co-operative Brewery in 1904, a competitor to the Carlton & United Breweries, it finally merged and was taken over by CUB in 1925. Abbots Lager, Melbourne Bitter Ale Abbotsford Stout, Extra Double Stout, Sparkling Ale and Dinner Ale were original products, and at one time Abbots was more popular than Foster's Lager. Part of the site had also been occupied by a distillery that used riverwater in the manufacture of their whisky (a Yarra whisky, imagine).

Malted barley to make the beer at Abbotsford comes from Barrett Burston. Their concrete silos downriver at Punt Road

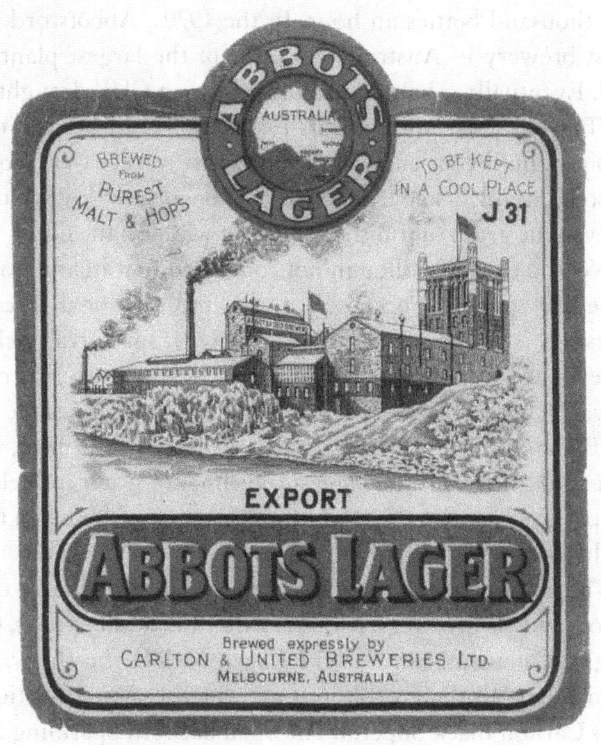

The castle of beer, Abbotsford. Church Street off right. Below-street-level basalt buildings are still visible riverside, although they are now battened off; the storeys above were razed and the site rebuilt on.

reached iconic status supporting the neon Nylex clock, but Burston of Richmond have been malting Melbourne beer for nearly a century and a half.

By the 1950s, Abbotsford brewery was handling packaged beers for the whole CUB group, refilling more than ten thousand bottles an hour. The different beers were then standardised, so that Foster's or VB would taste the same whichever plant it came from. This hadn't necessarily been the case previously—identically labelled beer might have come from Victoria Parade instead, or Carlton.

From 1962 the line ran 24 hours a day, turning out more than thirty thousand bottles an hour. In the 1970s, Abbotsford was the biggest brewery in Australia, and one of the largest plants in the world. Eventually it handled all the Victorian CUB draught beer as well. The old palace of beer (its castellations can be seen on early labels) was, unlike the current dry factory, very, very wet. Workers in their solid, wooden-soled, nailed leather boots were known to throw back even the green (unfinished) product while on the line.

Next to the river, though not connected to it in any way—and despite, or perhaps because of, its multinational presence—Abbotsford is still tied to Melbourne water from Yarra catchments. Wherever else its famous beers are brewed, they must first replicate that water, because otherwise they don't achieve the same beer. It takes five or so litres of water to make each litre of beer, and the Abbotsford brewery is the biggest consumer of water in Melbourne. They pay for it, and are restricted with everyone else when there's a drought on.

The plant now produces about two million stubbies a day, and ten thousand 50-litre kegs: Victoria Bitter (its number one), Carlton Draught, Crown Lager, Foster's Lager, Melbourne Bitter, Abbots Invalid Stout, all their variations and the occasional boutique line such as Carlton Black Superior Ale or Abbotsford Sparkling Ale.

CUB (the name altered to Carlton & United Beverages in 2004) has expanded into the Foster's Group which also owns one of the world's leading wine companies, Beringer Blass, and this boasts in its portfolio several Yarra Valley vineyards such as St Huberts and Yarra Ridge. Over a century ago the greatest of its chief brewers, Auguste de Bavay, owned half a Valley vineyard at Woori Yallock, so there is no novelty in the association.

The vineyards of the upper Yarra Valley take water from the river's watershed, collecting it in huge dams and/or pumping from the river or its tributaries. The first Yarra Valley wine was produced in 1845, at Yering Station. Some decades later, hundreds of thousands of vines in three major vineyards—Yering, St Huberts and Yeringberg—were bearing fruit, and the wines were winning gold medals in Paris and Bordeaux, where a lot of the original cuttings had come from (such as Chateau Lafite). The industry was developed by Swiss settlers, one of whom, Ernest Leuba, honoured the river by naming his first child Yarra Eugenie in 1862. By the 1920s, due to various circumstances, including lack of demand in a nation more accustomed to tea, beer, spirits and English cuisine,* the vines were ripped out and it all turned to dairy country, staying that way for five or six decades.

The properties of the river's water and river soil affect the wine. In the 1880s, at St Hubert's, Hubert de Castella observed Birrarung and the 'mystic lake':

> By midnight...a dense fog, lying flat on the ground like a sheet of water—a silver lake—out of which the tall gum trees and the dark clusters of mimosas, marking the course of the Yarra, emerge in solemn silence...in a few hours...The protective fog is rising, the silver cloud is slowly creeping up the slope of the hill. Before the dawn of the day, the dense vapour will have enveloped the vineyard.

He believed the silver lake emerged from the warm river, wrapped around his vines and protected them from frost, also 'contribut[ing] to the good quality of grapes at vintage time'. Some believe that is how Gulf Station—another one of the original Yarra Valley runs, and now a brand of De Bortoli Wines—got its name. In winter, from the top of the Yarra Ridge, looking down past Mount Wise towards Highbow Hill, a white, soft, dense, flat, mystic lake rolls away to the peaks on the opposite side of the valley: there are islands, gulfs...

Of the three great Yarra vineyards established by these noble Swiss adventurers, Guillaume de Pury's Yeringberg is the only one that has stayed in family hands, passing down through the generations, although the original vineyard was ripped out in 1921 and the

---

* Writer Hal Porter recalled, 'Wine is, in the Australia of the nineteen-thirties, generally considered to be only one cut above methylated spirits...the tipple of no-hopers, blackfellows, poverty-stricken alcoholics, and swagmen.'

new plantings were not put in until 1969, the first in the area. Its summit view of the valley, trees planted by Baron von Mueller and extraordinarily innovative winery and cellars built by David Mitchell in the 1870s remain alive today: a private, precious family 'kingdom' as all these properties once were.

Grapes have been grown on various sunny slopes heading down to the river, from those covering the northern slope of Punt Road* hill, South Yarra, after 1851 (a remnant survived until the 1920s), to small river frontages in Kew and Hawthorn a hundred and fifty years later. Studley Park Vineyard, near the Walmer Street footbridge, is, at the time of writing, metropolitan Melbourne's only commercial vineyard. It lies on the opposite bank to another subdivided in 1859, its riverfront willows, it was said, 'looked upon as the most beautiful ornament to the finest river walk in Melbourne'.

'Diverters'—businesses such as vineyards that are licensed to take water from the river—are varied and numerous, from papermills downstream to plant nurseries, golf courses and orchards. Melbourne Water manage the system, and are themselves required to maintain a minimum flow in the river. A sustainable diversion limit is figured out for each catchment and subcatchment, and major users are metered. Some diversion licences have been seasonal, obtainable for winter or for winter and spring, but not summer and autumn. When Melbourne and its catchment areas are in drought—which they have been for years at a time—diverters and their entitlements are restricted or even stopped.

Around twelve hundred users are registered in the Yarra catchment. With the huge growth in the number of vineyards, more and more large private commercial dams were put into the Yarra Valley around the turn of the millennium: by then it had around a thousand. In a dry year, autumn or winter flows are taken up filling a

* Now the name of another Yarra Valley winery.

dam, leaving nothing for the waterway. Consequently farm and vineyard irrigation dams must now be licensed or registered so that future water rights—or bulk entitlements—can be monitored, shared and traded.

There are also illegal diverters, wannabe pond scum who throw the pipe in and pump everybody else's water away when they think no one's looking. Creeks have been pumped dry in this way, even by such wholesome activities as organic vegetable growing and marijuana cultivation.

Apart from actual diversions—water taken from the river itself—a lot of water is taken before it even gets to the main river system, affecting the amount of flow. Melbourne's marvellous water supply is one great beneficiary and downstream much is lost to other factors. By the time it gets to the city, over a third of the river's total flow has been diverted one way or another*—it's not possible to take any more water from the river and keep it sustainable ecologically. There is no longer enough water for all who want it as well as the rivers and creeks themselves.

Working the river's water is everybody's business and politics. As perceptive high school teachers† used to intone decades ago (though perhaps from a slightly differing viewpoint): water is the limiting factor in Australia. Only now are the full implications beginning to be realised.

Settlement of Victoria followed flows of water because sheep, cattle and people need a permanent supply. So it was with the Yarra and its tributaries. The first settlers were as tied to it as Wurundjeri, and the creeks on which they located their runs—Ruffeys, Glass, Gardiners—took their names.

Yering (the Woiwurrung name for the deep waterhole fringed by blazing wattles on the Yarra River nearby) was originally settled as grazing land. In 1837 the Ryries took up the 30,000 acres of

* Overly low flows have been complained about since the Upper Yarra dam went in.

† Thank you Mr Watson.

Yering,* the adjoining 12,000 acres of View Hill or Tarrawarra in 1845, and the 16,000-acre Dalry, also adjoining, the following year. Several years later the de Castellas bought them out. It was not the uppermost station on the river; for some time that honour went to Solitude, round Woori Yallock. Cattle stations ran from there downstream to Prahran.

Along the way, a use was found for the billabongs either as water storage or pasture. Drained and kept that way—dried out for grazing land—or dammed and stopped with riverwater pumped in to create a long winding reservoir, accessible for stock or cultivation, they were seen as useful separated from their natural state. The biggest Yarra Valley dairy farm in the nineteenth century was Olinda Yarra, which lay adjacent to Yering. They drained, cleared and channelled the regularly flooded river wetlands and teatree forest, creating rich pastured country. Fresh milk for Melbourne was despatched twice daily.

Suburban Melbourne had its own dairy farms along the river, the earliest in the Domain, and one on the Botanic Gardens site. Riverflats were grazed everywhere. Farms such as Kilby and Willsmere in Kew were worked until they were taken over by golf clubs in the early to mid-twentieth century. Before supermarkets and centralised logistics, milk was bought and home-delivered from a local dairy. The last suburban river dairy was probably the one in East Ivanhoe, sold around the turn of the millennium. There are no cows now, though the odd steer can still be found grazing there.

A lot of grazing land ignores the river as far as possible, or treats it as a manageable intrusion—like some suburban golf courses that still cut and fill to get every square metre of green grass they can right up to the river's sides. And unfortunately, the occasional landholder can also be found tipping fill into creeks, or bulldozing them to 'improve' pasture.

In earlier days, riverflats were big enough to be used as airstrips: from a small, private grassed landing path at Pendleside on the

* Yering Station today has about 2.7 kilometres of river frontage.

former Solitude run to primitive joy flights north of Humbug Reach, and the Commonwealth Aircraft Corporation test strip at their Fishermans Bend factory, down the street from GMH (now underneath the West Gate Bridge freeway approaches). In the city, the river itself is the site for a moored pontoon that does the honours as the central city Melbourne Heliport.

~ ~ ~

The names in the biblical rollcall of Yarra tributaries are markers of narrative in themselves. Emblems of long gone stories, many were first uttered in the gold rush. Spicks and specks of gold had been found along the Upper Yarra and various tributaries such as the Plenty in the 1840s but the big rush, and the official discovery of gold, started on Yarra waters, at Andersons Creek, Warrandyte* in 1851. It was just a few grains, washed out of the gravel in an old creek bend. The miners put it for safekeeping in the flimsy paper wrapper of a Seidlitz (bicarb) powder, and the find was small enough to blow away from that. Nevertheless, the communal fever began.

There was gold in every gully, and crowds of men worked reefs in every hillock for those veins crystallised in old flow, ancient river and creek bed. Walking miles, boots sliding and crumbling the clayey soil up the steep ranges of stringybark, miners followed those arteries too, tracing them back to once-secret gullies in the hope that something might get them pumping.

A century and a half later the old gold-rush sites are grassily pockmarked with sunken mineshafts in the flats. No shell craters in this country, but scars of another primary desire. Gullies, chutes, gorges and mullock heaps are mantled in lichen and grass. Sparse trees lift the eye from the fantastic forms under the skin: ant castles now, trenches, escarpments, embankments, a squared split of quartz lonely to stumble over; still glistening.

Large-scale machinery—quartz crushers that weighed tonnes—was dragged in by horses piece by piece, and massive earthworks took over from a man, a creek and his pan. Every year there were mini-rushes, even in the city and suburbs, with gold mined in such exotic locations as North Balwyn and Heidelberg. In the 1860s a hole was drilled nearly forty metres to the bed of the ancient Yarra in

---

* Warrandyte's 'rush' went on and off for eighty years.

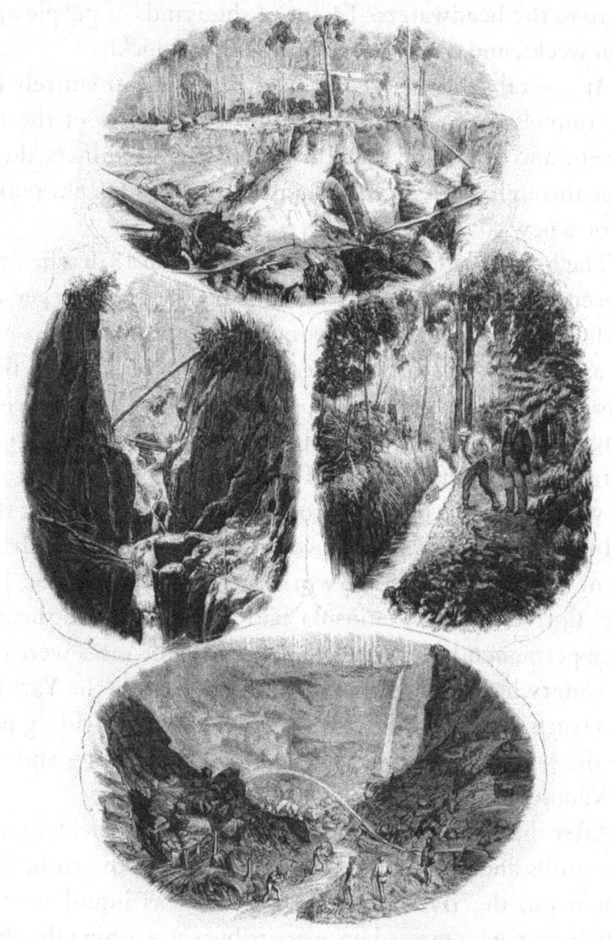

SLUICING FOR ALLUVIAL GOLD AT WARBURTON, UPPER YARRA.

1. WASHING DOWN THE CLIFF BELOW THE TOWNSHIP. 2. CUTTING THOUGH THE ROCK TO THE MAIN WORKINGS. 3. THE RACE A MILE-AND-A-HALF FROM THE WORKINGS. 4. THE FACE LOOKING NORTH, WITH THE RACE FALLING FROM TOP.

Collingwood, out the back of a pub on Hoddle Street.

Diggings in the Yarra catchment were to be found on every creek from the river up to St Andrews in the north, into the Dandenongs in the south-east, and from Warburton in the north-east way up to the headwaters. Towns of thousands of people appeared within weeks, and could disappear almost as quickly.

At several spots where the river loops almost entirely back on itself, tunnels were dug through the rock barrier of the ridge in between, and the river sent through. Chinese miners dug thirty metres through Little Peninsula at McMahons Creek, putting the river on a new course.

The biggest scheme was at Warrandyte in 1870 when the rush had been on for nearly twenty years.* The object was to get access to the whole five kilometres of Pound Bend, with its quartz and gold load, as drained and dry riverbed. Dammed with eleven thousand sandbags and elaborate bush carpentry, the Yarra was sent elsewhere through a 200-metre tunnel, but didn't give up great gifts. The celebrated Yarra mud was found to be fifteen metres deep in spots, a lot to wade or paddle through. Today, both tunnel and river flow.

In the late 1880s another company tried to get hydro power running there, which didn't work then, nor later in the 1920s. A tunnel upriver at Big Peninsula had about the same success rate, despite permanently diverting the river. Water-races were dug and huge waterwheels installed at various locations on the Yarra and its creeks (such as at Warburton and Warrandyte) providing power to drive the crushers. Some of the water diversion chutes and trenches were kilometres long.

After the gold, waterwheels were still used providing power to timber mills and even the odd pub; but during the rush, for miles downstream, the river must have seemed as liquid mud to the countless men who massed on every tributary, washing the clay away from the wished-for gold and into the body of the Yarra.

Any surrounding trees were cut for firewood or construction. Hoddle's 'barren scrub', Boldrewood's 'unredeemed stringy-bark desert'—that drear forest of bush complained about, cut down and burnt in every gully—has since reclaimed its spaces. It's now post-industrial stringybark (and upstream, myrtle, fern, blackwood

* An earlier scheme of 1859 had created a man-made island of another bend—Thomson's.

and mountain ash). But tracks cut by the Department of Mines in the nineteenth century all round the Upper Yarra persisted and were used later by walkers and naturalists before fire or water catchment regrowth removed them: Tanjil to Matlock; from the junction of the Yarra with Walshs Creek, along the Yarra to Mount Baw Baw; Aldermans Creek to Tanjil–Matlock; Contention Gully to Reefton; from the Yarra up O'Shannassy to the Yarra Track; up Starvation Creek to Big Pats Creek.

Sand or gravel for construction purposes were taken out from the river's surrounds at Fishermans Bend, Studley Park, Yarra Grange, Eltham, Warrandyte, Templestowe, and from the ancient river course at Kangaroo Ground—some of it went to build river bridges. Clay was dug for brickmaking on the north and south banks of the river in the city up till the 1850s, at South Yarra, Richmond and, much later, not far from the river at Bulleen. Basalt from the quarries at Burnley was shipped downriver to the Botanic Gardens for use as rockery.

From the early days of settlement the wattles that famously fringed the river's lower and middle reaches were stripped of bark to be used for tanning leather. The wattle or tan bark was taken in quantities large enough for export. The Ryries employed Wurundjeri to cut bark in the 1840s; round Warrandyte and Templestowe it was sold for local industry consumption in the late nineteenth and early twentieth centuries. They were cutting it in Christmas Hills and Yarra Glen during the 1930s Depression and tan bark was still being bought in the area in the 1970s.

Tall eucalypt forests along the upper reaches towards the source of the Yarra created a hardwood timber industry that would last for more than a century and a half. Yarra Junction's claim to fame was having more timber shipped through it than anywhere else in the world, except maybe Seattle. Even Richmond Flats, a couple of kilometres from town, were originally described as 'one great red-gum forest', with a few busy sawyers' pits in evidence on the land the great brewery was later built on. The north and south banks of the river were cleared of timber for firewood in the 1830s and '40s, troopers even being put on duty to stop any 'unlicensed wood cutting, brickmaking, &c.' Cutting wood to fire Melbourne's heating and cooking continued upriver for the next century.

Land surrounding the middle reaches of the river, particularly Templestowe, became devoted to orchards though there were also acreages of grains (wheat in the 1840s and '60s), potatoes—both in quantities big enough for export—and other vegetables, and later flowers on the rich river flats. During this period it was probably the richest farming land in the colony.

Apples were exported too, with most of what is now the outer middle belt of eastern suburbs covered in fruit trees. When they were knocked over for the suburban sprawl in the 1950s and '60s, some of the trees were a hundred years old. Pettys, established in 1911 and now publicly owned, is the oldest remaining orchard. They concentrate on organic production and heritage apple varieties, of which they have the largest number in mainland Australia. One of the many varieties is Batmans Tree, said to be a graft from the apple tree John Batman brought from Tasmania and planted by the banks of the Yarra far downstream in what is now the city of Melbourne. Many new varieties of fruit were developed in the area, including one known as Smiths—not to be confused with Sydney's Granny Smith—which was found growing by chance on the two-hectare Yarra River island west of Westerfolds Park.

Pettys Orchard was part of a family fruiting empire which probably ran to more than two hundred hectares in what became the eastern suburbs of Melbourne. The trees of the remnant originally ran to the river's edge—a thousand were taken out for the constrution of the Main Yarra Trail.*

---

* Cartoonist and Oscar-winning animator Bruce Petty, one of the extended family, explains the world through eccentric machinery such as his Environmentograph, Writeometer, Law Machine and Money Machine. His orchardist forebears similarly combined visual appreciation with innovative thought—the current proprietors remember them admiring the huge pink drifts of blossom down to the curve of the river. Their forebears invented radical new farm machinery to get the job done: Tom Petty a spray pump, and Frank and Herbert Petty an orchard disc plough. A younger Tom Petty is also an inventor.

Raspberries were grown on the rich land round the top of the valley before it heads up into the Divide. A lot of the fruit—berries and apples—grown along the river ended up downstream in the Rosella factory next to Cremorne Rail Bridge, where it came out in jams, preserves and sauces. For three-quarters of the twentieth century the smells of cooked and fermenting fruit emanating from Rosella wafted in thick drifts through entire suburbs.

Closer to town, Chinese market gardens could be found along the river in Ivanhoe, Hawthorn, Kew and Richmond in the last quarter of the nineteenth century, from pocket-sized areas up to larger spreads, intensively cultivated and watered; the furthest upriver was probably Warburton. Some gardens lasted till relatively recently in small perches near the river.

Hops were grown at the Aboriginal reserve of Coranderrk at Healesville in the 1870s and '80s. Kilns worked by Kulin and others living there were built on the banks of Badger Creek. The hops grossed good money, going to the highest bidders in the city and winning prizes at the Melbourne International Exhibition, but after the 1890s depression cut beer production, demand dropped off. Declining quality and the flood of superior Tasmanian hops after Federation finished them off. The Hay family, founders of the riverside Richmond Tiger Brewery, grew hops at their farm on the river in East Kew (the site of Hays Paddock). Hops were also cultivated on the opposite side of the river at Heidelberg in the 1840s.

Riverwater was used downstream by slaughterhouses, renderers, woolscourers and skin dealers, tanneries and dyeworks to wash away blood, viscera, fat, hair and grease in the process of creating their products. Soap and candle factories did the same. In the earlier days of settlement, the filthiest industries could be found right in the city and downstream from it. As Bernard Barrett and Graeme Davison have described, Richmond and Collingwood grew as solid working suburbs around these industries, stepping back from the river.

Other factories finishing goods, such as boots and shoes, made from these raw materials established themselves in turn there.

Hat factories, a big deal in the days when every man wore one, could use the river too for water and waste. The workers lived in tiny cottages on subdivided, subdivided, subdivided land patchworked through the suburb.

If CUB was the category killer in Australian beer for generations, APM did the same for paper and cardboard in this country. The first paper milled in Melbourne was made on the banks of the Yarra where Southgate is now. The foundations for the 1867 building were laid in earth moved from the Melbourne Town Hall construction site, in the hope of boosting the building up above river flood levels (it didn't make any difference, they still copped every big one). The plant machinery was bought and brought downriver from the paper mill at Dights Falls, which had been operating unsuccessfully in the middle of its intermittent career milling flour. Parts of the large machine used to produce the paper were still working a century later; the mill finally closed exactly one hundred years after it opened.

They made paper—at first brown wrap and newsprint—of a sort that's prized today, especially by artists, and paid for at a premium. Before synthetics, before plastic, before the words 'acid-free' and 'recycling' had even been invented, they milled paper out of old rags. The cloth, combined with a certain amount of used paper, was picked over, sorted, cut up, cleaned and boiled down to a big mash, then rolled out and dried.

The mill was sited on the river for the huge quantities of fresh water needed in the papermaking process. There was a pipeline, as well, to the billabong or lagoon on the Alexandra Gardens site. So when Coode's scheme blew away the Falls, the natural barrier to saltwater travelling further up the river, the mill, along with a lot of other riverwater users, was in trouble. It took till the close of the nineteenth century for an alternative water source to be exploited, with a quarter of a million gallons of Yarra water pumped from Dights Falls, just above the tidal reach, to the Princes Bridge mill every day. By this stage the mill was working day and night, on twelve-hour shifts.

After World War One, the company built a big new mill upriver at Fairfield which still operates. Rather than rags, it took recycled paper, woodchips and straw, turning out various kinds of cardboard and, later on, finer papers. Newsprint made from eucalyptus was first tested at the Fairfield mill in the 1920s, though the Princes Bridge mill had experimented with paper made from native plants in the 1870s.*

Modern paper mills still need a lot of water. APM is now known as Amcor and the Fairfield mill sits on the banks of the Yarra and is the biggest individual diverter of this river's water, with direct intakes and outlets right where the rowboats go by. The water used as coolant comes out cleaner than it went in, but slightly warmer.

The riverwater is used again for cooling in the Newport Power Station, though it's largely saltwater down there. Situated at the mouth of the Yarra, the first power station, later known as Newport A, was built so that Melbourne's trains could run on electricity rather than steam—the first electrified rail service in Australia.† The first trial train ran between Newmarket and Flemington racetrack in 1918, and the last line to switch over from steam to electricity was Eltham in 1923.

Newport A generated enough power for the excess to be on-sold to the City of Melbourne, who also ran their own Spencer Street power station. It, too, used riverwater for cooling; so did the Richmond power station and terminal near the Burnley cut. The old station powered Melbourne's trams, including what was at the time the world's biggest cabletram system (some of the superseded cable-tramways parts were later used for timber tramways in the Upper Yarra region).

---

* Our newsprint today is mostly manufactured from pine woodchips, some recycled de-inked newspaper and a small quantity of eucalyptus.

† Later adjacent power stations (Newport B 1923, C 1945, coal-fired, oil-fired and resulting in a contiguous building approximately a quarter of a mile long; and D, the controversial natural gas-fired replacement now known as the AES Transpower Yarra Generation Plant) were run by the State Electricity Commission of Victoria, purely for the main grid.

Yarra Falls Limited woollen mills, once described as producing the best fabric in Australia, also used large quantities of riverwater and were sited next to the Johnston Street Bridge for that reason. Founded in 1918, the various divisions—spinning, weaving and, later, knitting—employed more than a thousand people, many of whom worked for the company for decades. The basement of the knitting mills was inundated in the 1934 flood, and the huge river wall built as a result dates from a few years later.

Now that we are part of a globalised economy, Australia's apparel is manufactured mostly offshore: we may grow the wool, but we prefer to let someone else add the value and buy it back later. At the turn of the twenty-first century the expansive red brick buildings began their post-industrial refit to white-collar offices and apartments.

Upstream, the Seventh Day Adventist community which was established on the river in Warburton at the beginning of the twentieth century actually powered their publishing and printing works through a sophisticated waterwheel on Rocky Creek (a Yarra tributary), and had enough left over for lighting their homes.* Yankee Jims Creek ran another waterwheel which charged electrical batteries used for limited lighting in homes around the district. Other smaller private wheels on the Don, and again on Rocky Creek, were also in use. Reportedly one farmhouse downriver next to Pettys Orchard got its electricity from a waterwheel too.

The Seventh Day Adventists set up Sanitarium Health Food Company—famous makers, from around 1898, of Australia's first peanut butter and Weet-Bix, the nation's most popular breakfast cereal—in Warburton in the 1920s. The factory was run on hydro power from Cement Creek for decades, even supplying the local electricity company occasionally, and not connecting to the grid till 1980. In the late 1930s Sanitarium Health Foods and its sister company, Signs Publishing, were moved out of Yarra flood range and into a complex on the south side of the river. The beautiful new moderne buildings, set in Edna Walling gardens and designed by a

* Parts of the Upper Yarra didn't get electricity till the second half of the twentieth century.

former student of Walter Burley Griffin's, Edward Fielder Billson, won the Royal Victorian Institute of Architecture Street Architecture Medal in 1940. They were still to be found on the main road even after the company had rationalised and gone in 1997, set for future redevelopment. In 2003 they again made a list of Victoria's best buildings.

Dights Falls are named after the flour miller who set up there in 1839. He produced the first local flour but the mill failed initially because there wasn't enough water pressure during low flow of the Yarra to drive the grinding wheel. An auxiliary steam mill was attempted, then the 1840s depression hit, then floods, then fire. Mid-nineteenth-century pictures show a fine three-storey bluestone and brick building with a large waterwheel.

The paper mill of the 1860s was yet another not-quite-successful endeavour. Various companies ran a river-powered mill there, with the last viable attempt made in the 1880s before a final run with a steam engine a couple of decades later. Fire put an end to it: only a mill race and turbine chamber remain, on the Collingwood side of the river.

Several other mills were constructed along the river. A small flour mill at Warringal, just below the confluence with Salt Creek, lasted a few decades until they stopped growing wheat on the riverflats after the 1860s floods.

The weir created by Dights Falls, repeatedly augmented since settlement, has been heavily worked for its water. In the early 1890s a million-gallon reservoir was constructed on the escarpment in Kew (bordered by Studley Park Road, Walmer Street and the Boulevard), and riverwater was pumped up from Dights Falls. It was then gravity fed through pipes laid across Richmond to the Botanic Gardens and another reservoir, crossing the river twice along the way. This was the scheme that supplied the Princes Bridge paper mill. It also watered the Botanic Gardens, filled Albert Park Lake, and powered hydraulic lifts in the city with a total of three or four million gallons (say a dozen megalitres) a day.

The reservoir in the gardens was first constructed in the late 1870s, pumping its water up from the Yarra on site, back when the Falls barrier still kept the saltwater at bay. Already then, water was pumped from one of the same stations down to Albert Park Lake, keeping that filled.

Dights Falls watered the Gardens until the 1950s, when they went onto MMBW mains. During the 1967 drought, recycled water was pumped back from the APM Princes Bridge paper mill to help save the trees in the gardens. Rather than the recycled 'grey' water we refer to today, it was actually multi-coloured from the variously hued paper products being milled.

The hydraulic lifts of 1880s Marvellous Melbourne made it possible for fabulous skyscrapers to be built—as tall as any in New York or Chicago, taller than any building in Europe, and certainly including the tallest building in this country: the twelve storeys of the Australia Building, on the corner of Elizabeth Street and Flinders Lane. But water pressure was a problem until a centralised system was constructed running on Yarra water. The pumping station was at Australian (North) Wharf, and about ten kilometres of pipes went through the city to major elevated buildings such as the Grand Hotel, now the Windsor. As the Melbourne Hydraulic Power Company explained,

> The advantages of obtaining a better light and air, and the greater quiet of the upper floors are eagerly sought after by tenants; and by the increased rent the cost is soon repaid. When hydraulic lifts have been provided, upper floors previously tenantless have been at once let at good rents.

Before that, of course, the only way up was taking the stairs. Reassuringly they stated, 'Water is chiefly taken from the Yarra, and, by being passed through a system of filters, all sediment is removed therefrom before it reaches the main engine pumps.' There would have been a lot of sediment, and quite a bit of sewage too.

The system went into decline in the early years of the twentieth century after the introduction of electric lifts, though some city buildings were reportedly still running their water-powered lifts into the 1940s.

Dights Falls pumping station and escarpment reservoir were demolished in the mid 1960s, the reservoir site becoming Sir Arthur Rylah Oval. Remnants can be found on the Kew side of the Falls.

Upstream, most importantly, riverwater is worked by filling Country Fire Authority tankers to save lives. Downstream, the Metropolitan Fire Brigade pumped riverwater up to its training college in Abbotsford. In the early days of Melbourne, when fire engines were merely insurance company horse-and-cart rigs, water was pumped directly out of the river too.

During the worst bushfires recorded along the Yarra, people survived by sheltering in the river—as they did on fatal, awful Black Friday 1939, when everything burned. In Warrandyte, Christmas Hills and Warburton, women and children sat up to their necks in the water, surrounded by flames and smoke. Some had to do it again in 1962.

Working has been against the river, too. In 1895, with the Yarra as barrier, the Hobsons Bay Main Sewer had to be tunnelled four metres beneath the river to get across to the Spotswood Pumping Station. It collapsed, and six workers drowned. Tunnelling the Richmond Main below the riverbed at South Yarra killed another five, when they hit a pocket of poisonous gas.

When the Melbourne Main Sewer had to cross the river south-west of the city grid a few years later, it was put in by the less risky trench-and-sink method.

~ ~ ~

Once upon a time there were more docks than Docklands around the river port of Melbourne, with many ships owned by Australian companies and crewed by Australian seamen. Thousands of people worked the river.

The first ships direct from London arrived at the beginning of 1840. A year previously, the first ship exporting wool departed. But the steamer *Firefly* was the first boat to work the Yarra regularly. Rolf Boldrewood's father brought her to Melbourne stowed on another ship, and she paid her dues as a ferry for people or cargo, even towing sailing ships up to the docks. She was not universally appreciated, however: Garryowen described her as a 'half-rotten, incommodious old tub, more disposed to buzz than to fly, with more smoke than fire in its composition'.

There was a real problem in the early days getting people and cargo upriver from where sailing ships arrived in the Bay to the main settlement of Melbourne. Freight costs could be the same for that trip as for the previous one halfway round the world. Horses were used to tow vessels along the river at one point. No one could sail at night because there were no navigation lights on the river, and nothing deeper than a metre or two could clear the entrance mud bar at low tide.

Eventually, however, the bottleneck loosened. Private wharves were constructed in the city—Raleigh's Wharf, later Cole's,* was the first on the muddy banks, running about forty metres along the river at the bottom of William Street in the 1840s. In the 1850s it was made public, renamed Queens Wharf and extended down to Spencer Street, but in the beginning ships were still mooring to the nearest tree stump or stake, sometimes a dozen or more at a time.

* Cole, who married into the McCrae family, also owned the *Vesta*, a paddle steamer that ran from Melbourne down the Yarra to Williamstown, Geelong and various Bay destinations in the 1840s.

By the gold-rush era, this wharf was being used for passenger and mail boats. River traffic was probably at its peak then, with people pouring in from all over the world and so much cargo waiting to be unloaded, and no facilities or men to do it, that masses of expensive goods were just dumped on the nearest bank or shore. Hundreds of sailing ships would be moored at the same time, many deserted by crews on their way to the goldfields. On the Upper Yarra, flat-bottomed boats would take supplies for the goldminers from Launching Place up to Starvation Creek.

Little Dock had gone in before the gold rush, a rectangular cut next to Queens Wharf and parallel to Spencer Street just below where the bridge is now, on the current World Trade Centre site. It was filled in during the 1930s but in its heyday was used for small Bay boats bringing lime up from the Peninsula for building cement. From there, downstream, the Australian Wharf stretched for more than half a kilometre. First put in during the late 1850s gold rush, it became North Wharf in 1929, and was the main dock along the north bank of the river. Along the south banks and docks downstream of what is now Pier 35, hardwood sheet piling was put in during the 1890s (piles are reinforcing, so to speak, put in along the river's soft edges). These wharves were originally for ships carrying timber, pine from Oregon and from the Baltic, carried across the world for Marvellous Melbourne's building boom. Behind South Wharf and Duke & Orrs dry docks, spreading into South Melbourne, were various marine mercantile industries engaged in engineering, repairs and supplies. Boats were built there from the 1840s. Upstream, a boatbuilding yard was to be found on the river in South Yarra until floods made it untenable.*

By the turn of the nineteenth into the twentieth century the giant Victoria Dock and Coode Canal Scheme alterations were in place. Sail was on the way out and larger coal-fired steamships coming in, though 'tall ships' were working in the 1920s still. About a third of a kilometre of South Wharf went in around World War

* Savages, next to Church Street—by the 1930s moved to Hobsons Bay in Williamstown.

What once was. Looking upstream: ships at North Wharf, the Little Dock where Spencer Street Bridge is now, Queens Bridge the first bridge from the sea; sailing ships; and the curved dockshed (now the Maritime Museum) before it was shifted downstream. Teahouse upper right.

One, to be extended downstream the same distance again in the '20s. Reo concrete sheet piling began to be used instead of Australian eucalyptus hardwood, and there were lots of coal bunkers. Coal was a huge trade. It fuelled the ships and the power stations creating the city's electricity, and became gas for Melbourne's stoves and heaters back when gas was a manufactured product rather than a primary industry arriving 'natural' via pipeline. The gasworks were also on the river, facing North Wharf (opposite the Mirvac Yarra's Edge apartment complex site).

In the first years of the twentieth century, ninety percent of everything imported into the State of Victoria came through Victoria Dock and the river wharves. By the 1920s just about every dock was full, as well as adjoining cargo sheds. The lower reaches of the Yarra were lined with ships. (Imagine—nearly six kilometres of docked ships. It's very hard to now.) Excavation for Appleton Dock, at the entrance of Railway Canal/Moonee Ponds Creek on the north bank of the river and opposite the extended South Wharf, also began in the

1920s; part of it went over where the original Yarra had been, and the Railway Coal Canal. It took till the late 1950s for Appleton Dock to be complete and ready for use, then mainly as a coaling terminal.

The great vision, the engineering marvel of the Coode scheme, was finally in place after decades: and unfortunately somewhat irrelevant to the transport revolution that was coming. When Swanson Dock, just upstream of what is now the confluence with Maribyrnong River, began to be cut out in the 1960s, the age of containerisation was beginning. Its infrastructure included the surrounding reclaimed land for storage and turnaround of containers. Number One West Dock there became the first container facility in the country. The world's first purpose-built ocean-going container ship—a tiny thing called the *Kooringa*, made in Australia—was introduced in 1965 by the McIlwraith McEachern line* (a company based on the Yarra wharves) for the run between Melbourne and Fremantle.

Containerisation didn't just change the method of shipping, it changed the docks, the ports and the cities they were in. Instead of loading and unloading the vast multiples of individual cargo at every change of storage and transport, the actual items were only loaded once. The modular unit they were put in, the container—whose standard size fits every truck and ship and crane and dock right round the world—was shifted.

Men weren't needed to handle sacks or bags, lifting almost their bodyweight on their backs hundreds of times a day. Suburbs of dock workers weren't needed any more. Flour, wheat, sugar, cement, chemicals, cartons of cargo: all went to bulk handling by tanker or hold, or into containers. What used to take days and many hundreds of man-hours now took maybe twenty, with not much physical exertion.

Melbourne became the largest container port in the southern hemisphere, and ninety percent of waterside workers' jobs disappeared

---

* McIlwraith McEachern gave their ships Aboriginal names beginning with K: *Kooringa*, *Koorawatha*, *Katoomba*, *Kooralya*, *Kanimbla*. The last of these functioned as an auxiliary cruiser during World War Two: the present HMAS *Kanimbla*, which has served so valorously, was named after her.

within the next few decades. Money went into fitting out the docks—container handling needs huge specialised cranes, bays, aprons and mechanised systems. The amount of capital invested keeps paying off, because the amount of cargo turned over per ship and per berth increases exponentially—well over a million and a half containers a year through Melbourne at the start of the twenty-first century: two-thirds of the city's total trade turnover. Melbourne is Australia's largest container terminal. The port is much smaller, stopping at Bolte Bridge (though in its entirety it still takes up nearly five hundred hectares of land with river frontage), but much busier. One day there may be no wharfies, merely technicians.

Holden Dock, dedicated for tankers, went into the Yarraville riverbank near the oil companies' fuel dumps. Prior to that the tankers docked at Newport and the phosphate ships at Yarraville. The British Imperial Oil Company had put its acreage of fuel tanks into Spotswood in the middle of World War One. After World War Two, about half the docks adjacent to their respective terminals and factories were specialised for cargoes such as fuel, coal, iron and steel, cement, gypsum, liquid chemicals, grain and sugar. Certain wharfies skilled up in particular cargoes.

Sugar Australia—formerly CSR, the Colonial Sugar Refinery—can produce 42 tonnes of sugar an hour at the 130-plus-year-old Yarraville site. Like the CUB brewery on the river in Abbotsford, like the Port of Melbourne, the refinery was transformed by automation and now needs only handfuls of workers, compared to a thousand. They use riverwater as a coolant as the Amcor paper mill does. In the old days, the sweet sugar would be in the air, heavy drifting through clothes and mixing with the pungent sulphur fumes from the superphosphate terminal and processing plant next door.*

Holden Swinging Basin, just upstream of the dock at the (modern) confluence of the Maribyrnong and Yarra, is a deepened,

---

* Its products would be spread on Upper Yarra paddocks, with the excess running off back downstream; cropdusting started there in the 1950s.

widened section of the river, designed to be big enough for oil tankers to turn, keeping them separate from the rest of the shipping. About a hundred thousand tonnes of petrol, jet fuel and diesel can be stored in turnaround at the dock at any one time. Coode Island, used for bulk liquids (food and chemicals), is served by Maribyrnong No. 1 Dock. In 1991 more than two dozen of its petrochemical tanks were consumed by a huge industrial fire, ingesting and spewing forth toxic material which swirled through the residential, commercial and retail air of Melbourne for days.

The Holden named here is actually a Melbourne Harbor Trust official, not the car manufacturer; however General Motors-Holdens, a subsidiary of the American multinational, did purchase fifty acres nearby, on the bank opposite at Fishermans Bend. An incentive for the port authority was the amount of river wharves and harbour dues they would account for on Lorimer Street/South Wharf, literally over the road from the plant.

'Australia's own car'—the Holden, first to be made and designed here—came from the banks of the Yarra, too. Some of their aspirational advertising even displayed the cars with the river—albeit somewhere much more beautiful upstream—as backdrop. By the mid-1960s one in every three cars on the road in Australia was a Holden; in 1974 the three-millionth Holden rolled off the line. The low-rise '30s Detroit Deco offices of the GM factory were later rationalised off into a separate business park; the hell of its engine plant replaced by a slick new production line, turning out V6s for the local Holden Commodore and other models in the world group.

Wharfies, and ship painters and dockers, worked in the port doing honest graft under appallingly hard, dirty and dangerous conditions. Some died on the job, handling explosive or dangerous cargo, or much later from the after-effects of poisonous materials surrounding them. In the 1920s and '30s some were found to be suffering malnutrition. One former shipping-line employee of the 1950s and '60s has said, 'They were treated like animals.' That was the other side, the background, for the corruption of the Painters and Dockers union.

Many men have been sailors and visited the working river. A Polish seaman called Conrad Korzeniowski, later known as Joseph Conrad, came up the Yarra captaining a cargo ship in the late 1880s and worked the Australian coast for a while. A photograph in one of his biographies shows the sailing vessel at South Wharf with Conrad (purportedly) on deck. The Tea House is behind, and they are moored at the same dock shed—curved to fit round the river's bend—that now sits slightly downstream. The shed was relocated in the 1970s and is part of the National Trust Maritime Museum. After returning to the Thames, Conrad started writing, in English, and his next upriver trip was into the Belgian Congo, the Heart of Darkness, where he began the great literary river journey upon which the film *Apocalypse Now* is based.

A plan put together for the Melbourne Harbor Trust in the late 1960s foresaw the port industrial area expanding so much that it took over the suburbs of Port Melbourne and Garden City. The consultant's suggestion was to construct four islands in Port Phillip Bay to which the inhabitants, at that time from a lower income demographic, could be relocated.

The future turned out to be a complete mirror image. Most of the old docks are gone, razed; the space has been taken up by people who either own or occupy expensive high-rise apartments. North Wharf is crumbling, petite pigface pushing up through the cracks. Maybe the pretty pink flowers are descendants of that 'belt of magenta fire' that flamed around Blue Lake nearly two centuries ago. The twenty-first-century Port of Melbourne is expected to be handling three million containers a year by the second decade, and to expand north over Footscray Road, connecting with Dynon railyards. The biggest ship handled so far has been around three hundred metres long, almost a third of a kilometre.

A maritime dispute in 2002—seen by some as symbolising the end of Australian shipping—ironically centred on a ship named *CSL Yarra*. A bulk cargo cement carrier, owned by Canadian Steamship Lines, it had once been part of the (later privatised) Australian

National Line. The company wanted to spin it off to CSL Asia, put it under a flag of convenience, sack the Australian crew, and replace them with half-price Ukrainians. At that time there were less than fifty Australian ships left working the seaports of the entire nation. (In the early 1960s McIlwraith McEachern alone—through Associated Steamships—had around that number running out of its Yarraside berths: regular interstate passenger vessels, tugboats, specialised cargo such as CSR sugar from Queensland and general shipping. The Tiger Beer they stocked their ships with came from upriver at Richmond, and was loved before it became CUBed.)

In a globalised world, the country with the largest coastline—Australia—might end up with no seamen or ships of its own. But lingering remnants of the old working river may be found in the post-industrial Maritime Museum at Duke & Orrs dry docks on the south bank, where once men busted their guts.

~ ~ ~

Not-working the river is a grand, unacknowledged tradition: from those carrying their swag on the wallaby with a Wagga blanket* to these days of stashed polyester on corrugated Amcor or Visyboard. But there was, at regular intervals, some back-breaking labour involved in not-working.

The Coode Canal scheme diverting the river started in the 1890s depression with a lot of cheap unemployed labour. So did the enormous Board of Works scheme sewering Melbourne. The old road from Warburton to Reefton, along the river then up the spur towards Cumberland Junction, was also done on susso at the same time (the newer Reefton Spur road on top, beloved of motorcyclists, was asphalted and beautifully curved some decades later).

Susso (or sustenance payments, a primitive work-for-the-dole scheme) was the biggest long-term effect on the river of the 1930s Depression. Port workers did their susso on Fishermans Bend, shovelling sand from high bits down to lower bits, levelling, raising and reclaiming the land for the GM Holden factory site, among others. They found it a lot easier than what they had been doing down at the docks. Some waterside workers took to the swag. Alan Marshall, in the 1930s, described the '"Seagulls" [who] live on food thrown over from ships'. (They were people who waited for ships' cooks to lower buckets of scraps to them.) In Collingwood, people tried fishing the Yarra with eucalypt branches as boys in the bush did.

The river boulevards and parks of Richmond, South Yarra and Kew were built by men in shirtsleeves, waistcoats and hats, with pick, shovel and wheelbarrow, digging roads out of the banks for susso programs that coincided with the Centenary program celebrating Melbourne's beginnings. A lot of funding was donated by Sir

---

* Sewn from woollen scraps or the hessian sacks that were used to package drygoods before containerisation and shrink-wrapped pallets.

Sidney Myer, community-minded philanthropist and hugely successful department store founder. Yarra Bend or Studley Park was developed then too (although it had been a park since the 1870s), with susso relief workers putting in paths and landscaping.

Susso beautification seems to have a recognisable style based on rustic basalt borders, although now it is mostly found unmaintained and in decay, the 'beauty spots' often scattered with rubbish. The style may have hit the tiny Gothic heights of municipal design in the corner of Fairview Park, Hawthorn, where a narrow footpath zigzags up a corner precipice to Riversdale and Wallen Roads above, with half a dozen perfectly detailed blocks of nineteenth-century bluestone thrown into the mix. Community schemes of the latter twentieth century consisted of native plantings, wooden 'wetlands' boardwalks,* benches and gravel paths, which generally fell into disrepair due to lack of maintenance once political photo opportunities had passed.

The disaffected and the affected, future prime ministers and past ministers, worked and not-worked the river, too, as soapbox orators—Yarrabank speakers. It was a great Sunday's entertainment in the days when wowser Melbourne didn't have any.† Before television, computers and the internet, public debate was exactly that: literally out in the open. Originally to be found, among other places, along the river at Queens Wharf, at Studley Park or on the south bank near Princes Bridge, this venue of ferment settled at the Yarrabank on the north side, south of the formerly much-larger railyards, in 1899. This was at the politically geographical behest of Alfred Deakin (at one point prior to Federation a Victorian police minister; later Australian prime minister), with the aim of concentrating dangerous radicals away from the general population of the metropolis.

---

* The first boardwalks near the river were probably those of the 1860s connecting Emerald Hill (or South Melbourne) with the city and St Kilda Road. Built over wetlands lower than the river itself, they were reportedly more than a metre wide and a metre high, with a single handrail. They differ generally from the late-twentieth-century boardwalks in that they are functional and go somewhere.

† Once upon a time there was no Sunday cinema, theatre, restaurants, cafes, casino, football, drinking, shopping...You could go to church, but.

It became a destination for marches through the city centre. Various speeches would be made simultaneously, each to their own supporters or detractors. The mounds speakers stood on have now been reinstated as a historical design element of Birrarung Marr, the new park between Federation Square and the Tennis Centre.

Crowd numbers ran into the thousands and discussion could become heated; some speakers would untie their shoelaces beforehand in case they (the shoe-wearers) were thrown into the river. The biggest Yarrabank crowds were up to a hundred thousand, in the anti-conscription days of World War One. John Curtin, one of Australia's greatest prime ministers and the nation's leader during World War Two, began his political career there, and is said to have remarked, 'The Yarra Bank was my university.'*

Another intense, risky but completely dishonourable form of not-working the river also has its long past. With Melbourne being founded in 1835, smuggling on the river was recorded in 1836. Gallons of rum were brought in without duty being paid. Though the activity has romantic historical connotations, today it's as charming and simple as bringing in heroin, a port activity which expanded greatly in the 1970s along with the waterfront wars.

The docks were the place for petty crime. Reportedly rife from the early 1840s on, it used to be budgeted for as pilferage or 'pillage' and searched for by the pillage squad.† Traffic in sly grog, cigars and cigarettes, stoushes, two-up and other betting for entertainment were also activities. In the days before legal state-sponsored gambling and 24-hour alcohol, these were all criminal acts. General graft, favours and people on the take made the wheels go round in every aspect of waterfront society: shipping companies, unions, customs and police. It could be as trivial as a couple of bottles of hard-to-get-whisky out

---

* As a union officer Curtin toured the Upper Yarra for the Timber Workers, organising to beat their terrible conditions. He finally left Melbourne by the river, on a McIlwraith McEachern steamship to Perth, where he later became a Federal Labor politician.

† 'Shrinkage' is the more modern economic term.

of the company store (for the union office) or via one of the two-weekly London air services (for shipping management). Jobs were routinely given to friends and relatives of those already on the waterfront.

Serious underworld machinations and rackets were the province of one organisation: the notorious Federated Ship Painters and Dockers Union.* Finally, in the early 1980s, they were the subject of a Royal Commission. When in 1973 State Secretary Pat Shannon was shot and killed in a busy South Melbourne pub,† no one saw a thing. It was that kind of organisation. Ditto when another well-known Painter and Docker had his head taken off by a shotgun on the riverfront at South Wharf. There was only a small two-person toilet, but twenty to thirty men thought they may have been in there, out of sight of the action, at the crucial time. Either that or they'd been looking the other way, despite blood and brain spatter arguing the contrary.

At one point, every official of the union had criminal convictions, as well as a large proportion of the membership. There was the usual thieving; plus murder, firebombing, standover and protection, drug dealing, gaming or SP bookmaking and armed robbery; plus participation in a top international shoplifting gang. The union specialised in the immaterial: invisibilising homicides, manufacturing false identities and 'ghosts'—workers who were on the payroll but didn't exist. Another dockie or official would pick up the extra paypacket(s), tax refunds, social security, dole or compo: for example, on one 39-worker payroll, twenty men would collect all the pays between them.

As Commissioner Frank Costigan reported, apart from their traditional area of 'street crime' union activities ranged 'from murder

---

* During the 1980s, one of Melbourne's cult bands was named after the Painters and Dockers, who were fellow drinkers at their Port Melbourne local. One of the band's catchy tunes, 'You're Going Home in the Back of a Divi Van' (sic), was later dedicated by the Dili All Stars to General Wiranto, Indonesia's (allegedly) criminal military commander.

† Druids, in the early 2000s the young and fashionable Water Rat.

to company manipulation'. The scams were incredible, the stakes huge; money laundering and tax evasion were particularly popular, the latter delivering 'profits comparable only to the heady days of the Victorian gold rush'—at the time, hundreds of millions of dollars.

Those professionally involved dissected legal precedents 'with an attention to detail which would have done credit to...medieval theologians'. Various companies, unusually, had as directors violently well-known Painters and Dockers whom nobody, least of all the mild-mannered public servants of the Taxation Department, wished to upset. This style of corporate personnel management was a stroke of genius, as the Commissioner remarked. Some dockies retired very rich, then put their money into shares. It was a long way from the river.*

Generally, members of the Painters and Dockers only murdered each other, averaging a dozen a decade. 'We catch and kill our own,' was the famous comment of one federal secretary. Billy 'The Texan' Longley went to prison for Pat Shannon's death, and was protected from a similar fate by fellow Pentridge inmate Mark 'Chopper' Read. Protagonists left standing, still on the outside and wanting to expand their commercial activities, went on to become very hard men indeed and general gunnies for hire. In the post-modern world, some finally became 'consultants'. Career criminals from Melbourne's most infamous families have worked on the docks.

* The half-kilometre-long Melbourne Exhibition Centre close to the old South Wharf, colloquially known as Jeff's Shed after Premier Jeff Kennett, occupies space once taken up by the Painters and Dockers' union offices.

Bridging it III

Through the barriers

Charles Grimes Bridge killed the upper North and South Wharves, and Duke & Orrs dry docks. Like other city bridges, it has clearance of only a few metres at high tide, and the start of its construction stopped shipping going any further upriver. When first built in 1977–8 it was called Johnson Street Bridge, then renamed in 1980 after the first white man to travel and map part of the Yarra.

Before this, and before West Gate, small ferries ran workers from the west at Francis Street to factories such as GMH and Commonwealth Aircraft along the Bend. In the 1920s, long rowboats were used to carry wharfies over between Yarraville and Port. An even earlier ferry was McCallums of the 1850s and '60s. Charles Grimes' more recent twin-bridge eight-lane structure arose out of its demolition, reconfiguration and reconstruction in 2000 as part of the Docklands infrastructure redevelopment, with new orange detailing contrasting perfectly with the green aquatic life clinging to the concrete at the waterline. Critics saw it and the connecting Wurundjeri Way as new barriers between the city, its people and the waterfront.

~

Apart from West Gate, each city bridge has rerouted north–south vehicle traffic and stopped river shipping traffic upstream. Spencer Street Bridge, built in 1930, has the lowest clearance of all. Tides vary by about a metre, and the bridge has only three metres clearance even at low water. This was the bridge that cut off the Turning Basin, where ships had first moored to settle Melbourne, that half of the saltwater/freshwater access equation which led to the siting of the

A ship turning in the Turning Basin when they could still do that. Teahouse upper left, Queens Bridge, Flinders Street and railyards; Melbourne Fish Market tower upper right.

city. The Turning Basin wasn't actually filled in for carparking until the 1950s, however; and then it was redug later by the Council in an award-winning reinstatement, though it may seem now like a visual forecourt for the Casino.

Until the 1970s, this was as far downstream as you could cross from the northern and western suburbs to the south by bridge. As a belated part of the Coode Scheme, the river was doubled in width before the bridge was built. Its construction ended the ferries which had run since the 1850s,* and forced the filling of Little Dock.

~

The Kings Bridge approaches were rebuilt in the 1990s with the development of Crown Casino. On the south side, one actually drives

* During the gold rush, the area was full of ferries, five running between the Falls and Clarendon Street alone (Queen and Spencer streets).

dramatically through the middle of the Casino building and down to cross the river, though the greater excitement is probably that provided occasionally by the exploding sculptural fireballs on its promenade. Originally built in 1960, Kings Bridge opened in 1961, then cracked up and closed the next year: another Yarra bridge with its own Royal Commission, but at least there was no tragedy involved, beyond a broken steel plate girder and a million-pound repair bill for Premier Bolte. Strengthened and pre-stressed, its six lanes reopened in 1965.

~

Bridges haven't just carried horses, carriages, cars and people. Main utilities such as water and gas have to cross too, usually unseen below. Some Yarra bridges have been built purely for utilities: Fairfield Pipe Bridge is probably the largest. It laid on Yan Yean water to the eastern suburbs of Kew and Hawthorn with several mains in the 1880s. Only when the third main was added was a walkway provided. The bridge didn't survive the 1934 flood, but was rebuilt in 1937 and restored in 1982. It now has open public access as part of the Yarra bike and walk trail network.

~

Banksia Street Bridge, Bulleen to Heidelberg, is the site of the fourth water main crossing the Yarra from Yan Yean to the eastern suburbs, on a direct route of some thirty-odd kilometres. The main came in 1891, on its own beautifully formed redbrick and render piers alongside the road bridge (then upstream—the current bridge is downstream). At crossings with multiple bridgings such as this one, layers and chunks of history can be found—literally where they have fallen or been abandoned. Ghost bridges may leave firm traces: an abutment and approach endpost here, precisely cut bluestone footings there, waterlogged timbers and mossy splatters of agg concrete somewhere else. Bridge building occurred here in 1860, 1890, 1911, 1960, 1974; in the 1840s there was a punt just upstream and, prior to that, a ford.

~

Walmer Street Footbridge, Burnley to Kew—near the Skipping Girl sign—was another built as a pipeline in 1891, like the Banksia Street

Simpsons Road punt, where the Walmer Street footbridge is now.

main. It carried millions of gallons of Yarra water up over the river from Dights Falls on the way to the Botanic Gardens and further; the Morell Bridge was where it crossed back. Previously, back when Victoria Street was still known as Simpsons Road, there'd been steps down the bank to the Simpsons Road Ferry, a rowboat taking passengers from the Kew or Studley Park side of the river over towards the vicinity of the Burnley and Victoria streets intersection.

~

Footbridges have gone from madness to beauty. The other Kew Footbridge, also known as the Zigzag Bridge (Bellbird picnic area site), ran between the two lunatic asylums of Yarra Bend and Kew. Despite being serially damaged and patched high and low as a result of flood—ultimately zigzagging several levels—it was not demolished until the early 1930s. The bridge had earlier been used to shift stone quarried in Yarra Bend for the new Kew buildings, and then for the movement of staff between the two institutions; also, later, Fairfield Hospital staff.

A bridge on what's now known as Kanes Bridge site, about two kilometres and half a dozen bends downstream near the Yarra Bend Boathouse, also earlier gave access to the original lunatic asylum. Another bridge washed out by the 1934 flood and rebuilt, Collins footbridge to Collingwood, is adjacent on the Studley Park side to some large old European trees reputedly planted by Baron von Mueller when the site was being considered for Government House, before the Italianate pile next to the Botanic Gardens appeared in the 1870s.

~

Mac Robertson Bridge was one of four major gifts from chocolate manufacturer Sir Macpherson Robertson* to the people of Victoria during the 1930s Depression, honouring Melbourne's centenary of settlement. Joining Grange Road, Toorak, to the edge of Hoddle's old Surveyors Paddock in Burnley, the Sidney Myer-funded susso-built Boulevard and (further on for pedestrians) Richmond rail and tram lines, its centre span was some hundred or more metres. Like the Church Street Bridge, its northernmost arch has to straddle the Monash Freeway, now perched there on the riverbank: the extra span was added and matched to the original bridge for this purpose. The bridge was built without rivets, saving thirty tons of steel.

Twickenham Ferry had operated at this location since 1865, and the ferryman lived and worked there on a 99-year lease (though people of the era do remember rowing themselves across when no one was about). His family only left when the lease was up—the same year the freeway was built and thirty years after the end of their original business.

~

Hoddle Bridge, more familiarly known as Punt Road Bridge, was of course the site of a paying punt, too, as well as various rowboats, from the mid-nineteenth century. Its official name honours Robert Hoddle, the government surveyor who traversed to the very source of the river so many miles upstream. The first bridge was a two-span

---

* Mac Robertson had started his illustrious career riverside, apprenticed to the Victorian Confectionery Company (the site was later known for the Allens Sweets neon, next to Princes Bridge).

steel footbridge built, long before there were cars, to carry a water main. The current concrete road bridge, a diagonal crossing with what seems to be the traditional standard decorative concrete pylon lantern style, replaced the 1890s pedestrian bridge in 1938.

~

Swan Street Bridge was built in the same era as the Upper Yarra Dam and suffered similar logistical problems in its construction: projected before the Second World War, it was consequently postponed to a time when postwar shortages of manpower and materials were causing problems for all kinds of building, from dams to bridges to houses. The first pile was driven in early 1947 but the bridge didn't open until 1952. Before that Branders Ferry was the original method of crossing the site, along with the nearby Botanic Gardens footbridge.

The crossing is another built on the diagonal, and the bridge is designed to give central clearance for rowing regattas, with side arches spanning both the river's edge and the traditional path for rowing coaches' bicycles. (All bridges on the main rowing route are mapped and their arches are identified as down or up, or closed to the boats.) Unlike Princes Bridge, Swan Street Bridge was not designed to carry huge pedestrian crowds as it now must, connecting parking, the Botanic Gardens, the Tennis Centre, the MCG and other sporting and entertainment facilities.

~

In the late twentieth century and the early 2000s, footbridges were designed to delight and please. Southgate Footbridge, with its curve, triangle and angled decks, was designed to take a small growing tree and ended up having an outdoor cafe on the island around one of its two piers. Opening in 1990, it connected Southgate to the city via Flinders Street Station underpass.

Webb Footbridge, designed by artist Robert Owen and Denton Corker Marshall (DCM) architects, which opened in 2003, was built on the base of what had been the Webb Dock freight rail bridge. Part of Docklands redevelopment, the six-metre-high superstructure was hooped like the Gunditjmara eel traps of western Victoria, a spatial gesture of bridging and reconciliation between white and black form.

Pleasure & Pain

On the billabong known as Wrights Swamp, next to the Yarra River, a pleasure park was constructed: Cremorne Gardens.* The gold rush had lured the bankrupt proprietor of London's Cremorne Gardens to Melbourne in the hope that he could recoup his fortune. In 1853 under patronage of, among others, Mayor John Hodgson (the same John Hodgson who ran the punt), events in the magnificent acreage unfolded—acrobats, dancing, fireworks, a concert—all as a hospital fundraiser.

In 1856, the Eight Hour Day movement† ended its inaugural procession there, and the illustrious George Coppin was the new owner of the gardens. The billabong had become an ornamental lake over which tightrope walkers danced, and Spectaculars took place, such as

> the Bombardment of Sebastopol, extra brilliant Fire Works, consisting of Water Rockets, Water Fountains, Fiery Dragons, Golden Rain, Bomb Shells, Sky Rockets & c.

---

* On the site of the Rosella Factory, now bounded by Balmain Street, the Sandringham rail line, Monash Freeway / Yarra River and Cremorne Street.

† 8 8 8 = eight hours work, rest and play. Melbourne had the eight-hour day before anywhere else in the world.

> Explosion and Blowing up of the Malakoff Tower, the Town on fire & c. And Also, a Grand Water Piece consisting of a Horizontal Wheel, discharging innumerable Rockets, with every variety of Beautiful Bouquets of Roman Candles...

Other performances illustrated the Eruption of Mount Vesuvius over Naples and the Battle of Waterloo: anything historical that involved explosions and pyrotechnics, and a semblance of instructional narrative. The illuminated backdrops, between the former billabong and the river, were extraordinary panoramas three metres high and nearly eighty metres long.

Coppin was a showman born and bred. Cremorne had rosebeds, wizards, gaslights, glassblowers, a menagerie, a maze, bellringers, Punch and Judy, fountains, grottoes, skaters, a shooting gallery, bowling alley, lovers lane, opera, fortune teller, clowns and sideshows, a Swiss Family Treehouse, ballet, a performing elephant and billiards. Admission tickets doubled as lottery tickets for a while, with prizes of gold nuggets or jewellery. Waxworks included the explorers Burke and Wills—Coppin had hoped to provide camels for their expedition. There was a theatre, the Pantheon, with pantomime, vaudeville, concerts and benefits; and luckily, 'The boxes...are kept rigidly select and ladies need be under no apprehension whatever of meeting with persons they would rather avoid.'

It was evidently a timely reassurance. 'The gardens were frequented by fast men and women having money to burn,' was the opinion of a local historian. Reputedly all kinds of women could be met on the 2,000-person dance floor. Future politician and prime minister Alfred Deakin had an 'escapade' there as an adventurous four-year-old, being frightened off by roaring lions in the menagerie (the first lion cubs in Australia were born there).

The art could be found outside: 150 lifesize plastercast and cement copies of ancient Greek and Roman classical sculpture which, after Cremorne's demise, were relocated along the pathways of Fitzroy Gardens. They—or what was left of their overpainted, patched and occasionally limb-deprived selves—remained there until the 1930s. Arthur Streeton, the painter, commented in a letter to the editor of the *Herald* in 1934,

> Civic authorities of those days, finding the statues looked dirty; gave them a coat of white oil paint; repeated coats of paint eventually thickened and obscured all the features of heads, hands and feet; the statues actually became large and grotesque in appearance...So much for vandal control of the gardens!...thus the statues, owing to barbarous, philistine treatment, assumed a sadly comic appearance. But the original casts were heroic and beautiful.

The first time a manned balloon took off over the Yarra was also the first time anyone had been in the air over the entire continent of Australia; and yes, it was a Coppin spectacle from Cremorne Gardens, and a sensation. Two English aeronauts, Captain Dean and Professor Brown, were imported in 1858 for the ascent. There was only enough buoyancy for one man: Dean went up first above the twists and turns of the river, drifting to Heidelberg. Brown went up two weeks later, unfortunately coming down among the uncouth working-class savages of Collingwood Flat who attacked him and the air conveyance. A flight they made together a month later from Cremorne—this time their balloon held enough gas—almost ended the same way at Batmans Swamp, but they kept going to the safety of Emerald Hill.

Coppin went broke and Cremorne Gardens closed in 1863. Even Cremorne railway station had closed by then.* The pleasure gardens and their buildings, including what had been Coppin's own house, became Cremorne Lunatic Asylum, a Private Retreat for the Insane and Inebriate, the only one in the colony. The proprietor had previously been Superintendent of Yarra Bend Lunatic Asylum. When the owner retired in 1884 he sold the land for subdivision, and it was cut up for small workers' cottages by none other than old Tommy Bent, MLA. Bent Street, Richmond, runs right through the

* It had opened while Coppin was chairman of the Melbourne and Suburban Railway Company, whose line ran past the gardens (it's now part of the Sandringham line).

middle of what was Cremorne Gardens. A big engineering factory went in during 1939, and during the 1960s (what was to become) the Monash Freeway went straight over the top of (what had been) the Gardens' river edge.

Touristic balloons still sometimes drift overhead, but these days they mostly travel over the Yarra Valley vineyards far upstream. In 1870, after a somewhat unsuccessful career, aeronaut Charles Brown was found as a floater in the river, there at Richmond.

One might have arrived at Cremorne in its heyday via the river. The first pleasure boat to ply the Yarra was built to ferry customers from the riverbank north-east of Princes Bridge. Until Coppin got the railway through, the *Gondola* (a paddlesteamer with a high decorative prow matching its name) churned along carrying up to a couple of hundred passengers a load.

Long after Cremorne closed, other tea and pleasure gardens opened along the river, offering slightly more passive recreation. Picnicking riverside in the Survey Paddock, Richmond or at Studley Park was most popular in the nineteenth century—hence Pic-Nic railway station on the Burnley circus site, close to the Survey Paddock, which was described in 1866 as 'the elysium of cockney picnic parties on Christmas and New Year's Days'. Cross-river ferry spots such as Twickenham Ferry* and Branders Ferry† also boasted mini-zoos for general amusement. They were the bustling outdoor cafes of their day, the equivalent of late-twentieth-century Melbourne latte society, except that one would arrive and depart by rowboat, canoe or ferry. Hawthorn Tea Gardens, on the Leonda site at the end of Swan Street, was about three-quarters of an hour by river from Princes Bridge. Ferries regularly called there with other stops along the way, such as Botanic Gardens. An earlier tea garden in Hawthorn was the Glen, near the Gardiners Creek confluence, opposite the Survey Paddock. For a while, boats would run as far up

---

* Mac Robertson Bridge site.

† Swan Street Bridge site.

as Studley Park, where passengers could hike over the hill and down to Burns Boathouse.

Known originally, when it opened in 1863, as 'Riversdale', Studley Park Boathouse is the oldest continuously operating boathouse on the Yarra. A solid row upstream—or a short trip by small motorboat—might have ended at Rudder Grange,* another wonderful boathouse with refreshment rooms, a fountain, a small pleasure garden and afternoon teas, then a further stretch upstream, perhaps under the Outer Circle bridge where the Chandler Highway now crosses the river. There were several other large boathouses, all of which, at their 1920s and '30s peak, had canoes for hire, Devonshire tea and rowboats with gilt names on turned, varnished wooden backboards.

Fairfield Boathouse was built in 1908 and approachable by river. After falling into severe decrepitude, becoming a most romantic and desolate spot, it was restored and reopened in the mid-1980s. Macauleys Boathouse in Kew, opposite Yarra Bend, is now a private riverside home. It opened in the 1890s with changing rooms and a kiosk added later, only closing after half a century. Chipperfields at Connors Creek confluence† was originally a house with boatshed underneath and a popular destination from downstream boathouses, with a floating kiosk on the river.

Ferries were still popular in the 1940s. An old Richmond Brewery barge was configured as a dance club, and would cruise up and back with its own special floor and live band. The decline came in the 1950s and '60s, when everybody got a car and turned away from the river; Hawthorn Tea Gardens closed. River ferry pleasure cruises didn't come back until the general renewal of the river and its environs took off in the 1980s—when Southbank and the walking and cycle trails were built.

For those lucky enough to have their own boat, there are public moorings at various spots downriver from Dights Falls. For those

---

* Between Alphington Street and Yarraford Avenue.

† Underneath the Eastern Freeway.

lucky enough to have river frontage homes, that's at the bottom of your garden. For users of public (river) transport, regular ferry services have run intermittently: from the city to Punt Road, for example, before there was a road bridge, and downstream to General Motors at Fishermans Bend.

Serious boating, that is, serious rowing along the Yarra, was exemplified by two major events. Like Cremorne Gardens, both were inspired by—or imitations of—Thames-side pursuits: Head of the River and Henley Regatta.

A rowing contest between the top private boys' schools evolved into the Head of the River. Beginning in the 1860s as a race between Scotch College and Melbourne (Boys') Grammar, it expanded annually by taking in other schools and became, with its tens of thousands of spectators, such a huge event that it was deemed out of control (and hazardous to the boys' overinflated egos). So in 1946 the race was moved from the Yarra to Barwon River, Geelong. Just over a decade later, Hawthorn Rowing Club, itself more than a century and a quarter old, inaugurated the Head of the Yarra, a race from their club to Princes Bridge.

By the early 2000s, competition numbered well over a hundred crews, including Melbourne 1956 and Sydney 2000 Olympians, several of whom counted the river as their home stretch. Gold medal Olympians of 1992, the 'Oarsome Foursome', came out of a Yarraside club. After personnel changes they went on to win gold twice more, at the Atlanta Olympics (1996) and in Athens in 2004 after training along the Yarra River.

Clubs and regattas date back to the 1860s, though in the very early days regattas were held downstream of Princes Bridge, heading towards Footscray. The boatsheds upstream of Princes Bridge have been there since before the old lagoon or billabong was filled in for the Alexandra Gardens and the river embanked in the latter part of the nineteenth century; the foul state of the water then doesn't seem to have affected the amount of traffic on the river. Bicycle tracks worn by yelling coaches still parallel the Yarra's course upstream.

Early corporate entertaining—the heights of Henley Regatta. Location: Swan Street Bridge; Government House tower to left.

The river's curves and loops provide extra challenges compared to a straight course, as well as a certain amount of weather protection, though perhaps that is balanced by the current.

Henley Regatta began in the early 1900s and was as big a public event as the Melbourne Cup. Or not quite: it never got its own public holiday. But by the 1920s more than a quarter of a million people would crowd the riverbanks to watch.

Held on the Saturday afternoon before the epic horse race, it had similar social structure. The Henley equivalent of the corporate box or luxury car-boot was the houseboat, built and decorated for the occasion on a pontoon base. With prizes offered for best decoration, all kinds of wonderfully turned-out spectator boats moored near the eight-hundred-yard straight with their flower-covered canopies and their pennants and flags flying.

Canoes would contain a pretty girl reclining in a sea of shirred satin cushions, one gloved hand holding a parasol over her hatted curls as she gazed up at her manly boatman. The Miss Henley competition was hugely successful for several decades from the 1930s, finally morphing into the Moomba Queen title in 1955.

As with the Cup, the fashions of the field were at least as important to many participants, some of them completely oblivious to the reason they were nominally there, to watch the rowing race of the year. Henley was a good excuse for general gorgeousness: frocks, a flutter and a flirt; the spectacle of it all. White trousers, dresses and hats were worn, and in the background, palm court orchestras played.

The judges' box, built in 1930, still stands over the finish line on the south bank of the river, halfway between Boathouse Drive and the Swan Street Bridge (which at that time did not exist). The box was completely submerged in the 1934 flood. Silvertails—if they couldn't get a possie on anything actually afloat—were to be found along this stretch, the south bank reserve area. The more humble punters would stand or sit for free on the north bank. Pre-empting Moomba—a street parade and festival beginning in 1955 with river events such as waterskiing* held in the same location—and perhaps dating back to Cremorne Gardens, the evening would end with fireworks on the riverbank. Princes Bridge closed, and a river flotilla glowed and twinkled with light.

In angling pursuits, the biggest fish caught in the Yarra have probably been Murray cod, some forty years old and huge. Strangers from Millewa, these 'Kings of the aquatic food chain', which can grow in length to the height of a man, are some of the biggest freshwater fish on the planet. The ancient species, traceable back millions of years, was first introduced to the Yarra in the 1850s. On the Murray-Darling, some believed that each giant fish's skin contained within it a natural map of its river home.

The largest hauls of modern fishing have most likely been taken at the Warmies or Hotties in the warm water outfall from Newport Power Station, where tailor congregate. In the late 1960s fish counts

---

* In the glamorous heyday of Moomba Masters waterskiing, television starlets could get their start there—such as Rosemary Margan, one-time weathergirl and ad-read foil to Graham Kennedy and later radio's Neil Mitchell. The Birdman Rally and the amusement sideshows in Alexandra Gardens added to Moomba entertainment; later there were Dragonboats.

were netting about twenty kilos of fish per river acre at Eltham. The most common fish taken from the upper Yarra in the nineteenth century was the native blackfish, whose numbers have dwindled in proportion to the amount of LWD or snags removed from the water—it uses woody areas in the water to spawn.

Another large aquatic creature, the dolphin, has also been known to visit the river from the Bay. There have been recent sightings in the city's Turning Basin, but historical reports list them as far up as Richmond.

Bunyips—not strangers but fearfully strange—were a mystery. Charles La Trobe, Superintendent of the Port Phillip District, wrote in 1847 of the constant rumours 'of some unknown beast'. He was convinced of their existence and various Kulin provided sketches for him of this very large billabong- and river-based creature, somewhat resembling a plesiosaurus. La Trobe stated, 'It is pretended that before the Europeans arrived the Yarra near Melbourne possessed many of them.' Sightings were also reported at Tooradin, which is posited as the prehistoric site of an earlier Yarra River's entrance to the sea.

The more adventurous canoe and kayak down the river. Depending on flow and water levels, you can paddle from Reefton, not far from the Upper Yarra Dam, to Port Melbourne, with some portage and rapids and a few set courses and clubhouses along the way. There used to be a canoe club at Twickenham Ferry that raced, but in the Henley era there may have been more canoodling 'under the willow trees with a girl and a gramophone on board' on appropriate stretches all the way upstream.

There have been various canoe clubs. Fairfield was formed in 1919. In the 1970s the rapids near Watsons Creek round Bend of Islands were immortalised in TV advertising as rough and tough enough to provide a challenge for Solo Man, a very butch kayakker who fought his way through the white water to a well-earned can of fizzy lemon squash, which he chugged down under his fast-bowler moustache. (Then he crushed the can.)

~

Swimming was originally described as bathing, for that is what people did. In the 1840s, a floating 'baths'—a screened swimming platform about twenty metres long—was moored below the Falls in town (going adrift only once). Bathing in the river during daytime was against council by-laws. In 1850 a man and boy were heavily fined for bathing naked hidden under the river wharves. People in Richmond would wash in the Yarra because there were no baths in the houses they lived in.

'Bathing' probably began to metamorphose into 'swimming' when those basic facilities became more available, and the river and municipal baths were visited for amusement rather than cleanliness. Melbourne City Baths, where one could bathe for cleanliness and swim for pleasure, opened in 1904.

Bathing—elegant, proper, English—became swimming—rough, energetic, Australian. Even if that's not exactly what you did, but rather sank your toes into warm mud, lay in a rapid stream, did bombs off an old canvas firehose or ship's hawser tied to a gumtree, shot baby rapids in a rubber innertube, then swam, briefly, before sitting back, knees bent, sculling water, determined to build a raft and set off downstream on the big adventure…at least until the next bend.

Wurundjeri swam in the river, extremely well. Garryowen described Kulin as being natural swimmers, learning to swim as soon as they could walk.

> They could perform wondrous feats in swimming and diving, and the mode of water-travelling was unlike the European system, as the swimmer instead of lying flat on the water, went on his side with hand struck out from shoulder as a steering apparatus, and the other hand and feet acting as powerful propellors.

There are still swimming holes all along the river. Below Dights Falls, in the tidal river, swimming is not allowed because of boat traffic, though not everyone takes notice: the odd long-distance swimmer, champion tennis player* or kid looking for somewhere to do a bomb can be seen.

There used to be suburban river beaches and pools, dug-out surrounds, semi-concreted in like Sydney's sea-baths. The Ivanhoe, Alphington and Fairfield stretch was described as equal in popularity to St Kilda beach in the late 1920s. It included Wilson Reserve, Ivanhoe; Fairfield Park next to the Boathouse (the children's pool was finally filled in during the 1980s); Rudder Grange; and Alphington, just upstream of the paper mill—built by locals in the 1920s, lasting until the 1960s and now partially restored. There was also Deep Rock at Yarra Bend, a curve upstream from Dights Falls and River Avenue, Willsmere or North Kew (complete with change-rooms until the freeway arrived).

Less formal but just as popular spots included a diving platform at Mullum Mullum Creek confluence in Templestowe and many places at Heidelberg, Warrandyte beaches, Kangaroo Ground and Christmas Hills.† Yarra Glen had a picket enclosure. Warburton had a diving board at Willow Pool and an early waterslide down a dropped log at Chinamans Pool behind the first Signs Publishing building.

In Richmond they swam at what is now Herring Island. It used to be called the Sandy, as it was on a bend that collected a beautiful beach each spring. The old quarries opposite were also a very popular spot for Tigertown boys—anywhere along the river was, despite the fact that it was filthy: bridges were for diving off.

Serious swimming took place in the Yarra, too. In 1905 Annette Kellerman was still in her teens when, as champion swimmer of Australia and one of the best long-distance swimmers in the world, she swam from Johnston Street to Princes Bridge—about ten and a

---

* Jim Courier's coach said he would jump in the Yarra if Courier won the Australian Open: Courier said if he won he'd join him. Courier did win the 1992 Open at the Melbourne Tennis Centre and ran straight across the road to dive into the river.

† Bert Tucker photographed and Neil Douglas described Sid Nolan diving in the Yarra at Heide, Bulleen: 'He would run as fast as he could down the hill and launch himself into the air much too soon so that we thought his stomach would be ripped open, a human missile shooting past us as we sat...I've never seen anything like it.'

Yarra-trained Annette Kellerman—the woman with the medically-certified perfect body—shows London and New York how to do a bomb.

quarter miles or sixteen and a half kilometres—in just under five hours using the 'trudgeon and double overarm stroke'. She had become crippled (reportedly with rickets) when she was a child, and used swimming in her recovery.

As a schoolgirl she did a mermaid act at Princes Court funfair, now the Arts Centre site, and also did shows swimming in a tank at the Aquarium. She became a sensation overseas with more of the same: swimming further than any other woman ever had, high diving, vaudeville, stunts and the movies. In 1952 there was a Busby Berkeley Hollywood biopic of her life called *Million Dollar Mermaid*, starring Esther Williams.

Kellerman published two books in 1918: *How to Swim* and *Physical Beauty—How to Keep It*. In the latter Kellerman uses the analogy of a river flowing well and purifying itself, as compared to stagnating and being unfit for any use, to describe the human bloodstream 'which must flow pure and strong'. In *How to Swim* there is a useful illustrated description of the Australian splosh ('doing a bomb') and unfortunately her opinion of the Yarra, in which she could do two and a quarter miles in 46 minutes: it was a 'dead river', she thought, and 'very difficult to swim in'.

Deep Rock Swimming and Life Saving Club formed in the early 1900s, and took advantage of a naturally deep, wide pool of the river just up the bend from Dights Falls by putting in concrete terracing, a kids' pool and a diving tower. (Deep Rock would compete against other river-based swimming clubs including Fairfield, Ivanhoe, Willsmere and Alphington). In 1918, deciding they needed a sensational event for a patriotic fundraiser at their swim carnival, they convinced Alick Wickham to go for the world high dive record. A tower was built on the high cliff (Studley Park side) opposite the Deep Rock club (Clifton Hill side).

These days, even without the tower, standing atop the escarpment looking down at the Yarra can induce vertigo. The wisping treetops are way, way below, the river is flat in front of you, rippling, strong, brown: that wet solid-wall image. The problem—Wickham's fear—was getting away from those treetops and jagged rock faces.

Sixty thousand people arrived to see what would happen. Luckily, Wickham was the most exciting diver in the country, if not the world. A Solomon Islander whose father was English and mother Polynesian, he introduced the Pacific Islander style of swimming to Australia, from where it evolved and became popularised around the world as the Australian crawl. As he climbed the tower—two hundred feet, more than sixty metres, the club claimed, above the water—the crowd went crazy. An army bugler, from the forces sent to fight and die in Europe, played a call. In the sudden silence Wickham, now at the top, steadied himself and on the second bugle call, leapt.

It was a swallow dive, and perfect—except that the force of entry ripped off his costume and left him naked, unwilling to leave the water until provided with blanket coverage. The speed of the dive (timed at two and a half seconds) was described as thrilling and even terrifying for the spectators. Wickham himself apparently described the sensation as like descending in a lift (except, presumably, you're going down head first, not exactly sure what it's going to be like when you hit bottom).

Notorious gambling czar and swimming club president John Wren* rewarded him with a hundred pounds, a fortune in those days (and just as well, he'd done it for free). Like Annette Kellerman, Wickham worked the vaudeville circuit, the tonight-show equivalent

* Wren lived up over the ridge in John Hodgson's old house, Studley, which he'd rebuilt in 1919, but preferred to swim near his Collingwood turf. He had already sponsored a lot of the club's outdoor infrastructure. Wren had various business interests sited near the inner city river.

of its day, and earnt good money. Deep Rock was destroyed when the river was rerouted during construction of the Eastern Freeway but the club itself had closed in 1953.

The big river swim, which started in 1913, was the Victorian Amateur Swimming Association's Yarra River Three Mile Swim, from Grange Road, Toorak at the Mac Robertson Bridge or Twickenham Ferry site, downstream to Princes Bridge. An annual event for half a century, it drew hundreds of entries and thousands of spectators. Despite the odd scandal or scamming by competitors, it was treated as the state long-distance title event. Various other meets were run. Abbotsford swim club's two-mile handicap of 1935 was at the time reportedly 'the most gruelling of its kind ever held in Victoria'. The riverwater was so cold that less than a third of those entered finished (two-thirds had started). The course was from Studley Park Boathouse one mile upstream and back. None of the placegetters in the Yarra Three Mile Swim that year could cut it. Those successful were described as having superior knowledge and experience of river swimming, or rather racing.

The flatness of the river flood plains made them ideal for amusement and games; some even evolved around that factor. Steeplechase at Yarra Glen, straight races at Heidelberg, picnic races at Wesburn and Woori Yallock, trotting and cars at Fishermans Bend, foot races and rifle ranges at Kew and Fishermans Bend, archery at Bulleen and North Kew, ponies at John Wren's Richmond course and private racetracks (1930s North Kew, now in the Yarra Valley) are or were once all to be found. A drive-in cinema opened at Bulleen in the 1960s, but no one had considered old Birrarung itself—the mists rising up from the river behind the large screen: it was another element that made the business never quite as successful as it might have been.

When the first Australian Rules football was played in the open space near what is now known as the G* in the 1850s, the land ran clear through to the river. As Geoffrey Blainey has explained, the

* The Melbourne Cricket Ground or MCG: still the game's spiritual centre.

irregular open spaces provided by the Yarra River flats, the local climate's effect on the winter ground and the big river redgums—some of which are still to be found—were all elements in the development of the game. (For example, limitless space with occasional obstruction led to the size of the playing field not being set, but shifting according to the particular ground: it wasn't until the 1870s that it was played inside contained grounds such as the early MCG.)

Marngrook, the Aboriginal game played with a ball of sewn-up possum skin or possum-hair twine, was about high marking and kicking long, features of what became Australian Rules football. A version of it was probably played earlier on the same site as the G, which is on Woiwurrung meeting and corroboree ground; it was certainly played at Coranderrk.

Rolf Boldrewood, as well as making various observations about the river, also played for South Yarra against Melbourne FC in 1859, in one of the first set Australian Rules games. Melbourne Football Club's first home, on the Friendly Society grounds, was ruined when the river was rerouted for the Botanical Gardens Cut in the late 1890s: it was then that they moved to the MCG.

Australian Rules is the most popular type of football in the world, with more people in total turning out in Melbourne each round as spectators than in any other city on the planet. Per-game attendance is still higher for American gridiron, but the Aussie Rules average is higher than any European soccer game.

There's always been a place for bread and circuses along the river. The node on the south bank of the river west of Princes Bridge has long been such a spot. A touring circus of the 1870s visited first, with amusements reportedly including a steam piano and the sideshow of a woman threading a needle with her toes.

The funfairs settled, and by the early 1900s Princes Court, later Wirths, had a skating rink, shooting gallery, waterslide, cinema and Japanese teahouse, as well as performing humans and animals. From the 1920s, dancing was the feature, with famous venues the Green

Mill, and later the Trocadero, fronting the Snowden Gardens which sloped down to the river.

The tradition of spectacle probably began in 1849 with a ropewalker crossing the river twenty feet (about six metres) above the water. It took him twenty minutes to go a hundred yards (or metres, near enough). In 1854, another gentleman tried walking across the river near Princes Bridge using 'water-boots'. American Harry Houdini, the greatest escapologist and showman of all time, toured in 1910. As a promotional stunt, he dived off Queens Bridge while chained, padlocked and cuffed. Despite a crowd crush, no one was killed watching him, though he was lost to sight as soon as he entered the muddy water. In fact, it was reported that he complained later of having to stand in mud up to his armpits at the bottom of the Yarra while manipulating his way out of the aforementioned constrictions.

The Great Levante, another chained escapologist, jumped off Princes Bridge in the 1940s with other spectacular divers as part of a learn-to-swim display.

Allens Confectionery built a new factory in 1925 on the Southbank site which later featured a huge extravaganza of flashing rooftop neon illustrating their explosive taste sensations. This may have been the artistic highlight of the view from Flinders Street Station, St Kilda Road and Princes Bridge for decades. Later (continuing to the present day) there was the added thrill of the Moomba Birdman Rally; in which entrants grasp on to putative flying contraptions and leap off Princes Bridge—the aim being to see how far you can go before plummeting into the water.

The Victorian Arts Centre eventually replaced Snowden Gardens and the old amusement sites, opening for business in the 1980s. The interior wall treatments of its Concert Hall were inspired by the colours and striations in the rock cuttings along the Eastern Freeway, the geological formations that had determined the river's location.

Federation Square,* the redevelopment of the the Princes Bridge Station site, contains the National Gallery of Victoria's

* Celebrating the centenary of Australia's federation in 1901.

Australian galleries, a magnificent attraction. The buildings' costly, fractured, computer-calculated zinc and glass surface patterns and interior angles were controversial, likened by some critics to the visual schema favoured by unmedicated schizophrenics, or psychotic feng shui. A marvel of steps leading up from Flinders Street to the unseen main square formally echoes the tiny natural fractal sandstone 'staircases' formed by intermittent creek flow to the river, upstream along the escarpment at Studley Park. The sight of the wondrously tiled, undulating square itself is exhilarating (that is unless you're elderly, frail, in a wheelchair, with a child's pusher or wearing high heels: though possibly doubly exhilarating if you're a public liability lawyer).

The much-vaunted new connection of the river to the city was not immediately apparent. What faced the Yarra directly below Federation Square was the heritage-listed bluestone vaults of the approaches to Princes Bridge. Well after the square opened, they were being squatted in by young sniffers of assorted solvents who would taunt the middle-class tourists as they lined up for their river boat trip.

Perhaps one day a portion of these state mega-budgets can be found to restore the already existing and iconic Flinders Street Station building, the city's face to the north bank of the river—fabulous ballroom and all.*

Downstream on the opposite bank, Crown Casino complex opened in the 1990s: half a million square metres of gaming complex (Australia's biggest) fronting two city blocks' worth of river, with upmarket shops, hundreds of hotel rooms, cinemas, nightclubs, scores of restaurants and bars...right down to two-cent pokies for the pensioners on its half-kilometre of gaming floor. It would be amazing if you couldn't find something you wanted to do in its World of Entertainment®.

---

* Flinders Street was designed to house the Victorian Railways Institute as well as Melbourne's main metropolitan station, and provided classrooms and social facilities for VR employees: the concert hall which doubled as a ballroom, a library of (by 1960) more than 40,000 books, reading rooms, a billiard room, a gym and so on, as well as—briefly—a children's nursery for mothers visiting the city.

It was the single largest building project ever undertaken in Australia. Various people objected to the alliance of government and big business taking huge profits from punters, as well as the overlapping interests involved in getting the two-billion-dollar project up to that point. Homegrown-later-Hollywood star Rachel Griffiths bared her breasts—uninvited—in protest at the opening of the gambling venue.

By the early 2000s Crown was listed as one of the biggest casinos in the world: the redistribution of wealth* was massive. Asian high-rollers were the cream of the market. The true luck of the draw—life—didn't seem to have an analogy in the state-sanctioned losses incurred by lower-demographic punters on the automated gaming machines now also found in their home suburbs. Pain, and pleasure no doubt, were to be found in greater extremes than ever before on the Yarrabank.

* Or perhaps that should be accumulation of wealth: apart from the massive ongoing government rake-off which paid for some of the nearby waterfront redevelopments, Crown was now owned by Kerry Packer, richest man in Australia.

~ ~ ~

Wherever there was pleasure there were artists. S. T. Gill painted a view of Cremorne Gardens from Paul de Castella's father-in-law's place on the opposite side of the river. Nicholas Chevalier depicted the Survey Paddock at sunset. Everybody did Studley Park. Poor Ludwig Becker, who died on the Burke and Wills expedition, did old Princes Bridge. Many painters arrived along with the general populace in the gold-rush years of the 1850s, when there was more money for the superfluities of art.

As Tim Bonyhady has pointed out, river landscapes were painted with eyes only for the notion of Beauty, ignoring the realities of industrial and human waste floating or festering nearby. Even critics of the time remarked upon this extraordinary facility. As with the rowing, people seemed able to ignore what was under—or even up—their very noses.

Eugene von Guérard's first commission was a homestead just upstream of what would become Rudder Grange—*The Farm of Mr Perry on the Yarra*, painted at Fulham Grange in 1855. (The Perrys were rumoured to have a hundred thousand fruit trees of more than 180 varieties by the peak of their empire.) Fulham Grange, Alphington, became the northernmost rail station on the Outer Circle line, just north of what is now Chandler Highway Bridge. Von Guérard, who sketched at Heidelberg and other Yarra Valley locations, also later travelled to the other side of the river's headwaters in Baw Baw with Chevalier and Howitt, the gentleman who was to record Barak's knowledge for posterity.

Louis Buvelot arrived in 1865 and painted along the river for several decades, from Fishermans Bend, and the Survey Paddock, up to what is now Yarra Glen (then Yarra Flats) and into the lush catchment of Fernshawe. His bucolic *September morning, Richmond* of 1866 shows some of the original river, a bend that is now gone with its river redgums, and countryside that became Punt Road/

Anderson Street hill. *Winter morning near Heidelberg* of the same year, looks across a steep riverbank with LWD (large wooden debris) eroded out, to two men and a woman putting timber on a fire.

Buvelot's painting *Summer afternoon Templestowe* of 1866 probably had the greatest impact. Frederick McCubbin described it as 'thoroughly Australian', which was both a compliment and a new concept. Arthur Streeton, one of the original Heidelberg School painters, thought it 'the first fine landscape painted in Victoria'. In 1889 he walked from the rail line down the valley, across and up the river to its location, then painted his own *Road to Templestowe*. It was on the way back that he met the owner of the Eaglemont estate which would become the base of the famous Heidelberg School, Australia's impressionist painters, the first to truly depict its light and landscape.

McCubbin and Tom Roberts had both been Buvelot's pupils and were greatly influenced by him. McCubbin grew up in West Melbourne, studied under von Guérard at the Gallery School and depicted urban riverside Melbourne, as well as the bush at and beyond Studley Park: Old Falls Bridge at twilight; the Sunday afternoon passing parade at Branders Ferry wine garden; a woman walking through dappled sunlight on the bushland riverbank, wholly concentrating on reading a letter; a wharf panorama of Melbourne's spires and towers rising profiled behind belching steamships ready to go; and Princes Bridge topped by the triumphal Federation arch, when the city was the continent's capitol.

Tom Roberts was born in England, arriving in Melbourne as a child. When he was an old man, his son remembered, one day in Studley Park he said that, 'for the first few years his memory of England prevented any appreciation of the Australian landscape until a view of the Yarra above the Falls suddenly made him realise its beauty'. Before Heidelberg, he and other painters such as McCubbin went on sketching expeditions along the river to various locations like Richmond paddock, Studley Park, and from Merri Creek up to Darebin Creek. Roberts was a great portraitist, and painted George Coppin in the sitter's old age.

Arthur Streeton went to Punt Road State School, took McCubbin's classes at the Gallery night school, and went painting in the open air, along the river and docks as well. It was from a review of his work that the term Heidelberg School came, and the artists' camp at Eaglemont in 1888, where, on the paddocks along the Yarra, European Australians were shown how to see their country as it was rather than as an approximation of somewhere else.

Still glides the stream, and shall for ever glide (a line written by the English Romantic poet William Wordsworth) is one of a series of paintings to which *Golden summer, Eaglemont* and *Spring* also belong. These distant views to blue Corhanwarrabul (the Dandenongs), across the golden-paddocked river valley, are opposite to the twilight shadows of the previous year's *Between the lights—Princes Bridge*.

Spring shows young men bathing on Sills Bend, Heidelberg (where people still swim), with foreground details of insects and flowers in the grass. This painting was owned for a few decades by Baldwin Spencer, that intrepid explorer and photographer of the Upper Yarra, its creeks and waterfall. It depicts a landscape quite contrary to the wild and weird country he battled through near the river's source at around the same time Streeton painted the work.*

John Mather in 1895 painted Billibellary's lake, the flood of Yarra water in the Yering basin as *Wintry weather, Yarra Glen*. Mather owned at least one of Barak's drawings.

Other artists to paint at Heidelberg, visit the artists' camps or work in the open air within cooee of the river included David Davies (*Moonrise*), Jane Sutherland, Arthur Loureiro, E. Phillips Fox and Charles Conder (*The Yarra, Heidelberg*, like Streeton's *Spring* and *Boys bathing*, depicts a still-used swimming hole). Walter Withers was also at the Heidelberg artists' camps, and after a couple of years

---

* Louis Buvelot's *Winter morning* and *Summer afternoon, Templestowe*, Penleigh Boyd's *The breath of Spring*, Arthur Streeton's *Spring* and John Mather's *Wintry weather, Yarra Glen* can be seen with many other treasures not far from the river at the National Gallery of Victoria, Federation Square.

took over Charterisville* as an artists' colony, later painting at Warrandyte (the old bridge), then Eltham.

Withers, and McCubbin at the Gallery School, taught Clara Southern who became a Warrandyte landscape painter in the early 1900s. She had been to the Eaglemont camp, later centring a cluster of artists at Warrandyte, and lived overlooking the river there. Like Withers, she too depicted the old Warrandyte bridge, as well as the wattles and river itself; *Evensong* and *Cool corner* are both identifiable river locations.

Penleigh Boyd was another whose artistic world focused on the Yarra. His parents, Arthur Merric and Emma Minnie Boyd, were both exhibiting painters, and knew McCubbin, Withers and Conder. The family had bought a farm with river frontage at Yarra Glen—within sight of the long trestle bridge—and a lot of their watercolours were executed there. Penleigh was already at the Gallery School in his mid teens, and had his first work, *Grey day, Yarra Glen*, hung with his mother's. On the weekend he would bring along other young painters such as William McInnes and sketch on the river. He painted the city dockside as well as more familiar valley scenes, still painting in Yarra Glen even after the family moved back to town. He too painted *The old bridge, Warrandyte* also known as *Bridge and wattle at Warrandyte*. Pre-war, the wattles are sidelined, framing the picture.

In his early twenties, Penleigh Boyd married Edith Anderson, an artist in her own right and a model for E. Phillips Fox. She was described by an English cousin of Penleigh's as having 'river-coloured eyes'. The couple built a house and studio above the Yarra at Warrandyte.

---

* Charterisville was one of the big original river estates described by Rolf Boldrewood. Hubert de Castella, Yarra Valley winemaker, also owned it at one time. In 1906 the world's first feature film *The Story of the Kelly Gang*—illustrating bushranger Ned Kelly's exploits until his capture—was partly shot on location there, as the director's wife's family then had the estate. The several actors playing Ned wear his actual armour.

In 1915 Penleigh enlisted to fight. At Ypres in 1917, in the trenches of World War One, he was gassed and permanently affected. By 1918, he was painting again, on the river (*Wattle gatherers*). The pictures of 1919 are his most extraordinary (*Wattle blossom*, *Spring fantasy*, *Yarra River*), *The breath of Spring* his most famous, and later *Golden fires of Spring* and *'Twixt shadow and shine*.

These large paintings of Yarra wattles are amazing celebratory images, antidote to trenches 'heavy with the odour of rotting corpses and foul gas'. The trees burst with sunlit blossom—ethereal above the muted flow of earthed water—centrepoints of innocent figures tiny in comparison to the vigour and splendour of the golden world towering above them. The river at base grounds but still reflects the incandescence, Yarra mud the colour in flow.

The previous year, Boyd wrote,

> Mud...the chief enemy and misery of the soldier. Mud, soft and deep, that you sink into, vainly seeking a foothold on something solid; or stiff and clinging, gripping boots so firmly as sometimes to drag them off. Mud, that coats men, horses, guns, rifles, and all in a thick camouflage, so that they become almost indistinguishable from the ground. It clings to men's bodies and cracks their skins, and the slimy horror of it soaks their souls and sucks their courage...

...but was still able to write in a letter home to his wife from France, 'spring suggests life & vigour and ambition'. It is in early spring that the muddy Yarra flow is lifted with flooding rains—an exhilarating sight after drought—to swirl and meet the golden wattle blossom mid-branch.*

There is attributed to the great French chef Escoffier, sensation of pre-war London, a recipe for wattle (acacia) blossom fritters, soaked in sugar and cognac liqueur. Arthur Streeton had written to a friend more than twenty years earlier of 'the wattle intoxication at

* During World War One groups of wounded veterans were taken on outings to Warrandyte. Halls and automobiles were decorated with wattle in season: for pleasure and patriotism.

Heidelberg'. The memory of blossom soft on the skin was the fragrance of childhood sunshine. Each of the Boyds who had grown up at Yarra Glen held the images of wattle blossom throughout their lifetimes. Helen, the youngest, described 'the river…lined with the golden flowers of the wattle trees just like fairyland'; Martin, later famous as a novelist, wrote in his memoirs of burying his face in the blossom during an idyllic boyhood.

Wattles begin to bloom after the coldest and darkest period of the year, blazing hope and renewal during what might be one's bleakest time. Some start in winter, others run to spring. They are heralds and vouchsafes, reminders of hope—there is death and remembrance—there is and will be new life in the midst of cold, wet, mud. In the grey darkness, there is blissfulness, sweet scent, golden light: redemption is as far as the riverbank. Reminder, perhaps, of another more spiritual place, in this plane or not, above in the sky world, Tharangalk-bek.

For Barak and his father, the wattles were calling time. These are the silver wattles that lined the River Yarra before the beginning of settlement, blazing every year, the wattles titling a biography of Barak* (that venerable Wurundjeri headman and son of a Batman treaty 'signatory') because he believed he would die when they were in bloom again, as his father had: and so it happened. Old folk stories, of Kulin and settlers both, say wattle—so beautiful—is bad luck in the home: never bring it inside.

Penleigh Boyd was killed in a single-vehicle accident on a country road in 1923.

Penleigh's brother Merric also found his artistic vocation while the Boyds lived at Yarra Glen, though when much older. He, too, was taught by Frederick McCubbin, and he started exhibiting sculpture and pottery in his early twenties. After Yarra Glen, Merric went to Murrumbeena and, with his wife Doris (also a riverside sketcher), built on land adjoining the southern end of the Outer Circle rail line.

---

* Shirley Wiencke's *When the Wattles Bloom Again*.

As a studio potter, Merric used Australian flora and fauna as motifs and forms. The 'Arthur Merric Boyd' pottery produced in the mid-1940s was actually made by a group of artists working under the one label. They included Merric's son Arthur Boyd, John Perceval (who married Arthur's sister Mary, herself later to marry Sidney Nolan) and Neil Douglas.

Arthur had exhibited as a painter in a Penleigh Boyd studio group show maintained by Penleigh's widow while still in his late teens. Decades later, in an English art magazine, he related how on his Saturday afternoons off from working in his uncle's paint factory, aged fifteen, 'I would take my paints on the cable train and go down to the River Yarra. The banks had a lovely rocky and clay ground—a magical space. I'd always done that whenever I could get away.' By the late 1930s and early '40s, even when he was in the army, he went further upstream to Warburton and Launching Place. He painted at Warrandyte, too, *The old waterwheel*, just near the bridge. Some of his allegorical pictures also include the river.

Perceval later painted the Yarra downstream (*Ship in the River*) and beyond, at Williamstown, as well as many landscapes in its watershed. One of his commissioned ceramics, an earthenware coffeepot, depicts in the glaze the mists of the River Yarra which rise near the Kangaroo Ground home of the owner.

Neil Douglas joined the pottery as a decorator in 1944, and became a partner in 1950. He led the way in understanding and depicting the Australian bush in ceramics and pictures. After the AMB partnership ended, he moved back to the other side of the Yarra in the late 1950s. Over the next few decades, he painted many locations along the river, from a snow landscape and the forest of the Upper Yarra, to Yarra Glen near the Boyds' old house, and the bush close to his own home at the Bend of Islands, Kangaroo Ground.

He thought the great Australian artists were really 'paddock painters', and espoused a personal pictorial theory of the 'disarray' of the bush, which is exactly what one finds along the Yarra watershed. There is not necessarily a clear visual path, as Hoddle and Baldwin Spencer knew. 'If it's curious and ancient and very old as Australia is,' he said, 'it doesn't conform to an English type of realism or beauty, it conforms to a new, yet hardly painted, and different kind of motivation.'

He would retell the story throughout his long life of being criticised as a fuddy-duddy landscape painter for painting the wattle; but like hakea and grevillea, he said, it comes, 'from primeval times and is a response to the extraordinary light of Australia...If we have strange forms in Australia, in our wildflowers and in our rocks—well, then, they look like a new sort of sculpture.'

For one commissioned exhibition of the Yarra Valley, Douglas walked in to what he identified as the river's source (actually one of the headwaters, Falls Creek: the place Baldwin Spencer travelled to). Describing it as a magic pilgrimage, he found a tiny spring and underground waterfall in a wild bush garden.

The Yarra's landscape in the country in which Douglas lived can be recognised today as looking like one of his paintings because the reverse was true. He captured the experience of being in the bush—both in his illustrative ceramics and the best of his paintings—by his sense of place, knowing the turn of a swamp wallaby's silhouette as it bounds away, the highlight pink of heath and yellow of wattle in their landscape forms, smooth earth glow of an opposite hillside distant in sunlight.

In the late 1930s, he was the gardener at Heide, that most famous artists' haven on the river at Bulleen (the opposite bank to Heidelberg), and John Reed told him he'd never be a painter. Douglas was considered old-fashioned, not being at the cutting edge of figurative painting as the artists around him were. Douglas himself said, 'They thought I was a gifted gardener, but they laughed at my paintings.' In 2003, however, during an exhibition of his work by Heide Art Gallery, there were Douglas paintings and ceramics displayed in every room of Reed's old house.

Heide was the home, from 1935, of John and Sunday Reed, cultural benefactors and patrons. Sidney Nolan did his Ned Kelly series of paintings there,* as well as immediate landscapes, and Albert

* Nolan's policeman grandfather was one sent up on the Kelly chase, as Barak was.

Tucker and Joy Hester also lived and worked there for some time. Three Heidelberg School Streetons hung in the house, plus a McCubbin and three Emma Minnie Boyd watercolours.

While Nolan was there during World War Two, he reproduced on the roof one of his most contentious paintings, *Moonboy*. A very simple flat image of a large yellow circular shape on a neck against a dark rectangular ground, it was ordered destroyed by Air Force Intelligence as potentially being a Japanese rising sun symbol near an object of strategic importance (that was, the Banksia Street Bridge over the Yarra, carrying main road and water utilities as it did).

Heide I, the old farmhouse, and modernist showpiece Heide II, built in 1965 of limestone and glass, now function as a house museum and art gallery.

Other modern artists painted the Yarra. Clarice Beckett depicted the atmospheric boulevardier river of the 1920s and '30s: Alexandra Avenue, the new gleaming, dreamy white Church Street Bridge of Harold Desbrowe-Annears, late sun reflecting, lights ablaze; the tea gardens, and Princes Bridge where at that time lots of little boats still moored and the very old, tall, vertical palms still stood.

George Johnston, writer of the great Australian novel *My Brother Jack*, described in its sequel:

> leaning on the granite coping near Flinders Street, where the attenuated palms sullenly survive the slow asphyxiation of train smut and the wrong climate, I watched the engines of the goods trains in the yards breathing white like old men on frosty mornings, and looked down on lovers welded in sculptural lumps in dry archways.

Sybil Craig, while a war artist, painted a view towards Princes Bridge, showing Catani's original standard street lamps. Lina Bryans painted the river in its factory setting at Abbotsford, Spencer Street Bridge, Fishermans Bend in the 1930s, at Banyule, Darebin and Alphington in the 1940s, and the Warrandyte bridge in the late 1950s (as a girl, she'd skipped school to sit by the Yarra and read). She, too, painted the wattles on the river at Warrandyte, many times, as well as the heath and eucalypts. Her studio home in an old pub on Darebin Creek, shared by other artists such as Ian Fairweather, later became a research lab and offices for APM from the Fairfield paper mill.

John Brack's landscape painting as a teenager where Tom Roberts had his revelation produced what he reportedly later described as 'those terrible riverbank things'.* His visits to Studley Park as a returned soldier Gallery School student saw him looking above in a Cezannesque manner, depicting the Boulevard and its cutting around the river's bend.

Fred Williams followed in some of Tom Roberts' other footsteps, painting Kew Billabong. In the early 1970s he did several views of the river from the heights of city office buildings. Within a few years he moved from the river's mouth (*Williamstown*) upstream to produce *Yarra at Abbotsford*, *Yarra in flood*—the Abbotsford Convent aproned by a sweep of brown water around the treetops—*Dights Falls*—the escarpment and factories opposite to the skyline—and *Yarra at Kew* with the dual chunky solids of the Willsmere towers over the horizon. At one point he hoped to work along the river right up to its source.

The Kew Billabong series of the mid- to late 1970s, done while the Eastern Freeway was being put through, are the most interesting. Intense repeated observations within an enclosed world, they have downward views, water edges, reflections below the once-was riverbank, natural forms as tiny gestures growing through, and detritus from that cosmos or man's, in the old waterway-to-tip progression. The billabong has survived; the paintings too, vivid, alive.

Innumerable artists have depicted the Yarra River, many more will.

---

* Brack's father was located a bit further down the river: he was a worker in the Abbotsford brewery.

~ ~ ~

From the very beginnings of alcohol in Melbourne, people have been falling dead drunk into the river; sometimes just dead. A waterside worker recalled spotting floaters of all origins at the rate of one a week in the 1920s (which they might save up for their least-favourite copper to retrieve by tying the body to a wharf—the putrescence would make it float there). In the early days before bridges, people would cross the river by swimming and sometimes drown. Falling out of boats, especially when inebriated, has also been hazardous. Corpses have been found fully clothed, still seated in the river, just underwater. Jumpers have been jumping since there's been something high enough to jump from. Before that they just threw themselves in, bereft of swimming skills, with no hope for the best or worst left.

The highest point into the river has been the West Gate Bridge. To off oneself from the West Gate must be rather like jumping into a very large, huge, solid, muddy brown wall. A permanent outcome is not guaranteed, depending on degree of difficulty and angle of entry.*

A hundred years ago, Princes Bridge in the middle of the night might have seemed like a good—though not so sure—spot to exercise the will to not live. The Vagabond (journalist John Stanley James) arrived in Melbourne broke and despairing in the 1870s, and reportedly tossed a coin on Princes Bridge to see whether he would kill himself. Life won, and he died decades later, semi-destitute again, having recorded for posterity the low underbelly of the city and the high beauties of Fernshawe and other upriver places.

The wild country round the upper reaches of the Yarra has its share of bodies, and on the extremely odd occasion, stashed loot. Old

* BASE jumping—doing the same thing but with a parachute for the undoubted thrill—is something else, though not if the parachute fails.

mine shafts are particularly useful, but not always accessible when you need one. Some people, it seems, drive up to the bush and, finding themselves in blackness as deep and vast as that wrapped around their own souls, think they are indeed in the middle of nowhere. Which is why they keep topping themselves in the same old spots, blowing their brains out or sucking exhaust, leaving the same old coppers and towies to deal with the remains. A few search out private spots of great beauty, anywhere on the river, where they take their last breath.

Those with opposite predilections and a deeper visceral blackness end up dumping the bodies of others in obvious places; in shallow graves close to tracks or dirt roads used by locals. Finding body-shaped mounds now overgrown or good quality blood-stained clothing hacked up in old quarries is not unknown.

Career criminal and author 'Chopper' Read told the story of being made to dig his own grave near Warburton in the 1970s. Cuffed in the boot of a Holden Monaro, listening to Dean Martin's 'Everybody Loves Somebody' through the back seat, he was taken from town and beaten up first for good measure. Hip-deep in the grave, spade in hand, he mounted a surprise counterattack and won out narrowly over a bad handgun: it was another body that got buried. Read writes of the spookiness, then, of hearing someone or something moving around in the bush. Probably a wild pig, as he states.

Barak believed that one's spirit, when one's body was either dead or asleep, could wander at will round country, and up through into sky-country.

Doubtless there have been a lot more dead ones dumped *in* the river close to town than *near* it upstream. If you were, say, a psychopathic drug-dealing criminal living in Cremorne, the easiest option would be to dump the bodies into something down the end of your street, even if you did have to muck around with a hacksaw, a cement mixer and a 44-gallon drum. Especially if you had a reputation for killing people in your loungeroom.

For upper-middle-class low-IQ naifs heading for Upper Yarra

bush, hiring a trailer for the family corpses might get you into trouble: it would be better perhaps to go with that first simple thought of 'Dump them in the river'. As the Painters and Dockers found, near enough can definitely be good enough—over the side of the wharf, in a car or otherwise, required much less effort.

The river has an irregular rocky bottom, silt-settled, its depth varying from an average of three metres to ten in the dredged-out lower reaches. Always deep enough to drown in, definitely deep enough to hide bodies in and soft and dark and sucky enough to bury evidence in (stolen cars, the odd cracked safe, guns…).

Once, on the way home after an underworld murder, the prime suspect was said to have thrown an empty Maccas bag over the side of West Gate Bridge. Suspiciously heavy-looking, it plummeted to the Yarra's maximum depth below. Police divers could find no trace: the murder weapon is still missing. The reverse has also occurred, with divers locating more 'evidence' than was helpful. One alleged weapon contained (it was unfortunately found in court) bullets made after the crime was committed. Young 1970s Communist (Marxist-Leninist) Party members dumped their guns in the river too.

Squizzy Taylor, that weasel-like gangster of the 1920s, first made the acquaintance of the police as an eleven-year-old, picked up walking along the Yarra at Burnley with a sack over his shoulder. He tried to dump the bag in the river but didn't get away. Down at the station they gave him a beating, but Squizzy wouldn't give up anything about the sack's contents—bread, a hammer and nails and a tin of jam—which was probably the pathetic haul of a domestic Tigertown B & E.

At the end of the nineteenth century, a page-stopping murder sub-headed 'The Yarra Mystery' kept Melbourne enthralled for weeks. The naked body of a young woman was found in a boot-trunk floating on the river. As she was unknown, her severed, putrefied head was publicly exhibited at the Yarra Bank Morgue* in

* Later Batman Avenue, Birrarung Marr site.

the hope of an identification. A large sum of money was offered and for days a steady stream of people filed through from morning to night. The *Argus* noted,

> So many family parties dotted the Yarra Bank road, including children, to view the head in the preserving jar...2,000 visitors, only 100 of which were police...the vast majority seemed to be actuated by no other desire than to see the horrible object that had caused so much talk and discussion.

Further comments related to the 'puerile attempts' of reward seekers. Two people were charged with the young woman's murder, a 'futurist and palmist' who had performed an 'illegal operation' on her and a 'land and estate agent...responsible for her condition', both of South Yarra. They had gone down to the quarries on the river at the bottom of Como Estate (the Herring Island site) to dump the body, crushing and doubling it to fit the boot trunk, which was weighted with stone. Somehow, there can seem to be greater horrors than death.

The river itself can be weapon or illusory sanctuary: from the murder/suicide by drowning of a mother and her daughter a century and a half ago;* to the young men who leapt in recently to escape being macheted and were then taunted and menaced, forced to stay there until they disappeared, choking to death on the turbid waters.†

Parts of *Mad Max*, that post-apocalyptic Mel Gibson road movie running on adrenalin, are set in a grimy, nineteenth-century redbrick building—the Halls of Justice, where near-future cop Max is based. In actuality it was mainly the old Spotswood Pumping Station, which used to push away the dark river that runs below the Yarra—not to an underworld but to the brilliant sunlit plains extended of

---

* As recorded by Garryowen: a woman threw her two daughters, aged eleven and nine, in to drown, and then disposed of herself the same way. Only the younger girl survived.

† Viet-Australian gang warfare: the river was the endpoint from a South Yarra nightclub glassing, avenging a previous incident at Crown Casino.

Werribee sewage farm (the domain not of Hades but the Melbourne & Metropolitan Board of Works). Other Halls of Justice exteriors were shot at Port Melbourne.

Like the Heidelberg School painters upriver to the east a century earlier, director George Miller showed us for the first time one of our own landscapes, only this one was west, post-industrial and automotive, and involved a lot of carnage. Not everyone recognised it. An undertow to the wave of Australian period films then being made with that nineteenth-century Heidelberg-golden-summers look, it had big problems getting funding.

Streeton and Roberts, and George Miller and Byron Kennedy, all looked selectively at what was in front of them at the time. Kennedy, the film's producer, had grown up in the Westie high car culture; Miller MD had seen a lot of road casualties. He described *Mad Max* as 'about the dark side of ourselves'. The film's mythology is classical: the hero warrior, forged through suffering, battles the underworld (the same eternal story that will continue to evolve as the roles of our police and soldiers do). The state government later resisted the notion of reserving 'MAX'-prefixed numberplates for its own warrior-class of Victoria Police—for cars with a bit of grunt—instead pastily putting them onto an assortment of Camryesque government-issue vehicles.*

Today, every Victoria Police squad and branch can be called to work on the River, though it is Search and Rescue that sees it from belly up. Members have saved many people from drowning in the river, whether they wanted to be rescued or not (jumpers on bridges and drunks on buoys at 3 a.m.), and been variously commended and awarded.

They retrieve corpses too: the oft-repeated floater story had two young constables finding a body in the Yarra on their night beat. All for reporting and bringing it in, they were counselled by two older, wiser Ds, and advised, since the end of their shift was nearing, to let

* Police in other parts of Australia have been known to quote decades-old Miller/McAusland dialogue back to the original actors after picking them up in the street (as big fans only, naturally).

it go—even, indeed, give it a little push. By morning, the tide would deliver said three- to ten-day-old dead one to the opposite bank, where another district's divvy van crew and station would have to deal with the hours of extra paperwork.

The Water Police were established in 1841, reporting to the Harbour Master, and mainly concerned with policing sailors, the conduct of the port and its regulation. In the 1880s they stopped steamers running down river pleasure boats. The Wharf Patrol was formed during the First World War, although it wasn't until the late 1920s that the Department for River Patrols bought a small open boat. It was stationed at Princes Bridge. Later a larger boat was obtained for the Dock Police and moored at the Victoria Dock station. From the 1950s to the 1970s a motor launch was based on the river at the Burnley MMBW Depot. Now off the river and with various craft, the Water Police cover anything in Victoria that floats: from yachts, motor boats, rowers and skiers to commercial fishing boats and ships, when in dock.

The Search and Rescue Squad was first trained to dive in the late 1950s, and brought in to find bodies, weapons, stolen goods and other evidence, even drugs secreted in the external cavities of ships' hulls. The practical component of the training course progressed from clear-water conditions up to the most ghastly and difficult (as reported by Victoria Police Public Relations Division in 1976): 'South Wharf on the lower Yarra, where visibility is usually nil, the water is deep and extremely filthy.'

Melbourne Water would say the water is no longer filthy—though it is perhaps extremely turbid and the Environment Protection Authority might rate it unsafe for swimming due to its bacteria count—but 'filthy' is still the term used colloquially by divers. Lavatories on the wharf were still emptying into the river in the 1970s.

Examples of squad river operations carried out in the past few decades include: diving South Wharf and recovering a gun used in a Painter and Docker killing; South Wharf again, for ship capsize survivors and bodies; Kangaroo Ground for canoeists stuck up a tree in the middle of a flood; diving Hawthorn for dumped safes (at least one is still there on the other bank, settling deeper); diving Kew for a stolen shotgun used in an armed rob. They've also tracked the river with sidescan Sonar, locating dozens of dumped stolen cars.

Zero visibility for divers means they're on the bottom of the river struggling with its currents, sinking mud and jagged rocks and can't see. The effect can range from a dense brown translucence to the kind of black you get pressing your palms over your eyes, except that their eyes are wide, wide open. Searching for something—a dead body, a gun with live ammo—is done by feel with the hands while crawling through what is described as a gooey, squelchy, underwater rubbish tip in the dark. Using no maps or charts, safeguarded against the possibility of disorientation by a tight line tied to colleagues above, they grid sweep till they get what they're looking for, which can take days.

Search and Rescue members are also all highly experienced in the bush, and traverse the wild reaches of the Upper Yarra valley looking for missing persons alive and dead.

Towards the end of the twentieth century, echoing Robert Hoddle's pursuit of the source of the Yarra Yarra in 1844–5, inverse urban expeditions began. To no economic purpose, merely for the thrill of adventure, a small group has for several decades mounted regular unlawful explorations of Melbourne's stormwater drains and tunnels. A Yarra underworld, designed for flow, the walkable kilometres of subterranean architecture heading downstream are round, arched, balloon-shaped, sarcophagus-shaped, egg-shaped, mushroom-shaped; stepped, rectangular, ledged, square; with cascades, waterfalls, rooms, chambers, slides, stairs, vaults; of redbrick, bluestone, cement, iron; named the Dungeon, the Great Stairway, Dwellers Tomb, Anzac…

The Cave Clan have a multitude of underground exploration routes at their fingertips and, as with any human group marking territory, everything is named and knowledge is passed on. Interesting to think of a creek named by Woiwurrung, named again in English by first settlers, then turned into an underground drain and given a code or generic name by the MMBW before finally being rediscovered and explored by the Cave Clan and renamed colloquially again. All names are true.

When it rains, the Clan don't do drains, and there is a seasonal break over winter for safety reasons. Their topside explorations have involved internal cavities of other riverside industrial architecture such as bridges and paper mills. Of course, their activities are illegal and dangerous (there was briefly—no longer—a $10,000 reward for dobbing them in).

Earlier anarchic individual exploration—by children who lived close to the river—took place through various decades of the twentieth century. By the next century, in old age, some were blaming their childhood meningitis and various illnesses on these adventures.

The biggest crime to do with the stormwater system, however, is probably the amount of filth delivered by it to the river. Every roof, every street and every footpath in multiple suburbs drains straight to the Yarra. Originally reckoned at one drain per 150 acres, the system was built big enough to take the average maximum rainfall in a ten-year period. (It was local government installation of larger drains that alleviated a lot of the flooding.)

Walking by the banks after big rain, one may hear the magnificence of a waterfall at the nearest large drain. That stuff you throw on the ground or wash away, the cigarette butts, plastic bags, old paint, drink bottles, dogshit, motor oil, six-pack collars, old chemicals, takeaway polystyrene, straws, cigarette lighters, syringes, detergent-filthy water: say hello to it again, flowing in the river. It doesn't go anywhere else, the sewerage system is completely separate.

Most of Melbourne (more than 4,000 square kilometres) is river land, and that equals river water.

~ ~ ~

'Are you going around the bend?!!'

This colloquialism querying the sanity of the subject originally referred to a trip around to Yarra Bend Lunatic Asylum. Hard cases, rumoured to arrive by boat upriver at night, were probably the ones most fully engaged in the actual physical 'round the bend' experience. Otherwise, it was in through the towering basalt front gates to a multitude of private purgatories.

As the incarceration objectives and institutions within this loop of the river changed, the gates stayed. Most recently they marked the entrance to Fairlea, Her Majesty's Female Prison. One column now stands forlorn in green surrounds next to playing fields on Yarra Bend Road, just north of and above the Eastern Freeway. 'Yarra' is also listed as antiquated slang describing the state of being mad: 'He's yarra, mate.'

Robert Hoddle determined the location of the asylum in 1844, the same year he made his Expedition to the Source of the Yarra Yarra River. It was slated for the place where the Corben Oval and Yarra Bend Public Golf Course Park now squat, where the river bends into a loop, because enclosing river bends make sites easy to secure and isolate. A few years later, in 1848, the Metropolitan Lunatic Asylum, Melbourne's first, opened there, to be renamed Yarra Bend in 1851.

Garryowen thought of that 600-odd acres as 'the romantic bend of the river at Studley Park';* and Bonwick, similarly, wrote: 'The Yarra Bend is nestled in woods, and looks like a sleeping scene of beauty rather than the dwelling-place of raving men.'

Buildings were added for the next forty years: cottages, dormitories, agricultural facilities. About twenty hectares was

---

* As it looks now, opposite Studley Park Boathouse, from Kanes Bridge.

Melbourne's first madhouse at its bucolic best: the lunatic asylum at Yarra Bend, now site of a popular park opposite Studley Park Boathouse.

farmed, and around seven hectares of the asylum itself was fenced off along the river. In the 1860s they supplied their own meat, dairy, eggs, vegetables and what The Vagabond, famous journalist of the time, described as a very fine beer, two thousand or so dozen bottles a year.

For certain people, perhaps the ones who queued to visit the unidentified severed head in the morgue downstream at Princes Bridge, a nineteenth-century Sunday drive may have included a big day out to Yarra Bend—again, for amusement: looking at mad people through the fence. A much bigger, more solid fence was soon built. Another aspect of asylum perimeter security, also used later at Willsmere, was the ha-ha, a high wall built in a deep grassed trench, so that it was hidden from view. The name is not an example of yarra-round-the-bend irony: the 'ha-ha' was a feature of eighteenth-century landscape design, from those large English estate gardens.

Yarra Bend Asylum was a debacle. The first resident medical officer, the remarkable Thomas Embling, noted in 1852, 'Donovan is the actual officer of this ward! and Donovan is both a lunatic patient and a paid attendant.'* Occasionally, the lunatics were indeed running the asylum. Some patients (the contemporary word was 'lunatics'; the late-twentieth-century term 'clients' supersedes the now-unfashionable 'patients') were registered twice, and some not at all. Embling noted of another officer, 'Highley again took his ride of about three hours—this man is hardly ever in any public lunic duty.' He observed, 'Mrs Walters going regularly to the ward at bellring that is mealtime and as usual dressed in lunatic's Clothing.' Unfortunately, Mrs Walters was no longer officially a lunatic.

A few other inmates didn't wear clothes. There were fights, brawls, someone getting king-hit, lunatics relieving themselves—or as Embling put it 'worshipping Cloaca'—all over the front paddock he had thought he would take walks in. When treatment was called for, 'I gave another pill and some sago and port wine.'

Given there were no psychotropic drugs available then to control the violently unhinged, an asylum could be quite a daunting place. Straitjackets, manacles and other restraining devices were in constant use. At the first government inquiry into the asylum, even the shower bath was described as 'an engine of torture'. The *Illustrated Melbourne Post* of 1862 thought the violent patients 'the worst of convicts, and brandy-mad diggers and others' and said that it was 'impossible at present to obtain a high class of attendants for the most repulsive of almost all occupations'.†

Despite the difficulty of obtaining good help, insanity was a growth industry. By 1870 Yarra Bend was one of the biggest

---

* Thomas Embling's diary and notes are in the manuscripts collection of the State Library of Victoria.

† It went on, 'Even in our domestic circles we are compelled to put up with such servants, and with such services as would in England be held altogether intolerable and incompatible with the ordinary requirements from those around us.'

madhouses in the world, with more than a thousand inmates. Towards the middle of the decade, another asylum opened on the other side of the river, overlooking Yarra Bend. Kew Asylum was 'originally intended for the reception of six hundred patients; but the growth of insanity in Victoria is unfortunately so rapid that the institution is usually overcrowded'. Soon there were a thousand patients amidst its ten hectares of shrubberies and flower gardens and its nearly twenty hectares of farmland. The entire reserve covered nearly two hundred hectares. There were exercise grounds and shelter sheds, carpenters', shoemakers' and blacksmiths' shops, a cricket ground, bowling green and concert room, and a library of 600 volumes. But security was stringent; the bluestone basement cells for the dangerously psychotic the most severe.

The first children's cottages were built in the 1880s. Patients on private money stayed in the front buildings with the river and city views. Until susso programs of the 1930s built the boulevards, the

The new palace of madness on the horizon (Kew, later Willsmere) which was eventually to replace Yarra Bend Lunatic Asylum, foreground left.

grounds ran right down to the Yarra and there was once a clear view straight across to Alphington.

Kew was a madhouse in both the literal and figurative senses, and there were Royal Commissions and Inquiries into conditions. The Lunatic Asylum—known from the 1950s as Willsmere Mental Hospital—was closed in 1988, in line with trends to deinstitutionalisation and rationalisation, and was renovated to become a private housing estate in 1993. The imposing towers of the asylum, visible from many parts of Melbourne, originally contained watertanks, headers for the institution's supply; now they are private apartments. The impressive entry gates had been removed some decades earlier to the site of the disappeared Connors Creek: Victoria Park, Kew, a few kilometres away.

Yarra Bend Lunatic Asylum itself had closed many years earlier, in 1925. In 1956 its bluestone and iron entrance reopened on Her Majesty's Female Prison Fairlea. It was the first women's jail in Melbourne. During the gold rush, women had been sent to prison hulks in Hobsons Bay; later they went to Pentridge (where Barak once worked), and also to Melbourne Gaol (where Ned was hanged). Fairlea operated for forty years. The women could hear the river. At the time it closed, to be demolished and replaced by a private enterprise 'correctional centre' elsewhere, most of its population could be reckoned as heroin users.

In 1904, the Queen's Memorial Infectious Diseases Hospital (not officially named Fairfield Hospital* until the 1950s) opened on nine hectares the government had carved off from Yarra Bend Lunatic Asylum's front reserve, in a creative variation on the state medical lockup theme. In the beginning it comprised one secure ward each for scarlet fever and diphtheria. By the 1920s there were 500-odd beds for measles, whooping cough, meningitis, polio and flu, besides the original dip and scarlet fever. There were beds for 700 patients by the 1930s, a total of 52 wards. Meningitis and whooping cough had

---

* The nurses' home was named Yarra House.

virtually disappeared, but typhoid was flaring.

The first iron lung was bought during the severe 1930s polio epidemic. Polio paralysed, crippled and killed. There was no vaccine then, and roughly one in twenty sufferers taken to Fairfield died of it. Boom kids of the 1960s never had to fear after free universal vaccination was introduced, though some of them later measured up for HIV/AIDS. But there was a time when it was common to see children and adults in iron calipers, or permanently dependent on crutches. Depending on the generation, they might have been TPIs* from the War or, like Alan Marshall the writer and John Perceval the painter, polio survivors. Sixty beds were available at Fairfield for long-term polio cases, some coming to live permanently in an iron lung.

In 1951, before streptomycin, two wards opened for pulmonary TB. We all got immunised for dip, and no one died of it anymore. Penicillin became available to ordinary people and did away with scarlet fever, among many other things—including the old VD hospital, Fairhaven, which had operated since 1927 in the infirmary of the recently closed Yarra Bend Asylum.† Prior to the development of those World War Two wonder drugs, sexually transmitted disease could be incurable and fatal but by 1951 the hospital was no longer needed and the building eventually became the basis of Fairlea Prison. When war hero Vivian Bullwinkel became Matron at Fairfield in 1961, she might have been forgiven for thinking the battle against infectious disease was all but over.

In the late 1960s the first injecting drug users with Hep B appeared; in the mid-1980s the first HIV patients. Fairfield led the way and became the main centre in Melbourne, caring for people whom—literally—no one else would touch. A garden was dedicated. Fine young men died, saying to their tough old dads (who'd likewise held the dying in wartime), 'Put me on the flowers.' Their fathers

* A veterans' disability classification: Totally and Permanently Incapacitated.

† The bulk of the buildings and grounds were demolished and converted to parkland, sports fields and a golf course.

might have passed through Fairfield themselves at the same age, coming back with a tropical disease after Borneo or Kokoda.

Many lives were saved at Fairfield: heroism and tragedy were commonplace. When the hospital was economically rationalised to close, finally, in 1996, its medical chief spoke publicly of anger, sorrow and pride.

In the twenty-first century the hundred-bed Thomas Embling Hospital opened on part of the old Fairfield/Fairlea site. If you're too much of a psychopath to make court or you're certified insane to get off murder, rape or child sexual assault charges, this is where you end up. More salubrious than those basalt and brick bottom cells at Willsmere, this madhouse prison (aka state forensic hospital) is for the hardcore, the most seriously dangerous cut snakes in the state (excluding a number of retired or still-alive-but-ageing gunnies. Who may, of course, be entirely sane.)

The name commemorates the old Lunatic Asylum's first medical officer whose work resulted in accusations against him of gross conscientiousness. After running the asylum, the next few things Thomas Embling did were: rally for the Eureka gold diggers in their struggle against the Crown, campaign for the Eight Hour Day, look after the poor on Collingwood Flat and become a member of the new state parliament, where he tried to get a thousand dead trees removed from the Yarra at Richmond and Collingwood because they were collecting too much absolute filth. Sadly, in the hope of encouraging industry Embling also tried to get any Yarra anti-pollution laws removed. The political choice perceived at the time was whether the banks of the Yarra should be used for providing jobs for workers or 'conserved for the residences of a few wealthy men'.*

He's sure to have been at the first Eight Hours rally at Cremorne Gardens in 1856, perhaps annually till Cremorne closed,

* The saga is detailed by Bernard Barrett in *Inner Suburbs*.

then over the river in the Botanic Gardens. If Thomas Embling inmates are ever outdoors, they might hear the river too: no hope of seeing it.

The river's isolation, and access, or lack of it, made it logical to put various secure stations along its lower reaches. A mid-nineteenth-century quarantine station held ships' passengers with cholera, measles and smallpox near Spottiswoods Ferry, near the Pumping Station site south of the Maribyrnong confluence. Ten years earlier the Border Police reserved the loop enclosed by the Yarra and Darebin Creek for their horses and only required a single fence to secure it. Hoddle took the large Survey Paddock loop at Burnley to keep the surveyors' bullock teams and other stock when they weren't in the country working.* Richmond Stockade (on the river close to Hawthorn Bridge) opened with the gold rush, and prisoners worked in the quarries nearby. After only a few years, the prisoners were transferred to the Hobsons Bay hulks and drunken police (convicted, not recreational) were the only inmates.

The hulks, another side-effect of the gold rush, were used for 'the most hardened and incorrigible' and the stockades for 'the less depraved'. Painted yellow and permanently moored, the old ships were surrounded with buoys and warnings, and shepherded by the guardship *Electra*, in the wash of the Yarra's mouth. By the close of the 1850s there were hundreds of convicts on the *Lysander*, *Sacramento*, *Success*, *Deborah* and *President*. The worst were manacled and shackled, held in dark, solitary, silent cells seven feet (just over two metres) below the waterline. Men went insane and died, buried ashore in their ball and chain.

The less depraved—such as Ned Kelly during his time on the *Sacramento* in 1873—were rowed ashore daily to work in gangs building up the bluestone waterfront at Williamstown. *Sacramento* was decommissioned in 1878 and scuttled along with the other

* Burnley College—Australia's first horticultural school—was later founded on part of the site with the help of Alfred Deakin in the 1890s.

remaining vessels (excluding *Success*) in Greenwich Bay, east of the Strand. What was left of the hulks was finally buried there under land reclamation around the turn of the twentieth century.

As with many of these institutions, the Abbotsford Convent of the Good Shepherd, which performed a function perched intriguingly between imprisonment and refuge, also contained and protected itself within a loop of the river.* On its western boundary the high, sheetmetal spiked fence pushes out and up in panels, to let through the brunt of Yarra floodwaters when they come from the east.

Irish Sisters from a French order established the convent in the 1860s, after being asked by the Catholic archbishop of the time to deal with some of the gold-rush fallout, taking in deserted women who'd become working girls after their men went off to the diggings. By the 1900s a gentleman's large riverside home had grown to a huge convent with an industrial school, commercial laundry and day school, and a farm big and fertile enough to make the nuns virtually self-sufficient. In the late 1940s the convent held a thousand (lay)women, girls and children, and 150 nuns. Inmates, known as 'penitents' were unfortunate wards of the state, 'doing penance' of hard work in the huge commercial laundry service for various Catholic bodies around town. Their sins may have been to be without parents, or perhaps unmarried. (The incarceration system of Good Shepherd laundries was infamous in Ireland.) For some, it was another clean dirty kind of hell on the river; others were helped. The convent closed in the mid-1970s and the farm became Collingwood Children's Farm late in the decade.

Only one religious order was left on the river by the twenty-first century. At Tarrawarra Abbey, a small number of Trappist monks practise the arts of silence, cattle farming and sacred reading, 'quarrying' the Bible for prayer. An Irish branch of the Cistercian Order, they established this Benedictine monastery in 1954. The

* It stands on the other side of the escarpment from Dights Falls and Yarra Bend Asylum; the northern boundary is Johnston Street and the bridge.

property has one of the largest pieces of riverfront (approximately 4.6 kilometres) remaining in the Valley. The Order's feast day is 15 August, the Assumption of Mary, also the anniversary of Barak's death in 1903.

The river, and especially its former religious institutions, has been sometime refuge for the drug-addicted and marginalised on either side of the wall. Secluded place to hit up, steal or deal though it is, these days there are probably more users inside nearby rehabs than out in the open. In the Upper Yarra there was O'Shannassy Lodge, where the young Queen Elizabeth stayed; at Lower Plenty, the monastery with its own bridge (the fathers had to get to church in town, and it was the only access in bad weather); the Salvos near Collins Bridge, Abbotsford; and the Warburton Sanitarium. By the turn of the twentieth-first century all had become rehab units with varying programs, fees and demographics.

The Sanitarium at Warburton was by the Seventh Day Adventists out of Dr Kellogg (operated by the same Sanitarium company that originally manufactured Weet-Bix there). It opened in the 1910s, bathed in mountain air, and the program was plenty of pure water (hot and cold; various baths), massage, outdoor exercise, fresh fruit, vegetables and dairy from the property. No meat, booze, smoking, tea, coffee—or swearing. The air is still fresh, and there is always a point, as you drive up the Yarra Valley, when it rushes into the car and you realise how wonderful such a substance can smell.

~ ~ ~

The greatest sources of pleasure—and sometimes of pain—are those entwined with the human heart: romance, and sex; not necessarily combined. The river can be the location of choice, by default sometimes, for the usual reasons: access and isolation.

You go to the river because it's romantic; it's convenient, you just can't wait. Or because there's nowhere else to go. Maybe you're too young, too poor, the wrong gender or with someone you shouldn't be. The river's free. And it's been that way for generations. Albert Tucker's *Images of modern evil* illustrate the mid-1940s era of the American soldier and the sexual promenade from Princes Bridge* to St Kilda (quick sex under the bridge). Working girls, and boys, have always cruised, from the docks up. Even at Cremorne Gardens it was rumoured that you could get what you wanted if you were prepared to pay.

More recently (as an unidentified rural youth from somewhere else was quoted in a national newspaper), 'The only things to do around here are drink, take speed, party round rivers, steal cars and root.' Downstream and upstream in the bush there's what archaeologists call a 'scatter' of condom wrappers and crushed alcohol cans (approximate ratio 1:20; found Kulin implements 1:5000). Once it was all freestyle and bareback and those cans were found only in the basic shades, red, green and blue.†

Young straight men living with their mum and dad, gay boys living with people who think they're not: the river seems to provide skin-mag privacy for those who want it. The straight mags discarded

---

* Counterbalanced by regular fights between Australian and American servicemen with reportedly the latter thrown into the river by the former.

† Melbourne Bitter, Victoria Bitter and Foster's from the Abbotsford Brewery downstream. Fading variations thereof provided a colour range big enough for artwork (as seen in 1979 at Mildura during the Sculpture Triennial).

after use picture by picture for public shock; the gay ones displayed within an empty car as invitation: 'the beat's here'.

Gay beats have a long history along the river. Until several decades ago, sex between men anywhere, including between two adults in their own home, was illegal. Beats—such as the city viaducts, Studley Park, Alexandra Avenue and Gardens, parks and bushland with sheltered toilet blocks next to easy anonymous street access—were and still are places to meet and have sex.

The story goes that on one occasion two men sentenced after being sprung under a South Yarra bridge were admonished by the beak for not only committing such an awful act, but doing it under one of the most beautiful pieces of architecture in Melbourne (it was probably Morell Bridge). Gay Day, in the 1980s, celebrated the first anniversaries of sexual law reform Yarraside, in Olympic Park.

Baron von Mueller loitered in his Gardens to meet a lady friend for an affair he never had. 'I waited on Wednesday and Thursday for about an hour at Yarra Bridge'; and again, 'I went on Thursday morning to the Garden Bridge on the Yarra and waited from 10 till ½ past 10. But you did not come.'

John Monash's whole life was stitched to the river. The family home he and his sisters inherited and lost was in Yarra Street. He worked on Princes, Morell and Outer Circle (Chandler) bridges (where he saw his life flash before his eyes in that near-miss accident) and for the Harbor Trust; he began a serious affair on the Hawthorn riverbank and was later busted by the husband in Studley Park, struggling all the way across Johnston Street Bridge. He finally proposed to the woman he married in another, more sedate, riverside location. He sought peace by the Yarra.

James Bonwick wrote in the 1850s of Studley Park:

> What charming little dells are scattered about it! How comfortably the Wattles shade where the straggling and nude branched Gums fail to screen from the summer's sun! How fantastically the rocks figure round about! How all the soft and genial emotions of humanity rise within one, and do homage to the spirit of rural peace and beauty! And how, too,

in suitable society, we do enjoy a ramble along its tortuous paths, or a lounge on its grassy, flowery banks, within sound of rippling waters...Many a time have we there caught sight of a pair of absent-minded ones, smiling in each other's faces, without a word to say. Hurrah for the Park Reserve!

Bridging it IV

Where the heart is

Morell is the jewel of Yarra bridges.

At the end of the 1890s, John Monash became one of the Australian agents for the new Monier method of reinforced concrete—which would become the material of the twentieth century. As an experiment Carlo Catani, then head of Public Works, decided to use reo rather than stone for the Anderson Street Bridge (renamed Morell in 1935). It was cheaper, thinner and stronger, and it could be moulded, with art applied. And here it was; beautifully.

Morell was built like a heavily engineered stage set. As part of Catani's scheme for the whole riverside area, including Batman and Alexandra avenues, the river was rerouted, which meant, he suggested, that the new Morell Bridge joining the two avenues could be constructed on dry land. And so it was that the bridge was built over an excavated channel, later widened to become the new bed of the Yarra River.

At its south and centre, the bridge sits on rock, but the north end rests on ironbark piles. On dry terrain, excavations for the piers could be done easily, and the arches constructed in stages with supports from below. Compacted earth fills the body of the bridge between the arches and supports a narrow two-laned roadway with footpaths. The form, three arches of around thirty metres each, is a match for Princes Bridge which at the time was the next downstream. But the style is light and decorative (also at Catani's suggestion) rather than dark, formal and heavy.

Even when finished Morell was still a piece of scenery, with a beautiful iron lace parapet, and bas-relief wyverns in the creamy spandrels.* The road approaches had not yet been built, and it connected nothing. Finally, the river reappeared fully underneath it, the avenues were connected, and Morell was real.

Right from the beginning it had a bit of sag, but nonetheless functioned to design for nearly a century. After some repairs and restoration in the 1940s and 1990s, it was closed in 1998 to anything heavier than an admiring fat man on a bicycle. It was the first major concrete reinforced structure completed in Victoria and nowhere near as brutal as reo could later become.

(The most marvellous reo construction of the early twentieth century in Melbourne is, of course, the great domed reading room of the State Library of Victoria, at that time—1913—the largest such concrete vault in the world.)

~

The Botanic Gardens Bridge Morell replaced was a pedestrian bridge only, but ideally sited for shifting crowds between the old Botanic Gardens railway station on the north side of the river (opened in 1859, south of the old MCG railyard pedestrian bridge site) and the gardens themselves. This rail line led to such other wonderful lost stations as that of Cremorne Pleasure Gardens and Pic-Nic,† on the river in Burnley. Of wrought iron lattice, sitting high above the water on stone piers, the bridge had been grandstand to river activities since 1860 when it replaced an earlier wooden footbridge. It had a centre span of forty-odd metres and two end spans of approximately a dozen which meant it wouldn't stretch to the larger width of the new channel cut to the south, and so it was destroyed along with the section of river it crossed. The new bridge was located to the east and south of the old one.

~

---

* A wyvern is a mythological winged creature, half dragon half serpent, with two legs and a barbed tail, described as a valiant defender of treasure. A spandrel is the space between the curve of an arch and the corner of the right angle horizontal and vertical it supports.

† Cremorne was before South Yarra on what became the Sandringham line, and Pic-Nic just before Hawthorn on what became the Belgrave line.

Walking away from Chapel Street. The Crimean War armoured bridge between South Yarra and Richmond, probably photographed around 1912. Old brickworks to the left.

The first Church Street Bridge boasted exotic origins. Bought as army surplus from the British Imperial War Office (a leftover from the Crimean campaign, where the names Inkerman and Balaclava come from), it was erected in the late 1850s to replace a ferry which had been plying there since the 1840s. Actually, it was only one span of a larger iron bridge—the other parts, frugally, were used to bridge the Barwon River and the Merri Creek. It measured about seven metres wide and sixty-odd metres long, with stone abutments. Its most curious feature was high, solid iron-walled walkways for pedestrians on either side: it was an armoured bridge.

A local historian, J. B. Cooper, writing in the early twentieth century, thought 'the footbridges acted like a magnet to morbid persons contemplating self-destruction'; also that, 'footpads lurked about the footbridge and garrotted their victims in the narrow passageway, and they added threats they would toss them into the river if they made a noise.'

The bridge had deteriorated towards the turn of the twentieth century, and eventually a temporary wooden bridge was constructed until the new bridge was built in the 1920s. Designed by renowned architect Harold Desbrowe-Annear,* it was another Monier bridge by John Monash. This one was made to carry trams as well, and matched the width of Chapel Street in the new widened-Yarra format of three spans crossing a hundred or so metres of water. Even before completion, the bridge survived a major Yarra flood, with workmen standing all night to manoeuvre a giant twenty-menacing-ton tree away from the formwork. Above each pier, on each face, ornamented concrete pylons, described as being in Edwardian Baroque style, hold a lantern of electric light.

Cooper thought the bridge would be in use in a hundred years, and mused philosophically:

> A bridge carries you a long, long way; it even suggests the mental indulgence in a dream of bridging time itself... Bridges have done more to bring people together than peace conferences; they have been more potent than even the ethical preaching of the brotherhood of man. The way of communication is the way to understanding.

Perhaps he had in mind the gulf between Prahran and Richmond councils, which had fought over funding for the bridge, or the social chasm between Tigertown and Toorak.

~

Some private bridges with restricted access still exist on the river, but there used to be many more. In Templestowe, a steel suspension footbridge was built and fenced off by the Church for access to the Blessed Sacrament Fathers Monastery in Lower Plenty. There were much earlier bridges on the site. One, recorded as decrepit by the 1920s, was washed away in the next big floods. Another, of the gold-rush era (the 1850s), washed away in the 1863 floods. In the 1930s, a

---

* Desbrowe-Annear had grown up near the Yarra and designed several treasured riverside projects including Ballangeich, the Macgeorge house at the junction of Darebin Creek, now owned by the University of Melbourne and used for artists in residence; and part of Chipperfields Boathouse.

flying fox* nearby was used to shift commercial sand across. Flying foxes or their remains may still be found along the river at various locations, such as Warrandyte, Collingwood and Yarra Grange.

The former monastery's bridge is now open and forms part of the Main Yarra Trail bike track that winds its way through parkland before crossing the river again upstream on Westerfolds Park Footbridge. This concrete arch was built in 1990 for the new-look Melbourne and Metropolitan Board of Works—not the monolithic corporation of the 1970s that pushed freeways into river valleys and had a chairman who hoped to ban bicycles, but the more enlightened body led by Ray Marginson who, by re-examining all aspects of the Board's activities, began promoting quality of life through natural and built heritage within its jurisdiction.

Of the private bridges, one built in 2003 connects two golf courses, and another nearby—at least seventy or eighty years older—provides access between farming properties. (One of the old farmhouses is an original Yarra Valley property, built of vertical rough timber slabs and bearing the name Yarra Glen before the town.) Before they got their bridge, the homestead's children would row across the river on their way to school. This bridge, being low and small, also disappeared in the 1934 floods and had to be rebuilt. Other bridges to farming property are at Doon Reserve, and O'Shannassy pipeline crossing.

~

It's impossible to know exactly how many Yarra bridges there have been. Apart from the pre-settlement crossings that will be forever undocumented, one-person bush-carpentry swing bridges have been thrown over between family properties over the years. In Warburton, Bramich Footbridge was first built in the 1960s when a millworker wanted a shorter way to the shops.†

The larger bridges of the Yarra, however, are monumental. Not

* A manual wire pulley system, fixed on either bank.

† It was rebuilt in 1993: old log facings are to be seen on its concrete piers.

simply lines from A to B, they are three-dimensional pieces of engineering, history and public suburban art that should be seen from below, from the riverside point of view, passing underneath and through as well as over. Look past any graffiti and US-style tags (just bad art by ageing kiddies who, presumably, stand there reminded by raw concrete of a city they've never visited); look past any filth and weeds. If we're going to have public art, skip certain sad artefacts with that designation and look at what we've already got: riparian cathedrals (the river as transept), an interface between the constructed and natural environment, modernist stage sets with planes, columns, arches and backdrops. These encrusted sculptures are only waiting for cleaning, maintenance and stage lighting (or perhaps settings for better artwork).

Some of the most wonderful nineteenth-, twentieth- and twenty-first-century built form in Melbourne is to be found awaiting viewing underneath the arches of Yarra bridges.

Home

In 1863, forty Kulin—men, women and children—including Barak and his cousin, Simon Wonga (Billibellary's son), walked across the Great Divide to get to their promised land: Coranderrk. Since Melbourne's settlement in the 1830s they'd been pushed from one reserve to another, most recently to Acheron Station on the Goulburn River.* A move to shift the Kulin onto the Mohican Run near Cathedral Mountain failed. Wonga, Wurundjeri headman, led them across the Blacks Spur—as it became known—to their new settlement on the Yarra at Badgers Creek which was, at the least, home ground.

Since the establishment of the first mission in the late 1830s,† however, the notion of home for the Kulin had been steadily whittled away. The original Yarra billabongs formed a constellation of Wurundjeri riverside sites as basic as the stars of the Southern Cross: the defining element of Melbourne or Kulin Woiwurung land. They were not only a rich food resource but also physically ideal for gatherings and ceremony, and were used by Kulin all the way up to Solitude (now Pendleside) in the Upper Yarra.

---

* Water falling on that side of the Divide finally ends up in the Southern Ocean near Adelaide, or it does when the Murray River is healthy enough to meet the sea.

† 362 hectares at South Yarra, on the upstream side of the Botanic Gardens site.

Kulin meeting ground then included several important pieces of country, such as the confluence of Merri Creek and the Yarra River just upstream of Dights Falls. There were big camps into the 1840s, and one source reports the last great corroboree there being held in the mid-1860s.

Another was Bolin-Bolin billabong. In the 1840s Wurundjeri were still home enough in their own land to have huge corroborees there—in December 1843, for example, nearly three hundred Kulin met for a week. Barak told of camping at Muddy Creek, the descriptive name for Koonung Creek which meets the Yarra just downstream of the Bolin-Bolin system. Plenty of fish, possum, murnong* and wild duck made it a little bit paradisial, like Yering, but it was the silver eel run that turned it into a banquet hall. It was a well-known feast. Observers described great piles of thrashing eels† by the side of the river, harvested with minimal effort and feeding hundreds of people to excess for weeks on end.

Around the 1850s, 600 or so hectares were reserved at Pound Bend, Warrandyte—again a place on the river recorded as being used by Wurundjeri for big long corroborees. This reserve lasted until the wattle tanbark strippers and then the gold miners moved through. A camp at Upper Yarra—just under 500 hectares between the Hoddles Creek and Woori Yallock Creek confluences—was gazetted in 1862 but never occupied. Land kept becoming too valuable to white settlers.

Bolin-Bolin—known as Lake Bulleen—was thickly banked with reeds and there were many river redgums on the grassy flats. The first settlers built a wattle-and-daub cottage and began draining the wetlands in 1840 to plant wheat and barley. They would sometimes find Wurundjeri canoes—cut from those river redgums and found also at Tarrawarra, Warrandyte, Kew, Fairfield, Burnley, Richmond, Coldstream and Templestowe—at the bottom of the drained 'lagoons'

---

* Yam daisy: the root the most commonly used Kulin vegetable, sometimes compared to the parsnip. Destroyed by European animals.

† Eels are born in the Coral Sea north-east of Australia, and swim all the way down to the Yarra River before turning freshwater. They return to where they were born to spawn.

and use them for stock troughs. By the 1850s the riverflats were dairy country, and by 1890 some of the farmers' descendants were in a boomtime two-storey house on the hill.

Around that time, the Heidelberg painters were walking, swimming, sketching and setting up their easels on the opposite bank, depicting those same trees. As for the eels, next century the poor, downstream on Collingwood Flat, would catch them and eat them stewed. Much later on, middle European migrants to whom they were a delicacy enjoyed them smoked—as had been the Gunditjmara (Western District) way.

Coranderrk's almost 2,000-hectare spread was part of the original Ryrie then de Castella Dalry Station. Named after the Woiwurrung Coranderrk (Christmas bush, or *Prostanthera lasianthos*) growing there, it was home, on average, to a hundred or so people housed in bark and, later, weatherboard huts. As with bush huts all over the colony, the interiors were wallpapered with pictures from the illustrated English and Australian newspapers. The land was used for grazing cattle and growing grain, vegetables and hops, all of which provided income. Traditional possum-skin rugs, baskets and other artefacts were also made, bringing in money for essential extras: horse gear, ammo, boots and hats. Hunting initially was good and the men were allowed to travel round the valley to do farm work, ride in picnic races and play footy.

It was a Christian mission—Presbyterian—and prayers were said twice daily. Barak had converted, Wonga (who had been initiated) too, though they both still practised their own culture. Rations, the great Australian colonial tradition, were doled out Mondays: 1½ lbs sugar, 3 oz. tea and 5 lbs flour, plus a little tobacco for the working man, with fresh meat on Tuesdays and Fridays. There was a daily morning muster (that is, a rollcall and headcount), new clothes and boots at Christmas, a time for everything and everything in its place.

But by the 1880s the land was getting even more valuable and the government wanted them off what was left of their country: the last of their country. There was no more. Wonga had died in 1874 and Barak was headman. There was a lot of death from measles and

TB. In 1886 the government changed its legal definition of Aborigine to include only 'full bloods', 'half-castes' over the age of thirty-four, 'half-caste' women with 'full-blood' husbands, and infants of same.* Anybody who didn't fit the definition had to leave the mission and go earn a living in the outside world. That didn't leave a lot of people to work the place, so the government did the logical thing and took about half the land back, now that it wasn't needed.

There was much struggle: the government had promised the Kulin they could always stay on the land which, after all, had been theirs in the first place. Thomas Embling was one of their supporters. But the Coranderrk population dropped, and eventually in 1917 all the state's Aboriginal stations were economically rationalised into one reservation at Lake Tyers on the east coast, where the water flows into the Tasman Sea. Groups that only a few generations before had thought of each other as the proverbial black snakes and barbarians were now all together in the same place.

The wife of the last manager at Coranderrk, Natalie Robarts (née Leuba), was the younger sister of Yarra Eugenie Leuba. Their father had worked as a horsebreaker at Dalry, Yarra Eugenie was born there and Natalie herself, prior to her marriage, worked there as a governess for David Syme, when he owned it. At the end of Coranderrk in 1923, after the clearance sale, half a dozen old Kulin were left. They were allowed to stay, still getting their rations.† A large part of the Coranderrk land later became Healesville Sanctuary.

The last child born on the Coranderrk mission grounds was Jimmy Wandin. He became headman of the Wurundjeri, and the oldest living Aboriginal league footballer—for the Saints, St Kilda.‡

---

* The act was pushed through parliament by Alfred Deakin on the same day as his remarkable new water rights legislation, which defined ownership of, among other things, the Yarra River.

† By now expanded to include oats, sago, condensed milk, golden syrup, candles, matches, split peas and rice.

‡ Jack Dyer, one of the greatest footballers and often held up as embodying the spirit of the game, started playing in bare feet at Yarra Junction nearby and ended up captain–coach of the Richmond Football Club.

~ ~ ~

High above the entire Yarra Bend loop, with large grounds running steep down to the river, was Raheen, which commenced construction in 1870 for Edward Latham of the Carlton Brewery. In 1913 it was bought to be used as the official residence of the new Archbishop of Melbourne, Daniel Mannix, whom great Catholic benefactor John Wren thought to be 'one of the greatest men living'.* If the archbishop, in his black frock and biretta, climbed the cast-iron stairs of the three-storey redbrick tower, he could look directly across into the windows of the Kew Lunatic Asylum, down below over the lunatics of the Yarra Bend Asylum and later the inmates of the venereal diseases hospital, later still the location of Fairlea Prison. No doubt some of them imagined seeing him.†

The great divide of Melbourne has been the river itself, separating basalt and sandstone, rich and poor, worker and boss, parishes, municipalities, police districts and football teams: a social divide between the high (south), and the low (north). On the upper bank: gracious gardens, views and solid brick houses. On the lower: Struggletowns—poorly drained river flats of overcrowded workers' cottages and factories, prone to 'miasmas' of bad, damp air and flooding. The mansions of Kew, Hawthorn and Toorak overlooked the cramped, dirty suburbs of Richmond, Burnley, Collingwood and Abbotsford laid out flat before them. The bosses could literally oversee their factories, and their workers. On the Kew side lived

---

* John Wren also supported the Caritas Christi hospice next door. When derros from the river below got a bit too close and annoying he had a wall built around it.

† Raheen was separated from the river by the susso work-for-the-dole Boulevard in the 1930s, and various acreages and subdivisions have been sold off since. The Church sold the house in 1981 and it became the Pratt family home. (Visyboard is one of the family's companies.) Richard Pratt, one of the richest men in Australia, has put much time and money into investigating the problems of rivers and irrigation in the nation.

brewery chiefs Auguste de Bavay, Emil Resch and Carl Pinschof, the paper mill's inheritor George Ramsden and shipping line owner Malcolm McEachern. Manning Clark in his *History of Australia* referred collectively to the powerful conservative governing forces of early twentieth-century Australia—moral, political and economic—as Yarraside.*

The landholding spread worked longitudinally as well as latitudinally. Various business barons with urban riverside mansions were also Collins Street farmers—Collins Street being the high-end city business address that was their familiar locale—with large river frontage farming properties in the Yarra Valley. (The Collins Street farmer is a phenomenon that continues in the valley. They may be the only ones who can afford the property.)

Even in 1960 Robin Boyd could observe by the riverbank, 'On the right...prosperity and comfort, on the left...depression, dirt and decay.' Or as Bonwick compared them in the 1850s, 'the dull, swampy, treeless flat' of Richmond, and Hawthorn's 'charming and wooded heights'. In 1866 Hawthorn was described as 'the favourite abode of many political and social celebrities'. An early local history of Kew describes it as having 'the distinction of being Melbourne's prettiest and healthiest suburb...doubtless due to its elevated situation...almost equal to the top of the flag pole on Government House tower'. It added, 'Kew receives no drainage from any other district, but passes on to its neighbour Hawthorn all storm water which does not flow directly into the Yarra.'

Any way you rated it, there were huge differences. The *Football Record* of 1967 commented in an article on recruitment zones,

> The independent commissioners will...consider the 'football mindedness' of the residents of those districts. By 'football

---

* Edzell, a grand house still to be seen high above the river in Toorak overlooking Burnley and the Boulevard, was built by a former Lord Mayor of Melbourne in 1891 reputedly with gun emplacements and cannon to deal with the threat of Russian invasion. No doubt the enemy would approach the centre of power by attacking upriver to the heart of Yarraside. As a later owner commented, the Russians ended up coming through the front door in the 1930s when Edzell was occupied by a successful immigrant family of Eastern European origins.

> mindedness' we mention for comparison the areas of, say, Collingwood and Toorak. One would expect to find the people of Collingwood, as a whole, more interested in football than those of Toorak.

As sports journalists noted when recollecting 1970—Hawthorn was a universe rather than just a riverbend away from Collingwood.

But that all changed dramatically in the decades that followed. Gentrification (the fashion for the inner city and the implied banality of the 'suburbs'), changes in lifestyle, environmentalism and greater public leadership led to a rejuvenation of the whole lower river and its parklands. Geoffrey Blainey could write in the early 1980s, 'I doubt whether more than a hundred people now living in Melbourne have walked along the banks of the river for more than ten miles in one day. It is strangely neglected and unknown, nor is it seen as vital to the city.' Alterations began with the riverside cycling and walking path, the first section opening in 1975 between Princes and Morell bridges. Since then a revolution has occurred, as cycling and walking traffic now attest every holiday weekend on the forty-kilometre Main Yarra Trail.

The price of an apartment in a former Abbotsford or Collingwood factory or warehouse might now easily match a bijou Kew or Hawthorn home. By the early 2000s President Eddie McGuire of the Collingwood Football Club (resident in Toorak, raised way northside in Broadmeadows) could state,

> Collingwood's not a suburb any more, it's a concept. When the club was born, Collingwood was the worst suburb in Melbourne, it was the place where the poor and the miserable lived. The football club became those people's badge of honour.

He was explaining how the club was to leave its home ground, Victoria Park, and move to better facilities at Olympic Park, to those Yarra riverflats near where football was invented.*

* It is a location not unknown to Collingwood supporters. John Wren, longstanding patron of the club, owned the Motordrome race venue there in the 1920s and '30s.

~

All over the western world in the late twentieth century disused waterways and ports such as London's Docklands were being overhauled and redeveloped as linear parks with public and private buildings alongside. Melbourne was no different but had perhaps a greater impetus, drawn from its refusal to identify as a provincial city within the 'Sydney or the Bush' power strata of Australian business and culture.* Several previously iconic city buildings had become demolition 'bomb sites'—the Southern Cross Hotel, the CUB Carlton Brewery at the top of Swanston Street and the Queen Victoria Hospital—lying idle for years while city retail activity was draining to the big suburban malls. The port area around North and South wharves and Victoria Dock was equally moribund.

In the early 1980s successful architects and developers such as Evan Walker and David Yencken† were either in or working for the state government. Yencken had started Merchant Builders, an influential firm constructing architect-designed homes, and was later head of the Australian Heritage Commission, the first government body to impose heritage controls on development. It was evident that the city was in urgent need of revitalisation but also that this created great possibilities. The Victorian Arts Centre was being constructed on the river's south bank bordering Princes Bridge. Design principles inherently found in some of the world's most desirable cities were going to be adopted for the urban river zone that became Southbank: building to the edge, no forecourts, six storeys maximum height on the riverfront and vibrant public use of ground-floor areas. Government did change things. But rough bluestone angled beaching of the banks became elegant hard-edged basalt embankments, riverside walkways with architectural lighting went in. Roads

---

* As 1980s treasurer and '90s prime minister Paul Keating explained in the 1990s, if you're not living in Sydney you're just camping out.

† Yencken described the Yarra then comparatively as an urban river with 'an intimate quality. You can develop a dialogue between both banks'. Walker, whose first job had been at the Princes Bridge APM paper mill, laid the precinct out like a 'four-poster bed': the posts were Flinders Street Station, the Arts Centre, the World Trade Centre and the Jeff's Shed site.

and land were repackaged and redesigned for urban redevelopment. By the mid-1990s Riverside Quay and Southgate were constructed, providing a mall of shops, offices and restaurants. The largest changes were the Melbourne Exhibition Centre and Crown Casino.

Riverside Southbank became the most popular part of Melbourne. An idea of cafe society had returned to the river after nearly a century—only now you didn't have to get a boat to one of the bucolic teahouses upstream but could stay in the city itself. The malls had come to town (minus free no-strings parking). It was delightful sitting outside drinking coffee and viewing the city skyline across the river; but after all this was a decade in which every conceivable enterprise in the entire metropolitan and rural area opened latte-set facilities.*

In the new millennium it was possible for the front cover of a junk mail catalogue to display a bedroom setting named 'Yarra' and describe it as a 'style statement'. All along the river's inner urban downstream length, industrial sites were being redeveloped for multi-storey apartments alongside cafes and shops, with views to the water now prized. Melbourne's city living population figures exploded, although a large segment was the new class category of overseas fee-paying students.

On Southbank in 2001 one of the world's tallest residential buildings began its ninety-odd-level construction. A smaller sixty-level tower in the same vicinity had a lawn planted on its tenth level. The developer was quoted as saying of the attempt to lure people from the suburbs,

> The recollection of the smell of freshly cut grass is important…It's that type of village feeling or emotion we're trying to develop on the banks of the Yarra…It's a recognition that the traditional home-owning values remain important in an apartment context.

~

* Immediate personal experience attests to an inner urban butcher's shop with cafe and a rural fringe chemist shop with cafe—both later closing the unsuccessful cafe areas to 'stick to their knitting'.

At the Royal Melbourne Institute of Technology's Landscape Architecture Unit in the late 1980s David McCubbin, great-grandson of Heidelberg School painter Frederick McCubbin, was leading a workshop on what later became Melbourne's Docklands area. Among other things, they looked at how historical anachronisms are part of the continuum of a city's vitality, and investigated the possibility of designing landscape using found objects—in which the degraded industrial wetland of Dudley Flats was particularly rich. McCubbin noted,

> The eerie sensation of being able to literally walk over the accumulated debris of the last 150 years within a landscape superficially unchanged in context (rather like Stonehenge, Hanging Rock, or Coles Bourke Street Cafeteria) is a privilege few Melbournians appreciate*...You emerge mud bespattered and weary with a photo-chemical euphoria that's deeply intuned to the nature of the landscape and ultimately a range of experiences more profound than a lifetime of Moombas.

Like his great-grandfather of the Heidelberg School before him, he identified a landscape and sense of place people hadn't readily acknowledged.

David McCubbin went on to quote Hal Porter's memoirs (dedicated to Sunday Reed of Heide), with a description of William Dargie's studio in Williamstown. It had, he said,

> a deep bay-window through the hand-made glass panes of which the silt jetties at the mouth of the Yarra are to be seen, and dredges and buoys and pilot-ships, and P. and O. liners, and yachts from the Royal Yacht Club, and seagulls and cormorants, the wastes of Fishermans Bend shimmering with noon-flowers in summer...At night the twinkling fires of a raffish encampment can be seen inland from Fishermans Bend—Dudley Flats, a squalid Alsatia of shelters made from

* Alas for those who loved it, Coles Bourke Street cafeteria and store are also long gone.

> packing-cases, fish-crates, oil-drums and corrugated iron in which the more gypsified and degenerate victims of the Depression and their own weaknesses re-enact Gin Lane, swigging methylated spirits from triangular bottles, gnawing Cornish pasties and shark-and-chips, and consuming goatish amours in nests of newspapers and sugar-bags. I often see these fuming stars of fires…

'Obviously,' McCubbin noted, 'Dudley Flats caters to a minority of the population.' He believed, however, that, 'An industrial landscape situated so close to the city, along our great waterway (the Yarra) must have special significance' and that perhaps they could 'develop a new vocabulary of design elements, [details] that really do reflect the surrounding landscape.'

The reality of Docklands didn't pan out that way. Like other such developments in Melbourne, it is possible to stand in a location one may have lived or worked in decades earlier and not recognise it. The entire sense of place has been vacuumed out and sealed up. (Literally, in some cases where they were forced to concrete over contaminated soil.) Rather than a true city's multiple layers of form and time being evident in its integrated buildings and landscapes, a homogenised facade is presented as a new brand, generic.* You could be anywhere in the world.

The freight of history that has come down the river and been played out along its banks is mostly only there in graphic inserts. The flotsam and jetsam, the dunnage, the accretions of the human story are largely gone. An emptiness remains, not just of derelict port buildings. Or at least, so it seems at the time of writing. No doubt all this will change upon completion of the huge project in 2015 when the expected 20,000 residents, 25,000 workers and 20 million visitors arrive (as per the site billboard).

~

* 'Disneyfication', as it's referred to in Kim Dovey's comprehensive analysis of Melbourne's waterfront redevelopment, *Fluid City*.

The vision of a waterfront connected to the city was no surprise to anyone living or working in Williamstown, Port or Yarraville. But at least initially the huge waterfront redevelopments created new barriers even as they opened the city up to the river. Through traffic, whether freight, rail, road, passenger or pedestrian was problematic, as was the cascade of changing deals and projects that didn't get up. Urban designers muttered about political leaders going for short-term payoffs (i.e. effective until about the next election) in impressive project announcements; apartment resale figures were said to be rubbery. At the start of the millennium the last remnant of natively vegetated riverside in the lower reaches area was offered up for removal to a more architecturally useful location.

Still, Docklands does link the city and the water. The traditional retail centre is a long kilometre away but Southern Cross Station (the inspired redevelopment of Spencer Street Station) with its truly spectacular architecture, may yet become the iconic lynchpin between the two.*

Future plans for the Yarra place it as central to the city of Melbourne. We live, work and play alongside it. The river is no longer the divide it once was.

* In an interview with architect Keith Brewis, the *Age*'s Joe Rollo described how the roof consists of natural shapes dictated by physics to allow for optimum venting of train fumes and steam, as sculpted by the prevailing winds: great design and architecture out of brilliant engineering and computer modelling by Kevin Winward.

~ ~ ~

Despite objections in the 1860s to the Yarra's banks being used merely for gentlemen's residences rather than job-creating industry (and no matter, apparently, that it was heavy-polluting industry), marvellous nineteenth-century homes were originally situated along the river's length from South Yarra to the upper reaches. All with river frontage and large grounds then; some with their own 'lagoons' or billabongs. When you find them today they are marooned in suburbia more often than not, some distance from the river.

Como, the flagship house museum of the National Trust in Victoria, had a kilometre of river and a large billabong which is now just another green sward.* Tivoli, Mount Verdant, the Waterloo Cottage† and Rockley‡ were other charming South Yarra riverfront properties and so was Toorak House, the first official Government House, residence of the Governor of Victoria.

Viewbank, the house of Robert Martin, great-grandfather of Merric, Martin and Penleigh Boyd, great-great-grandfather of Arthur and Robin Boyd, sat on nearly eighty hectares of riverfront upstream from Heidelberg, again above its own 'lagoon' or billabong. It had been a small cottage, but by the boom gold-rush years of the 1850s the house and gardens with ballroom and riverside orangerie were palatial. The house was demolished in the early twentieth century after becoming empty and 'haunted' and by the next century was an archaeological dig.

Adjoining was Banyule, once part of the same property, built in the 1840s. Robert Martin gave this mansion to his son as a wedding

---

* In the 1890s Como's wealthy owners became patrons of Arthur and Minnie Boyd, hanging their paintings in the ballroom for a three-day invitation-only exhibition that made the social pages. In 1910, Arthur and son Penleigh Boyd did a commissioned series of watercolours of Como including the view to the Yarra.

† The property is now the Melbourne Boys High School site.

‡ Its river frontage becoming part of Alexandra Avenue.

gift in 1874. With nearly 250 hectares of land at one stage, it sat on commanding heights overlooking a huge system of billabongs and wetlands, and is still incredibly impressive today, seen from across the water with the surrounding suburbs hidden from view.

In Hawthorn and Kew lie Swinton, The Hawthorns, Invergowrie and the now-vanished Blythswood and Rockingham, the latter both David Syme town properties (on the escarpment above Victoria Street Bridge). Syme owned the *Age* newspaper and supported Alfred Deakin as 'the most brilliant Victorian politician'. Syme owned three other country riverfront properties in the Yarra Valley at one point: Dalry, Killara (each bought from David Mitchell*) and Tarrawarra, which he gave that name in 1893—the earlier Ryries and de Castellas ran it as View Hill. By 1861 View Hill had briefly had its third owner: William Nicholson, one-time premier of Victoria, whose 1856 government was the first in the world to legislate for secret electoral ballots, now thought of as a cornerstone of democracy. In the 1870s they ran horses specially bred for military and police work, such as looking for Ned Kelly. The property stretched from Yarra Glen racecourse to Healesville racecourse and up to a thousand horses would run there after being droved down from up north, last open pasture before shipping off to the British Army. The King of England owned such a horse during World War One.

The Symes sold Dalry in 1916: it was later renamed Eyton on Yarra (not to be confused with the modern-day winery of the same name). Killara was completely self-sufficient with its own butchery, dairy, bakery, timber and fruit and vegetable gardens, which also supplied the city residences. Apples grown in its three hectares of orchard got the highest prices in London's Covent Garden market. It had a solid post-and-rail fence and its own railway station, a location still found on the Lilydale to Warburton Rail Trail.

* David Mitchell, Dame Nellie Melba's father, owned Dalry, Yering, Killara, Henley Farm and St Hubert's at various times.

David Syme carried out an early-twentieth-century version of firestick farming by carrying a 'box of Vestas' while striding over his property, dropping them alight in heaps of tussock grass and other unwanted inflammable piles of vegetation. Killara was ultimately subdivided and the homestead demolished.

Pendleside in Woori Yallock, a remnant Syme family property adjoining, sits on the original Solitude run—Stewarts Station—where Hoddle began his expedition to the source of the Yarra in 1845. The homestead with its Edna Walling garden was sited on the same rise as the first hut.

A link between succeeding styles and periods of riverside living can probably be found in the notion of a 'Boyd house'. The family's Yarra Glen homestead, Tralee, was in the 1910s, though comparatively small, emblematic in lifestyle of the marvellous nineteenth-century spreads (for those who were owners, not servants). The house appeared in Martin's novel *The Montforts* as Crosspatrick. He describes its location as 'only forty feet from the steep bank to the river', where 'clear water rippled over clean stones' and 'in June the bank of the river for miles and miles, as far as one could see, was a golden line of wattle blossom, threading its way through the middle of the valley'.

An idyllic childhood and youth was had there by the young Boyds, who remembered 'a place of perpetual sunlight—sunlight on the distant hills, sunlight filtering through the vines and nectarine trees that enclosed the verandah, and through the wattle branches on the river bank'.

The dining room was painted with a four-wall frieze illustrating the seasons and biblical text. In his autobiographical writings Martin Boyd famously recalled:

> We had our own ponies, and a mile and a half of river frontage with a private bathing-place. There was hunting and rough shooting and fishing if we wanted it. The fruit and cream were unlimited, and after dinner we could go into the orchard and stuff ourselves with peaches from the standard

> trees...I think that I was happier at Yarra Glen than I have been at any other time in my life. The country was beautiful in itself, and my imagination clothed it with poetic significance.

This was despite, or parallel to, the fact that at the time it seemed that 'England and Heaven were the two ultimate destinations of reasonable man.' At his death, decades later on the other side of the world, Martin Boyd had a photograph of Yarra Glen beside his bed.

By 1913, when the family had returned to Melbourne, temporarily leasing the farm and keeping the house for holidays, Penleigh, brother of Martin, was married and living in Warrandyte. He bought almost seven hectares near the river there, designing and building The Robins, an Arts and Crafts-style rammed earth, reo concrete home. The painting studio he also constructed was built from local materials. The Boyd family home at Yarra Glen was up the river from McPhersons Yarra Glen station and down the river from Gulf Station and Tarrawarra, each of which still have some of the oldest surviving bush carpentry and wooden slab building* in the country. After Penleigh Boyd's death in the 1920s the house was sold, but the studio was kept for some time and occasionally used for exhibitions (it was later destroyed by fire).

Stylistic inheritors of Penleigh Boyd's The Robins were the many artists who subsequently settled in Warrandyte, Eltham and upstream near the river, either building their own houses with material taken from the surrounds—earth for mudbricks or pise, local stone, timber—or experimenting with materials or design.

Artist Clara Southern's Warrandyte house overlooked the Yarra and used river stones for paving.† The most extraordinary was probably sculptural Stonygrad by Danila Vassilieff, expressionist artist and teacher at Koornong experimental school. Visitors

---

* Circa 1839.

† Yarra sand was also notoriously used for mortar in some South Yarra art deco apartment buildings of the 1930s on riverbank sites: the problems caused are still trickling out.

included Albert Tucker and Sid Nolan. Koornong was an award-winning modernist riverside design of the 1930s now existing as a group of houses in North Warrandyte. It had some remarkably eloquent students, one of whom proclaimed when the school was threatened with closure, 'We shall miss what all Australian schools should have: access to the Australian bush.'

The Eltham owner–builder rustic style of Whelan the Wrecker recycled, neo-European medieval mudbricks prevailed in quite a few riverside areas. The 1964 Bateman House had roof slates from Sir John Monash's home in Toorak. Eltham design went downstream with Alistair Knox and Ellis Stones, mudbrick builder and native landscaper respectively, when working on the former Macauleys Boathouse in riverfront Kew in the 1960s. Knox also did the Downing–Le Gallienne house on the river in Eltham, with occasional labouring by painter Clifton Pugh.

The culmination of this lifestyle is perhaps to be found in Australia's first official Environmental Living Zone, engendered by the activism of Neil Douglas and others in the 1960s and proclaimed in 1982. Previously threatened by a Board of Works dam, this 400 hectares round the northern bank of the Bend of Isles is bounded roughly by the Yarra River, Watsons Creek and the Maroondah Aqueduct. No new domestic animals nor fences are allowed on the residential bushland blocks (average size four to five hectares) and native flora and fauna are protected and promoted. Many of the houses are of mudbrick, and owner-built. Alan Marshall bought a riverfront block in support; Neil Douglas sold his Sid Nolan paintings to buy his block (a poetic comeback as it was he who claimed to have introduced Nolan to the bush as subject matter for painting). The Douglas house and surrounding landscapes appear through the family's books, paintings and other artworks.

Robin Boyd, born in 1919, was Penleigh Boyd's son, and his exciting work as a mid-century modernist architect may be experienced with joy in various houses along, or near, the river. The various levels and steep hillside of The Robins echo in many.

In his Boyer Lectures of 1967 Boyd spoke of a time, in the 1870s and '80s, 'when Australia responded to the idea…of being original'. He called it 'Australia's first age of ideas', citing the Heidelberg School and Melbourne's first skyscrapers—two seemingly disparate cultural moments but linked, as we've seen, by the Yarra River. The river, though unmentioned, runs through his thought as it ran through his early boyhood.

His 1955 Haughton James House, with steep river frontage at Kew overlooking Yarra Bend, was designed with a two-level floorplan in the shape of an eye, the iris the central staircase. Haughton James was in advertising and the house is remembered for fantastic parties. This was a Grounds Romberg & Boyd house—Roy Grounds went on to design the National Gallery of Victoria and the Arts Centre; Frederick Romberg lived near the river in the Heidelberg School area. It was a simple one-bedroom plus study, and fabulous.

The Clemson House nearby was built above a creek bed, landscaped by Ellis Stones, and beneath a butterfly roof with a translucent section, the first in Australia. The Handfield House in Eltham, a Boyd & Grounds design of the early 1960s, has a colour scheme based on surrounding manna* gums. From the top of the ridge you can see the city and Corhanwarrabul. Its base kitchen window frames the Yarra at your feet. On hot afternoons when a cooling breeze comes up the river, the house is designed to trap it and cross-ventilate. In the living room, there is a perfectly proportioned arrangement of sliding screens and full-length windows open to the river valley.

---

* Mannas were named for the manna that fell from their heavens, not just their leaves for koalas. George McCrae recalled of the manna forest that became Fitzroy and Treasury Gardens, 'we would often gather and devour the manna fallen from the milk-white boughs whose satiny bark exuded this eucalyptus sugar in all directions. It would drop in pieces large and small according to circumstances, and the grass beneath the trees during a good day (for the supply varied with the temperature and probably with the circulation of the sap) appeared as though someone had shaken a whitewash brush over it, or rather—if plaster of paris in knobby and "scrambled" fragments had fallen from above…when I found it perfectly new and just beginning to thicken (after exudation) the consistence was that of honey, and the tint either that of honey or of the paler kinds of olive oil. In this condition, which never lasted long, it was perfectly delicious.'

Robin Boyd designed various projects along the Yarra. Snowden Gardens, a pocket of 1900s municipal green, was the site of his wind fountain. Three successively larger flat circular pools stepped down from a plaza adjoining them south-west of Princes Bridge. The flow and height of the fountain's water were determined by windspeed: the stronger the wind the lower the water force. The fountain and gardens disappeared when the Arts Centre redevelopment began.

Peter McIntyre has been another architect whose career has been interwoven with the Yarra. His famous River House was designed and built in the early 1950s as the family home, a long horizontally-based triangle of two-level house hanging between a tall narrow A of steel frame at a sharp bend in the river at Kew. He was also one of the designers of the innovative 1956 Olympic Pool alongside the Swan Street Bridge, and was recalled fifty years later to convert it for Collingwood Football Club facilities.

Like Peter and Dionne McIntyre, in the late 1940s and '50s innovative architects all over Melbourne sat down with Board of Works maps searching for possible home sites near the river flood plain. Douglas Alexandra designed his 1960 Ivanhoe family home (near that of Frederick Romberg, Boyd's partner) to take modular floorplans without fixed internal walls. Theo Hammond, designer of Melbourne's first high-rise apartments for the rich and powerful, also built his 1960s family home in riverside Alphington with industrial construction elements and an entry facade similar to the quite extraordinary 1967–69 Boyd Featherstone house on Darebin Creek frontage, not far away. Clients who had more money and a little less daring simply built above it: the pocket of Kew from the Boulevard that was once paddocks looking up to Raheen and down to the river is studded with modernist architectural gems.

The most marvellous houses in Melbourne are to be found alongside river and creek land.

~ ~ ~

'Waltzing Matilda'—walking or wandering with a swag or blanket; 'on the road'—was something real once, and has a modern equivalent seen less through the eye of romance, and perhaps experienced by someone homeless camped by the river next to the Monash Freeway.

1850s gold-rush losers—the immigrant arrivals, those broke and back from the diggings, the dumped of the wrong sex or age—ended up at Canvas Town, which sat sprawled to the west of St Kilda Road, down from the later 1860s Victoria Barracks towards Princes Bridge. At the time, there was nothing much between it and the Yarra River. You could see straight through to the marvellous city of Melbourne on the other side. With hundreds of ships arriving in the Bay at once and their crews deserting in droves, there might be nowhere else to stay but in one of the tents lining its 'streets'. Named after famous London thoroughfares, they offered all manner of goods and services, from the wholesome if exorbitant to the severely dubious, before the whole place was closed down in 1853.

At its peak Canvas Town was home to 8,000 people. Antoine Fauchery called it, 'A floating city devoured by the sun, inundated by the rain and swept away by the wind when the latter is in one of its bad moods.' Andrew Garran later described it as where

> Men, women and children—those who had been gently born and nurtured, and those who had been familiar with a rough life in old countries; professional men, artisans, husbandmen from rural England, fugitives from justice in California, political refugees from France and Germany, escaped convicts from the other side of the Straits, and people who had quit the mother country with visions of becoming suddenly rich on the Victorian goldfields—were forced into a strange companionship, and were depressed to the same social level by the force of untoward circumstances.

Quite Australian.

The 'suburb' of Dudley Flats was located on reclaimed wetland in what is now part of Docklands precinct (on Moonee Ponds Creek at the end of Dudley Street). In the classic wetland or waterway rubbish-dump progression, it began as a nineteenth-century tip on the edge of West Melbourne Swamp. By the 1930s Depression, people not-working the river squatted there in shacks lashed together out of discarded packing materials (when packaging usually meant tin, wood or hessian sacks). They were left alone, on this land no one seemed to want or claim, to pick through junk and refuse which they would try to use or sell on. They had water views, but from a lot lower than the later Docklands apartments. Upstream, shanties reappeared all over old abandoned goldfield tributaries.

Sleeping under bridges and their approaches has evolved slightly from the nineteenth and twentieth centuries.* Instead of padding your clothing with straw or newspapers you've got a cheap used sleepingbag on a bit of cardboard, maybe with a poly tarp. No more tea chests and kero tins (they can be found fashionably distressed in inner-city interior style stores) but maybe an old vinyl lounge suite with the arse gone, a smashed-up coffee table, stretch of nylon wall-to-wall and, back-breakingly, an old unplugged fridge. Shelter courtesy of a Citylink bridge.

Or go to a bed of soft river dirt just off the asphalt of the walking track, under the old polychrome rail bridge, and sleep your way through the dawn chorus. Bellbirds, magpies, kookaburras don't bother you, nor the strong morning sunshine.

Only joggers and walkers come by in their Nikes and Reeboks, nigglingly wondering if you're dead and whether they should do something.

---

* Riverside parks were, and are, also used.

~ ~ ~

To see the best Fred Williams, Arthur Streeton, or Tom Roberts pictures in Melbourne, walk along the Yarra. You can scramble through them, live. The most beautiful landscapes in Melbourne today are in linear form along the river. Seen from the water or by foot on the riverbank, these microlandscapes—trees and rocks of the hidden Yarra—are some of our greatest secret treasures. Anthony Trollope, visiting nineteenth-century English novelist, observed, 'You might live in Melbourne all your life and hardly know that the Yarra Yarra was running by your door.' Even within ten metres of it you sometimes just can't see it.

James Bonwick wrote in the 1850s, 'Mile after mile of almost interminable beauty lead one round by the winding Yarra.' That was when bandicoots and quolls were still common in Studley Park. He describes how a rock formation there, 'exposed by the wear of the softer mineral, assumes the aspect of iron lace-work, with varieties enough for ladies' crochet patterns...the decomposition of the softer constituents has left some singular parallel ridges, like the cicatrices upon a Black's chest'. Barak's father and uncle, those Wurundjeri headmen, were buried north-west of that location.

The river zone—that land including the river's banks as well as land immediately affected and maybe protected by the river—is an environment that can be quite different from its surrounds, the country it sits in. The river zone has a greater variety of plants and animals because of the water; soil is richer. Like a linear micro-climate, it has lesser extremes of humidity and temperature. It operates as a safety zone and wildlife corridor, extending out from the river maybe tens of metres, maybe a kilometre if billabongs and wetlands are involved. A network of creeks may run right back from the river to national and state parks in the hills and mountains creating sanctuary 'highways' for native birds and animals to move around their own country.

Everything interrelates. Messing with any aspect of the natural river has a much bigger chain of effects than is immediately obvious. Maintaining seventy percent of the original tree cover along a riverbank stops destructive algaes and weeds from taking off: the shadows control heat and light, and the root systems hold the bank together, slowing erosion and minimising the amount of mud in the water. Food and shelter come down from the trees for those things living in or near the water. The trees and their LWD are homes, insects are food, for platypus, fish, turtles, frogs, lizards, birds.*

River redgums are big indicators of river health. Monarchs and kingdoms when alive, they may be found all along river flats. The sculptural dead ones, skeleton of flesh, still stand, or lie as fallen horizontal carcasses. Those in Westerfolds Park were five hundred years old when they were felled a century ago.† Many survived in Hoddle's old Survey Paddock site in Richmond. In 1965 the local council chopped down seventy-odd specimens it had killed there by turning the area into a tip (it was probably an old billabong location).

Breaking the flow by damming or pumping out water can stop the life cycle or physical movement of creatures along the river.‡ Cold water coming from the bottom of a dam as flow can also stop the trigger point of fish breeding. Many native fish need flood, for migration and reproduction, as well as all the habitats and conditions provided as part of a natural billabong cycle. Chemicals in the water from run-off or dumping may kill—insects, fish, their eggs—and then move up the food chain. Removing or changing one element in the river's schema affects everything else. Apart from the beauty, the health of the river zone is the river's health.

---

* The primeval platypus eats a minimum of a quarter of its own body weight every day in worms, yabbies and insects.

† Think of them as the buttresses of the only fourteenth-century cathedrals we have. The whorls and flows shrunk into their skin mirror the river's below: even in dead, cut trees, these patterns persist. They can still be seen in sticks of South Wharf near Jeff's Shed, bang up against a dying-in-drought European lawn and trees.

‡ Fish ladders at Dights Falls meant some native fish could get home upstream for the first time in more than a century.

The river zone is a squeezed and beaten sanctuary in places. Highly profitable retail plant nurseries on the Yarra that pride themselves on their box hedges and iceberg roses and the general gorgeousness of their facade, may tip and fill to within an inch of their lives down their backyard banks. Farmers and social clubs might squeeze in every extra possible square metre of foreign grass by pushing everything else over the edge. In some agricultural areas banks are collapsing from the last heavy-vehicle run of dead vegetation over the side, the soft riverflat soil washing into the water for a heavier, muddier sediment load. Blackberries haul up then, and only what can gain purchase almost vertically grows. In other places it's the natural steepness of the banks, and their inaccessibility, that have saved what metres there are of remnant bushland and original vegetation.

It wasn't until 1881 that the State Government of Victoria declared ownership of all river frontages. This, though radical, was a bit late. Most of the land along the Yarra River had already been 'alienated'—subdivided or cut up and sold off —with the boundary either along the river's banks, or in the middle of the river itself. Well over a hundred houses in Melbourne own actual river frontage right to the centre of the water because they are on old titles. In Australia, the states control the watercourses. Alfred Deakin, while he was the Victorian Minister for Public Works and Water Supply, introduced the law giving the state ownership of natural water in 1886. And it was 'the state' because there was no federal government until the same very astute Alfred Deakin helped form one a decade and a half later.

Yarra River frontage reserves were set at one and a half chains (about thirty metres) and its creeks or tributaries at one chain (about twenty metres). Long sections of rural riverfront belong to adjoining farms, even though they are Crown land reserve, because they've been leased to landowners.* In Warrandyte Crown reserves were

---

* Good old Tommy Bent brought in the legislation for this as a revenue-raiser in 1903.

incorporated into the State Park. Legally, ownership is a patchwork mess the length of the river. Most of the riverbanks are not publicly accessible;* privately owned pathways, used by the public for decades, become contentious issues when landowners decide to resume them. Agricultural landholders may also own to the centre of the river: a valuable and jealously guarded asset.

The golf courses, when they emerged as the new land-use phenomenon of the twentieth century, got kilometres of former farmland river frontage, because who else would want something so floodable? (And it was so much more scenic and rate revenuable for the councils.) At the time of a 1983 study, eleven kilometres of metropolitan Yarra River frontage were the province solely of golf courses. Fairways were seen to run to the top of the riverbanks, obliterating natural vegetation, and in the process destabilising banks. The study recommended there be no more golf courses, and that a passive bushland buffer of twenty to thirty metres be reserved along the riverbank. In the decades since, predictably, several more riverfront courses have gone in.

Some golf clubs are more notorious than others. There's the club that shoots native ducks because they leave droppings on the greens and cuts down native trees because they harbour the ducks. Not only would they prefer to forget about the river, they want everyone else to forget about it too, hiding it behind tasteful shrubs, cutting and filling as far as possible without falling in themselves, and marking the edges DANGER RIVER and TRESPASSERS PROSECUTED. Some golf clubs generously give over that last few metres they don't use to the linear river landscape, the riparian zone, putting in high Cyclone fencing to protect golfers and river wanderers from one another.

But attitudes shift, and so do demographics. Older public courses have computerised their watering and replanted with drought-tolerant grass and natives (because golf courses pump huge

* Bring back the billabongs. Give us back our river.

amounts of water out of the river for their cosseted greenery). The most recent development, in Wonga Park/Kangaroo Ground, felt compelled to advise publicly that it would be regenerating fourteen hectares of wetlands and planting 35,000 trees. They're rehabilitating old cut-and-filled farmland, providing gated public and wombat access to a fenced-off river zone, the path a platypus-safe distance from the water.

Concerns remain, however, that golf course developments such as these, with their extensive housing/resort components, are housing development by stealth within twenty-first-century legislated green-wedge zones.

Several decades ago community groups dedicated to caring for the river zone began to emerge. Helped by Melbourne Water and some of the large landholders, they have put in kilometres of planting and fencing. But there do appear to have been occasional cases of the baby going out with the bathwater in ridding the river's middle and lower reaches of exotic or foreign trees.

Historic plantings can be cultural heritage, sometimes more important than 'natural' environment: sixty-year-old poplars near remnant orchards, century-old fruit trees near former historic home sites, and occasional (ubiquitous) willows. Bonwick wrote in the 1850s of

> the celebrated Walk of Willows. These most admired trees border the garden of the lately deceased eldest daughter of John Batman...well shall we ever remember the stroll we had with that lady beneath that famous arch of foliage, listening to stories of the past...of her father's treaty with the Blacks, and of that father's last hours of suffering in Melbourne.

Labels of the original Abbotsford brewery showed just such large old willows edging the riverside building. One story has it that the willows along the Yarra all originated from a single cutting taken from Napoleon's grave site in St Helena. Willows are now classified as a Weed of National Significance for the damage they do generally

Famous Yarra willows one side, Australian bush the other. A beautiful view photographed by Charles Nettleton, Studley Park, in the 1860s.

choking Australian waterways: they are northern hemisphere erosion control. In California, conservation volunteers rip our eucalypts out of waterways and replant willow.

It's not hard, even now, to understand the colonial impulse, the clinging to an old home, that led to to the 'exotic weed' infestations in the first place. Melbourne's famous zoo, indeed, began as the

Acclimatisation Society* on the banks of the river opposite the Botanic Gardens. The society wanted to fill the entire continent with all the animals and birds they'd found so endearing at Home (England) and to get rid of the 'savage silence' of the Australian bush. They released or planted for the first time blackbirds, starlings, sparrows, Indian mynas, foxes, rabbits and blackberries, among others: most of those things now considered noxious weeds and pests, with a few decorative, contained exceptions.

George Coppin was given a pair of white swans, apparently the first in the colony, to float on the ex-billabong at Cremorne Gardens (the black ones are the real Australians). It was the zoological committee of the society that imported the camels for the Burke and Wills expedition: those camels Coppin himself offered may have developed 'showpony' traits at Cremorne Gardens; at any rate they were left behind.†

The Yarraside location opposite the Gardens was found too prone to being a billabong, so in 1861 the zoo moved to Royal Park, where the same cast of cultural thought and sensibility continued. As part of the centenary celebrations for the landing of the First British Fleet in 1788, a camp was set up with a family of real live Aborigines from Coranderrk in their bark miams, accompanied by dummy animals. These exhibits replaced earlier wooden models in the zoo.

An other notion of home.

---

* Leading members were Baron von Mueller, George Coppin, Paul de Castella and father-in-law Colonel Anderson, Rolf Boldrewood, Thomas Embling and Robert Martin: all inhabitants of wonderful riverside properties.

† Von Mueller was exploring the Baw Baws and returning along the Yarra's upper reaches while Burke and Wills were heading northward from Coopers Creek in 1860. In 1873 von Mueller traversed the Upper Yarra again to measure the tall trees.

~ ~ ~

The Main Yarra Trail runs from Mullum Mullum Creek down to the river's mouth. State Parks envelop the river further upstream; gradually, more properties are being acquired.* The Trail has been constructed in sections, and work continues. Locals in Warburton (a gang of sixty- to eighty-year-olds) 'own' their own trail section of the river—as Friends groups do in various locations—maintaining environmentally healthy and beautiful zones.

These are some of the greatest treasures to be found along the Yarra: people who have spent decades living near and observing the river. Other treasures are Victorian State Park rangers, guardians—where they can be—of the river zone. Hopefully one day they can care for it all.

In the river zone…

At Williamstown the beginning and end is marked with two buoys in the Bay: triangular red and green, port and starboard beacons to the channel marked RIVER ENTRANCE.

Looking up from the track opposite the convent in Abbotsford, there are 'outback' scenes on the river's steep banks.

At Kew, you wonder whether you're on the river now, or another billabong. In late afternoon sun, the golden hour, the water is still and brilliant with reflections, doesn't move. The surface ripples, even looks like it's going backwards in a drift of breeze. But no, at the speed of rolling molasses, the coffee-caramel-coloured mass can be seen slowly eddying. It is the river, not a billabong, merely twisting another double-back turn. (At Pigeon Bank, half the flow sweeps backwards in a curve.)

---

* Some of the places demolished in the reversion to bushland had contractors almost weeping at the loss of such beautiful riverside homes. Some of the houses were rumoured to be lived in just a little bit longer.

Round a bend from the shadowed glittery flow near Bolin-Bolin is a carpet of wattle blossom caught in a backwater, sheet-covering the river. Dusted golden in the sunshine and moving shadows it's so vivid it might be illuminated from within. Warm wind has blown it from the trees along the river's banks. A thousand times better than any abstract art, it pools, moves, changes with the flow, swirling in the eddies.

In the hour after dawn, through manna, box and stringybark, you pass a fat wombat digging, are observed by a mob of eastern grey roos and know you're a couple of hundred metres from a four-lane highway bridge to Eltham. Lorikeets flash past, a bronzewing on the opposite bank booms.

Walk through a forest of burgan wall-to-wall carpeted by thick moss. In Warrandyte, slow-step a narrow rocky path on a steep slope to the water shadowing an echidna. Up on its hind legs, snout probing into the melaleuca bark, legs splayed anchoring, claws hooked in at points, it is the original all-terrain perambulator. Backing backwards with clawed paws, it takes a mini dirt-surf down the bank on dry lichen and moss, then crosses the track at right angles.

At Wonga Park, rocky bluffs face the deep shadowed water. Huge trees grow right at the river's edge, LWD in the making. On the clayey way down, dusky pink gumleaves have fallen. A hot lime-green dragonfly passes.

Through swathes of years and tipped rubbish in Christmas Hills, you stride along the centre of an XYZ weave of twenty brown butterflies. You and a black swamp wallaby regard each other till one of you bounds away. Disturbing a powerful owl from its dark roost in a cherry ballart tree puts your feet next to some flowering tall sundews, native orchids with creamy blush flowers not as big as your smallest fingernail.

In summer, there's a huge red carpet of spent seed pods from the wattles at the reserve. Half a dozen firetails bob in midair, perched on seeding long paddock grass you haven't cut. The rare Yarra gum, found on the river flats between Kangaroo Ground and Healesville, is now saved; it's being planted out by the Tree Group. A pump clatters and chugs. Over the asphalt road along the paddock, a kestrel hovers, waiting to dive and kill for a feed.

A retreating billabong in Woori Yallock is filled with waterlilies. Paddocks are curved and carved with what once was, now ponds of demon thistle stand with giant manna gums and river reds, wattle and blackwoods blur close. You turn and see a wedgetail eagle standing with its back to you, so that for a moment you perceive it as animal, its sturdy legs so big, so unbirdlike.

Swim at dusk above the riverstones with a platypus in Warburton after the hum and whining rip of the sawmill finishes. Ten-metre-high treeferns stand sentinel: everything here is giant, even the weed scotch thistles cross nearly two metres at base. Fools gold glints seamed beneath teatree coloured shallows. A yabby, freshwater cray, moves slowly. Upstream in the fern forest, you can just about see the water forming tiny creeks as you watch. The platypus, like us, lives in towns and suburbs, at home in regenerated waterways, river and creeks, all the way down to Studley Park.

The Yarra is under 250 kilometres long, and catches water with its 3,000 kilometres of tributaries from more than 4,000 square kilometres of land, where about one and a half million people live—but most of the river's country is just that, country and bush. The entire catchment stretches from the Dandenongs to west of Mount Baw Baw, across to Mount St Leonard then Mount Disappointment and Mount Macedon, taking in everything from Port Melbourne to Ringwood, Gembrook to Toolangi, Kinglake to Lancefield, Keilor to Newport, and whatever lies between. It's most of greater Melbourne.

The Yarra itself is at home in nearly fifty towns or suburbs: Port Melbourne, Spotswood, Newport, Yarraville, Fishermans Bend, West Melbourne, South Melbourne, Docklands, Southbank, Melbourne, Jolimont, Cremorne, South Yarra, Richmond, Toorak, Hawthorn, Burnley, Abbotsford, Fairfield, Clifton Hill, Collingwood, Kew, Alphington, Ivanhoe, Eaglemont, Bulleen, North Balwyn, Heidelberg, View Bank, Templestowe, Lower

Plenty, Eltham, Warrandyte, Kangaroo Ground, Wonga Park, Bend of Isles, Chirnside Park, Coldstream, Yering, Christmas Hills, Yarra Glen, Tarrawarra, Healesville, Gruyere, Woori Yallock, Launching Place, Yarra Junction, Wesburn, Millgrove, Warburton, McMahons Creek and Reefton.

Down by your local billabong, you're dreaming, and so is the young brown snake in the sun you nearly step on. A pelican above soars stationary in the north wind.

Lovers lay and lie on fifty-degree angles, with stars and grass seeds in their eyes, ignored by sacred kingfishers and pausing rosellas. The river flows on.

Children have died here, been conceived here, been not conceived here. Wurundjeri were born here. Men have been buried here. Bodies washed away here.

The river flows on: *yarra yarra*.

The shape of this river echoes in its stories. There are meanders in the telling, billabongs, islands, snags, floods…

Acknowledgments

Tony Morabito, Land Victoria; Peter Knights, Office of the Surveyor-General of Victoria; Sheila Houghton, Field Naturalists Club of Victoria; Graham Rooney, Melbourne Water; Antoinette Smith, Victorian Aboriginal Corporation for Languages; Glenn Berrill, Jo Thompson, Thompson Berrill Landscape Design; Sabine Schreiber, Arthur Rylah Institute for Environmental Research; Jason and Marg Alexandra, Alexandra & Associates, Pettys Orchard; Rhonda Quaife, Carlton Brewhouse; Geoff Burke; Marvin Hurnall; Jennie Boddington; Ken Berryman, ScreenSound Australia; Rob McGauran, McGauran Giannini Soon; Paul Leahy, Monash University School of Geography and Environmental Science; David McCubbin; David Yencken; Oliver Streeton; Robert Greenaway, Victorian Beer Label Collectors' Society.

Victoria Police—Historical Unit, Water Police, Search and Rescue Squad.

Royal Historical Society of Victoria; Patricia Tibbits and Heidelberg Historical Society; Yarra Glen and District Historical Society; La Trobe Library, State Library of Victoria; Boroondara Library Service; Eastern Regional Libraries; Port Phillip Library Service; Yarra–Melbourne Regional Library Corporation; Prahran Mechanics' Institute.

Thanks

are mostly due to Mandy Brett, editor and great partner in literary process,
also to:
Andrew Otto
Karl-Heinz Otto
Murray Bragge
Nicola Otto Tragear
Chris Redfern and the extraordinary Avenue Bookstore community
and
Dean Putting
—from Highb[r]ow Hill to Mount Wise,
the last word…

Illustrations

p. 103 Abbotsford Lager label from the collection of Robert Greenaway, by kind permission.

p. 111 Samuel Calvert, *Sluicing for Alluvial Gold at Warburton, Upper Yarra,* June 14 1875, *Illustrated Australian News for Home Readers*. La Trobe Picture Collection, State Library of Victoria.

p. 138 *The Yarra, at Simpson's Road Punt* 1880? *Views of Victoria, South Australia, New South Wales and Tasmania*. By permission of the National Library of Australia.

p. 147 C. R. Gotts, *Henley-on-Yarra, Melbourne*, c. 1922. By permission of the National Library of Australia.

p. 152 Diagram from Annette Kellerman, *How to Swim*, 1918.

p. 178 Frederick Grosse, (engraver), E. R., (artist), *The Yarra Bend Asylum for the Insane*, May 23 1868, *Illustrated Australian News*. La Trobe Picture Collection, State Library of Victoria.

p. 180 *The Yarra Bend and Lunatic Asylum* 1880? in *Views of Victoria, South Australia, New South Wales and Tasmania*. By permission of the National Library of Australia.

p. 192 Church Street Bridge from John Butler Cooper, *The History of Prahran: from its first settlement to a city*, 1912 (rev. 1924).

p. 222 *Melbourne, The Yarra Yarra River* [assembled by] Benjamin Greene, 1866, *Travels in China, Japan, Australia, New Zealand, etc*. By permission of the National Library of Australia.

Photos on pp 83, 91, 124 from Benjamin Hoare, *Jubilee History of the Melbourne Harbor Trust*, 1927.

Sources

Allen, Jerry, *Sea Years of Joseph Conrad*, 1965
Allen, Max, *Yarra Valley Wineguide*, 1999
Anderson, Hugh, *Larrikin Crook: The Rise and Fall of Squizzy Taylor*, 1971
Anderson, W. K., *Fever Hospital: A History of Fairfield Infectious Diseases Hospital*, 2002
Archer & Beale, *Going Native: Living in the Australian Environment*, 2004
Ashton, Julian, *Now Came Still Evening On*, 1941
Aveling, Marion, *Lillydale: The Billanook Country*, 1972
Baessler, Arthur, *Südsee-Bilder*, 1895
Bagot, Alec, *Coppin the Great*, 1965
Barnard, F. G. A., *A Jubilee History of Kew 1803–1910*, 1910
Barnes, John, *Joseph Furphy*, 1963
Barrett, Bernard, *The Inner Suburbs: The Evolution of an Industrial Area*, 1971
Barwick, Diane, *Rebellion at Coranderrk*, 1998
Baxter, John, *The Australian Cinema*, 1970
Beardsell & Beardsell, *The Yarra: A Natural Treasure*, 1999
Beardsell & Herbst, *The Outer Circle: A History of the Fairfield to Oakleigh Railway*, 1979
Beatty, Bill, *A Treasury of Australian Folk Tales and Traditions*, 1960, 1969
Bell, Agnes Paton, *Melbourne: John Batman's Village*, 1965
Billis & Kenyon, *Pastoral Pioneers of Port Phillip*, 1932, 1974
Billot, C. P., *John Batman and the Founding of Melbourne*, 1979
Blainey, Geoffrey, *A Game of Our Own: The Origins of Australian Football*, 1990, 1993
—*A History of Camberwell*, 1964, 1980
—*Johns & Waygood Limited: One Hundred Years 1856–1956*, 1956
—*Our Side of the Country: The Story of Victoria*, 1984
Blake, L. J. ed., *Letters of Charles Joseph La Trobe*, 1975
Boldrewood, Rolf, *Old Melbourne Memories*, 1884, 1969
Bonwick, James, *A Sketch of Boroondara*, 1858, 1968
Bonyhady, Tim, *The Colonial Earth*, 2000
Boulton & Brock, *Australian Freshwater Ecology: Processes and Management*, 1999
Boyd, Martin, *Day of My Delight*, 1965
—*The Montforts*, 1928, 1963
Boyd, Penleigh, *Salvage*, 1918, 1983
Boyd, Robin, *Artificial Australia*, 1967
Brennan, Niall, *John Wren Gambler His Life and Times*, 1971
Brothers, C. R. D., *Early Victorian Psychiatry*, 1962
Brown, Richard, *The Story of the Alphington Swimming Pool*, 2002

Brown-May, Andrew, *Melbourne Street Life*, 1998

Bruce, Candice, *Eugene von Guérard*, 1980

Buckrich, Judith Raphael, *The Long and Perilous Journey: A History of the Port of Melbourne*, 2002

—*Melbourne's Grand Boulevard: The Story of St Kilda Road*, 1996

Burke, Janine, *The Eye of the Beholder: Albert Tucker's Photograph*, 1998

Cannon, Michael, *Life in the Cities: Australia in the Victorian Age 3*, 1975, 1983

—*Old Melbourne Town Before the Gold Rush*, 1991

Cannon & Macfarlane, eds, *Historical Records of Victoria:*

Vol. 1 Beginnings of Permanent Government, 1981

Vol. 2A The Aborigines of Port Phillip 1835–1839, 1982

Vol. 2B Aborigines and Protectors 1838–1839, 1983

Vol. 3 The Early Development of Melbourne 1836–1839, 1984

Vol. 4 Communications, Trade and Transport 1836–1839, 1985

Vol. 5 Surveyors' Problems and Achievements 1836–1839, 1988

Vol. 6 The Crown, the Land and the Squatter 1835–1840, 1991

Vol. 7 Public Finance of Port Phillip 1836–1840, 1998

Carroll, Brian, *River Yarra Sketchbook*, 1973

—*The Upper Yarra: An Illustrated History*, 1988

de Castella, Hubert, *Australian Squatters*, 1861, 1987

—*John Bull's Vineyard*, 1886, 1981

Clark, C. M. H., *A History of Australia* vol. VI: *'The Old Dead Tree and the Young Tree Green' 1916–1935*, 1987

Clark, Ian, *Aboriginal Language Areas in Victoria*, 1996

Clark & Heydon, *Dictionary of Aboriginal Placenames of Victoria*, 2002

Clark, Jane, *Sidney Nolan: Landscapes and Legends*, 1987

Clark & Whitelaw, *Golden Summers: Heidelberg and Beyond*, 1985

Clarke, Frank, *In the Botanic Gardens: Their History, Art and Design, with Stories of the Trees*, 1938

Colligan, Mimi, *Canvas Documentaries: Panoramic Entertainments in Nineteenth-Century Australia and New Zealand*, 2002

Colville, Berres Hoddle, *Robert Hoddle: Pioneer Surveyor 1794–1881*, 2003

Cooper, J. B., *The History of Prahran: From its First Settlement to a City*, 1912, 1924

Costello & Millar, *Wanna Bet?: Winners and Losers in Gambling's Luck Myth*, 2000

Costigan, Frank, *Royal Commission on the Activities of the Federated Ship Painters and Dockers Union: Interim Report V 1 No 3, 5*, 1982, 1983

de Courcy, Catherine, *The Zoo Story*, 1995

—*Evolution of a Zoo: A History of Melbourne Zoological Gardens 1857–1900*, 2003

Cranfield, Louis, *Golden History of Warrandyte*, 1982

Croll, Robert, *The Open Road in Victoria: Being the Ways of Many Walkers*, 1928

—*Tom Roberts: Father of Australian Landscape Painting*, 1935

Davison, Graeme, *The Rise and Fall of Marvellous Melbourne*, 1978, 1979, revised 2004

De Gruchy & Leigh, *Stranger's Guide to Melbourne*, 1866

Dingle & Rasmussen, *Vital Connections: Melbourne and its Board of Works 1891–1991*, 1991

Dixon & Blake, *The Aboriginal Language of Melbourne and Other Grammatical Sketches*, 1991
Dobrez & Herbst, *The Art of the Boyds: Generations of Artistic Achievement*, 1990
Dovey, Kim, *Fluid City: Transforming Melbourne's Urban Waterfront*, 2004
Downer & Phipps, *Victorian Vision: 1834 Onwards*, 1985
Dunstan, David, *Governing the Metropolis: Melbourne 1850–1891*, 1984
Dunstan, Keith, *The Amber Nectar: A Celebration of Beer and Brewing in Australia*, 1987
—*The People's Ground: The MCG*, 1962, 2000
Edquist, Harriet, *Harold Desbrowe-Annear: A Life in Architecture*, 2004
Edwards, Geoffrey, *Giant: Ancient and Historic Trees*, 2003
—*The Painter as Potter: Decorated Ceramics of the Murrumbeena Circle*, 1982
Eidelson, Meyer, *The Melbourne Dreaming: A Guide to the Aboriginal Places of Melbourne*, 1997
Ellender, Isabel, *People of the Merri Merri: The Wurundjeri in Colonial Days*, 2001
Escoffier, Auguste, *Escoffier Cookbook*, 1969, 1989
Fairfax, Vicki, *A Place across the River: They Aspired to Create the Victorian Arts Centre*, 2002
Fauchery, Antoine, *Letters from a Miner in Australia*, 1857, 1965
Fels, Marie Hansen, *Dandenong Police Paddocks: Early Use as Native Police Headquarters and Aboriginal Protectorate Station 1837–1853*, 1986
—*Good Men and True: The Aboriginal Police of the Port Phillip District 1837–1853*, 1988
Flett, James, *History of Gold Discovery in Victoria*, 1970
Forwood, Gillian, *Lina Bryans: Rare Modern 1909–2000*, 2003
Galbally & Gray, eds, *Letters from Smike: The Letters of Arthur Streeton 1890–1943*, 1989
Garden, Donald, *Heidelberg: The Land and its People 1838–1900*, 1972
Garran, Andrew, ed., *Picturesque Atlas of Australasia*, 1886, 1982
Garryowen, *Chronicles of Early Melbourne*, 1888, 1976
Gibbs, George, *Water Supply Systems of the Melbourne and Metropolitan Board of Works*, 1915
Gibson & Firth, *The Original Million Dollar Mermaid: The Annette Kellerman Story*, 2005
Gill, Edmund, *Melbourne Before History Began*, 1967
Gill, Herman, *Three Decades: The Story of the State Electricity Commission of Victoria from its Inception to December 1948*, 1949
Goad, Philip, *A Guide to Melbourne Architecture*, 1998
Grant & Serle, *The Melbourne Scene*, 1957, 1983
Green, Irvine, *Petticoats in the Orchard*, 1987
Griffin, James, *John Wren: A Life Reconsidered*, 2004
Griffiths, Tom, *Secrets of the Forest: Discovering History in Melbourne's Ash Range*, 1992
Grishin, Sasha, *The Art of John Brack*, 1990
Hall, T. S., *Victorian Hill and Dale: A Series of Geological Rambles around Melbourne and Further Afield*, 1911
Hansen, Brian, *The Awful Truth: The Inside Story of Crime and Sport*, 2004
Harrigan, Leo, *Victorian Railways to 62*, 1962
Heathcote & Douglas, *A Far Cry*, 1979

Hetherington, John, *Witness to Things Past; Stone, Brick, Wood and Men in Early Victoria*, 1964
Hibbins, G. M., *A Short History of Collingwood*, 1997
Hills, E. Sherbon, *Physiography of Victoria: An Introduction to Geomorphology*, 1940, 1975
Hitchings, Bill, *West Gate*, 1979
Hoare, Benjamin, *Jubilee History of the Melbourne Harbor Trust*, 1927
Hoddle, Robert, eds Scurfield, G. & J., *A Chapter on Port Phillip, Being an Account of the Settlement from Formation*, 1841,1991
Howden, Mary, *Yarra Grange Between the Wars: Gerald Phillips' Memories*, 1999
Howitt, A. W., *Native Tribes of South-East Australia*, 1904
Johnson, Joseph, *Billabongs and Birdies: A History of the Kew Golf Club 1894–1994*, 1994
Johnston, George, *Clean Straw for Nothing*, 1969
Jones, Colin, *Ferries on the Yarra*, 1981
Jones, Ian, *Ned Kelly*, 1995
Jones, Lewis & Peggy, *The Flour Mills of Victoria 1840–1990: An Historical Record*, 1990
Jones, Shar, *J. W. Lindt Master Photographer*, 1985
Kellerman, Annette, *How to Swim*, 1918
—*Physical Beauty: How to Keep It*, 1918
Kenyon, A. S., *Heidelberg: The City of Streams 1834–1934 Centenary: Its Story*, 1934
Keogh, Graham, *History of Doncaster & Templestowe*, 1975
Kynaston, Edward, *A Man on Edge: A Life of Baron Sir Ferdinand von Mueller*, 1981
Lacey, Geoff, *Still Glides the Stream: The Natural History of the Yarra from Heidelberg to Yarra Bend*, 2004
Lack, John, 'Worst Smelbourne: Melbourne's noxious trades' in Davison, Dunstan & McConville, *The Outcasts of Melbourne*, 1985
La Nauze, J. A., *Alfred Deakin: A Biography*, 1965
Leeuwenburg, Jeff, *The Making of Melbourne in Maps*, 1987
Lemon, Andrew, *The Northcote Side of the River*, 1983
Leppitt, Kilgour et al., *Melbourne's Parks: Their Natural Heritage/ Yarra Valley Park*, 1992
Lewis, Miles, *Melbourne: The City's History and Development*, 1995
Lindenmayer, David, *Life in the Tall Eucalypt Forests*, 2000
Lindsay, Andrew, *When Fish Had Feathers: Portraits of Collingwood's Older Men*, 2002
Lockwood, Rupert, *Ship to Shore: A History of Melbourne's Waterfront and its Union Struggles*, 1990
Lovett & Price, ed., *Riparian Land Management Technical Guidelines*, 1999
Lowenstein & Hills, *Under the Hook: Melbourne Waterside Workers Remember 1900–1998*, 1982, 1998
Lynn, Elwyn & Sidney Nolan, *Sidney Nolan—Australia*, 1979
Lynn & Armstrong, *From Pentonville to Pentridge: A History of Prisons in Victoria*, 1996
McCaughey, Patrick, *Fred Williams*, 1980
McCrae, Georgiana & McCrae, Hugh ed., *Georgiana's Journal*, 1934, 1966, 1992
McCulloch, Alan, *Encyclopedia of Australian Art*, 1984
McDonald, John, *The First 100: A Century of Swimming in Victoria*, 1993

McWilliam, Gwen, *Hawthorn Peppercorns*, 1978
Mackie, Elizabeth, *The Artists of Kew*, 1981
Magoffin, Richard, *Waltzing Matilda: The Story Behind the Legend*, 1983, 1987
Marriott, K. L., *The Yarra Valley*, 1975
Marshall, Alan, *Complete Stories of Alan Marshall*, 1977, 1982
—*Pioneers and Painters: One Hundred Years of Eltham and its Shire*, 1971, 1979
Massola, Aldo, *Bunjil's Cave*, 1968
—*Coranderrk: A History of the Aboriginal Station*, 1975
Millar, Ronald, *John Brack*, 1971
Mollison & Bonham, *Albert Tucker*, 1982
Morriss, E. E., ed., *Australia's First Century*, (*Cassell's Picturesque Australasia* facsimiles), 1889, 1982
Newnham, W. H., *Melbourne—Biography of a City*, 1956, 1985
Niall, Brenda, *The Boyds: A Family Biography*, 2002
Noble, John, *Port Phillip Panorama: A Maritime History*, 1975
Palmer, Maxine, *Tarrawarra: 130 Years on a Victorian Property*, 1967
Parkinson, Earle, *Warburton Ways*, 1984
Paynting & Grant, eds, *Victoria Illustrated 1834–1984*, 1985
Pearce, Barry, *Arthur Boyd Retrospective*, 1993
Peirce, J. Duncan, *Giant Trees of Victoria*, 1890
Perry, Roland, *Monash: The Outsider Who Won a War*, 2004
Pescott, R. T. M., *The Royal Botanical Gardens Melbourne: A History from 1845 to 1970*, 1982
Pike & Cooper, *Australian Film 1900–1977*, 1980
Pitkethly, Ann & Don, *N. J. Caire Landscape Photographer*, 1988
Plant, Margaret, *John Perceval*, 1971, 1978
Porter, Hal, *The Paper Chase*, 1966, 1980
Poulter, Hazel, *Templestowe: A Folk History*, 1985
Priestley, Susan, *South Melbourne: A History*, 1995
Read, Mark Brandon, *Chopper: From the Inside, the Confessions of Mark Brandon Read*, 1991, 2001
Reid, Alan, *Banksias and Bilbies: Seasons of Australia*, 1995
Robb, E. M., *Early Toorak and District*, 1934
Robertson, Jill, *Mac Robertson: The Chocolate King*, 2004
Rodgers, Helene, *Brown, Dean and Coppin, and Early Ballooning in Australia*, 1989
Rogers, Dorothy, *A History of Kew*, 1973
Ross, Lloyd, *John Curtin: A Biography*, 1977, 1983
Ruhen, Olaf, *Port of Melbourne 1835–1976*, 1976
Russell, Emma, *Fairlea: The History of a Women's Prison 1956–1996*, 1998
Rutherford, Jerie & Marsh, *A Rehabilitation Manual for Australian Streams*, 2000
Santamaria, B. A., *Daniel Mannix: A Biography*, 1984, 1985
Sayers, Andrew, *Aboriginal Artists of the Nineteenth Century*, 1994
Sayers, C. E., *David Syme: A Life*, 1965

Scurfield, G. & J., *The Hoddle Years: Surveying Victoria 1836–1853*, 1995
Selzer, Anita, *The Armytages of Como: Pastoral Pioneers*, 2003
Serle, Geoffrey, *John Monash: A Biography*, 1982
—*Robin Boyd: A Life*, 1995
de Serville, Paul, *Rolf Boldrewood: A Life*, 2000
Shillinglaw, John, ed., *Historical Records of Port Phillip*, 1879, 1972
Shirley & Adams, *Australian Cinema: The First Eighty Years*, 1983, 1989
Sinclair, E. K., *The Spreading Tree: A History of APM and Amcor 1844–1989*, 1991
Sinclair, Paul, *The Murray: A River and its People*, 2001
Smith, Val, *Wesburn (West Warburton): A Pictorial History*, 1994
Smyth, Dacre, *The Bridges of the Yarra*, 1979, 1991
—*Waterfalls of Victoria*, 1988
Smyth, R. Brough, *The Aborigines of Victoria: And Other Parts of Australia and Tasmania*, 1876, 1972
Sparrow & Sparrow, *Radical Melbourne: A Secret History*, 2001
Steenhuis, Luke, *Secret Places of the Upper Yarra Valley: Beauty Spots*, 1994
—*Secret Places of the Upper Yarra Valley: Historic Sites*, 1994
Stevens, John, ed., *Melbourne's Great Outdoors: Parks, Waterways and Trails Where to Go and What to Do*, 1993, 1996
Stirling, Alfred, *Old Richmond*, 1979
Strahan, Lynne, *At the Edge of the Centre: A History of Williamstown*, 1994
Sutherland, A., *Victoria and Its Metropolis*, 1889, 1977
Struthers, Peter, *Heide I: A Guide Book*, 2001
Swanson, Rex, *Melbourne's Historic Public Gardens: A Management and Conservation Guide*, 1984
Symonds, Sally, *Healesville: History in the Hills*, 1982
Tipping, Marjorie, *Melbourne on the Yarra*, 1977
Trollope, Anthony, *Australia*, 1873, 1967
Twopeny, Richard, *Town Life in Australia*, 1883, 1973
The Vagabond, ed. Cannon, Michael, *Vagabond Country*, (1885–88), 1981
Wiencke, Shirley, *When the Wattles Bloom Again: The Life and Times of William Barak, Last Chief of the Yarra Yarra Tribe*, 1984, 1988
—*Woori Yallock School and District: A Short History*, 1974
Woiwod, Mick, *Once Around the Sugarloaf*, 1992
Zable, Arnold ed., *The Industrial Yarra: Possibilities for Change*, 1976

~ ~ ~

Aboriginal History 1984
Diane E. Barwick 'Mapping the Past: An Atlas of Victorian Clans 1835–1904'
Australian Surveyor 1938
H. S. McComb 'Surveying the Yarra Yarra River'

Bulletin 1980
David Richards 'Dangerous Criminal Tells All'
—'How the Government Condones Waterfront Graft'
Proceedings of the Royal Society of Victoria 1911
J. T. Jutson 'A Contribution to the Physiography of the Yarra River and Dandenong Creek Basins, Victoria'
'The Structure and General Geology of the Warrandyte Goldfield and Adjacent Country'
Victorian Historical Magazine /Journal
1912 George McCrae 'Some Recollections of Melbourne in the "Forties"'
A. W. Greig 'The Naming of the River Yarra'
1927 James H. Watson 'Personal Recollections of Melbourne in the Sixties'
1940 J. Alex Allan 'The Story of the Yarra'
1941 & 1947 R. C. Seeger 'The History of Melbourne's Water Supply' Parts I & II
1942 Francois de Castella 'Early Victorian Wine-Growing'
1943 'Some Pioneer Lillydale Vignerons'
1955 L. R. Cranfield 'History of Warrandyte'
1980 Barbara Savill 'Cremorne Gardens: A Brief History'
Linden Rae Gillbank 'The Acclimatisation Society of Victoria'
1990 C. G. T. Weickhardt 'David Munro & Company, Melbourne'
1995 Mimi Colligan 'Cremorne Gardens, Richmond'
1996 Linden Gillbank 'A Tale of Two Animals—Alpaca and Camel: Zoological Shaping of Mueller's Botanic Gardens'
2001 Murray Houghton 'Warrandyte's Precious Commodity: Golden Days Amongst the Golden Wattle'
Victorian Naturalist
1891 'Report of a Visit to the Yarra Falls'
1908 obituary A. W. Howitt
1919 James Searle 'Gleanings of a City Naturalist'
1928 Geo. Lyell 'To Yarra Falls in the Eighties'
Walkabout
1967 John Currey 'Yarra Charm'

~ ~ ~

The Age
The Argus
The Australian
The Herald
The Leader
Lilydale Yarra Valley Leader
Mountain Views Mail
The Sun
Understorey
Warrandyte Diary
Yarra Valley News

~ ~ ~

2003 Guinness World Records

3AW *Breakfast* 'Ross Stevenson' and 'Sly of the Underworld'

500 Fridays: Ten Years of Contemporary Plein Air Painting, Geelong Gallery, 2003

Acclimatisation Society of Victoria: papers

At Home with the Artist Neil Douglas MBE, Schmeling Art Video, c. 1985

Australian Dictionary of Biography

Australian Platypus Conservancy Case Study: Melbourne Urban Platypus Program

Baw Baw Mountains and Past the Yarra Falls: Warburton to Walhalla c. 1908

Codwatch, 1995

Conserving Natural Rivers, Cooperative Research Centre for Freshwater Ecology, 2002

Contrary Modes: Proceedings of the World Science Fiction Conference, Melbourne, Australia, John Baxter, 'Max's Road: Some Structures in the Films *Mad Max* and *Mad Max 2*', 1985

Copping It Sweet: Shared Memories of Richmond, Carringbush Library, 1988

A Crystal Clear Yarra—Is It a Possibility? A. Mitchell, Soil Conservation Authority, 1980

The Day the Clan Stood Still or, How I Learned to Stop Worrying and Love the Clan, Cave Clan, 2001

The Docklands Heritage, Historic Buildings Council and the Docklands Task Force, 1991

Draft Yarra Catchment Strategy, State of Victoria Department of Natural Resources and Environment YarraCare Working Group, 1996

Effects of Water Resource Management from the Upper Yarra Dam to Warrandyte to 1994, Centre for Environmental Applied Hydrology: Brizga, Finlayson *et al.*, 1998

ESMap: Outer Melbourne Directory, 1991

Hard Yakka: 100 Years of Richmond Industry, City of Yarra

Healthy Rivers Healthy Communities & Regional Growth: Victorian River Health Strategy, draft/overview, State of Victoria Department of Natural Resources and Environment, 2002

Heidelberg Conservation Study Part II: Historic Riverland Landscape Assessment, Loder & Bayly; Marilyn McBriar, 1985

Hydrogeology of Melbourne—Melbourne's Underground Reservoir, Bruce Hutchinson, Royal Society of Victoria, 1999

In Celebration of 150 years of Victoria's Surveyors General 1851–2001, Surveying Victoria

Informing River Management Policies and Programs with Science, Edgar, Schofield & Campbell, 2000

Mad Max, dir. George Miller prod. Byron Kennedy scr. James McAusland & George Miller, 1979

Mainstream Melbourne: the River Yarra on Film, ScreenSound Australia, 2004

Melbourne & Metropolitan Board of Works publications:

Development of the Yarra River at Herring Island Strategy Report, 1981

Floods on the Yarra, B. G. Cargill, 1967

Historical Flood-Control Works and Flood Management Along the Lower Yarra River, Brian Ward, 1988

Lower Yarra Study: An Assessment of Environmental Opportunites, Llewellyn-Davies Kinhill

The Yarra Book: An Urban Wildlife Guide, Georgie Waterman, 1988

Yarra River Conference Proceedings, 1991:

Brian Finlayson, 'Geology and Topography'
Margaret Gardiner, 'Aboriginal Culture'
Tony Jones, 'Flood Plain Management'
Leigh Mackay, 'The Port of Melbourne'
Ninian Stephen, keynote address
(History segment, on video: Graeme Davison, Tony Dingle, Tom Griffiths, Colin Jones, Patrick Miller, Caroline Rasmussen)

Yarra River Study: Dights Falls to Burke Road, 1983

Melbourne Area District 2 Review Proposed Recommendations, Land Conservation Council, 1993

Melbourne Port Corporation: Whole of Port Environmental Management Plan, 2001

Melbourne's Parks & Gardens History, Features & Statistics, Melbourne City Council, 1984

Melbourne Water: Fluvial Geomorphology of the Yarra River, Brizga & Craigie, 1998

Melway Greater Melbourne Street Directory

Middle Yarra Timelines Calendar, Glenn Jameson

Neil Douglas: The Feather in the Flood, Somerville-Smith, c. 2000

Penleigh Boyd 1890–1923, Rodney James, incorporating *The breath of spring: images of wattle in the art of Penleigh Boyd*, Geoffrey Smith, 2000

A Project Dossier in the Monier Arch Bridge Series: Monier Arch Bridge at Anderson Street, Melbourne, the Morell Bridge, Alan Holgate, 1998

Public Hydraulic Power, the Melbourne Hydraulic Power Company

Register of the National Estate, Australian Heritage Commisson

Report by Sir John Coode, C. E., On Works of Improvement, Melbourne Harbor Trust, 1879

River Story, Nine Network, producer Daryl Talbot, story Jenny Brown, 1999

Securing Our Water Future: Green Paper for Discussion, State of Victoria Department of Sustainability and Environment, 2003

The Significance of the Eastern Freeway to North Kew, Jonathan Benyei, 1979

South Bank Architectural and Historical Study Volume 2: An Industrial Seed-Bed, Miles Lewis, State of Victoria Department of Planning, 1983

Strategy Directions Report, Water Resources Strategy Commitee for the Melbourne Area, 2002

Warrandyte Wattles: Despoiling of a Natural Treasure, Murray Houghton, 2004

Yarra Bend Park Trust Annual Report 2000/01

Yarra Care Waterway Series Discussion Paper No 10: Stormwater Drainage in the Yarra Catchment

Yarra Ranges Heritage Study, Shire of Yarra Ranges, 2000

Yarra Trail: A History of Richmond's River

Yarra Video Project Bulletin, ScreenSound Australia, 2003

Index